The Laurinbu

The Laurinburg Institute

*The Historic Black Prep School,
1904 to Today*

Elizabeth Munroe Jones

McFarland & Company, Inc., Publishers
Jefferson, North Carolina

LIBRARY OF CONGRESS CATALOGING-IN-PUBLICATION DATA

Names: Jones, Elizabeth Munroe, 1944– author.
Title: The Laurinburg Institute : the historic Black prep school, 1904 to today /
    Elizabeth Munroe Jones.
Description: Jefferson, North Carolina : McFarland & Company, Inc., Publishers,
    2024. | Includes bibliographical references and index.
Identifiers: LCCN 2024024087 | ISBN 9781476694160
    (paperback : acid free paper) ∞
    ISBN 9781476652214 (ebook)
Subjects: LCSH: Laurinburg Institute (Laurinburg, N.C.)—History. |
    African Americans—Education (Secondary)—North Carolina—Laurinburg—
    History. | BISAC: HISTORY / African American & Black | EDUCATION /
    History
Classification: LCC LC2803.L38 J66 2024 | DDC 373.22/209756335—dc23/
    eng/20240620
LC record available at https://lccn.loc.gov/2024024087

BRITISH LIBRARY CATALOGUING DATA ARE AVAILABLE

ISBN (print) 978-1-4766-9416-0
ISBN (ebook) 978-1-4766-5221-4

Front cover: Moore Academic Hall, Laurinburg Institute, 1909
(Durwood Barbour Collection of North Carolina Postcards,
Wilson Special Collections Library, University of North Carolina
at Chapel Hill)

Printed in the United States of America

McFarland & Company, Inc., Publishers
    Box 611, Jefferson, North Carolina 28640
    www.mcfarlandpub.com

In memory of Vera Revels Campbell
and Mable Ingram Ellerbee.

And in gratitude for John Ellery
and Blaise Ellery.

The Fervent Prayer of Black America

This spark of life, Dear Lord, protect,
In paths of righteousness direct,
When my poor heart would solely bleed,
Beset by prejudice and greed,
Let Thy good spirit reign indeed.

  Like Stephen stoned so cruelly,
  May I not ever bitter be....

Always grant me control of self,
To wrongs to act both blind and deaf,
Give youth an optimistic mind,
Then fashion in thine own design,
Democracy that's color blind.
For all the home I know is here,
And everything that I hold dear,
The many labors of my hand,
Sweat, blood and tears since life began,
And songs tuned to no other land.

  Show men Thy writing on the wall,
  "Together stand, divided fall."

—Ivory H. and Isabelle T. Smith
Laurinburg Institute Faculty Members
Life Lines: A Collection of Inspiring Poetry and Prose, 1952, 82–83

Table of Contents

Acknowledgments

Almost nothing in this account is original. I am grateful, therefore, to the many writers, historians, reporters and filmmakers who recorded what I have pieced together to make a 119 year history of the Laurinburg Institute. I also am grateful to those who met with me personally for lengthy interviews. President Frank "Bishop" McDuffie, Jr., was the first to inspire this historical account and to share his time and memories at the Institute campus on May 20, 2021, and, later, on March 1, 2023. Four other McDuffie family members, including Principal Cynthia McDuffie, Judge Fran McDuffie, Shirley McDuffie McCoy and Dr. Fran McDuffie Foster, contributed vital memories, particularly relating to the roles of women at Laurinburg Institute. Coach Chris Chaney offered key information about his role in leading the Institute to two national prep school championships in 2003 and 2005. Chris Everett supplied many photographs, which document the school, and shared his memories of summer camp experiences at the Institute. The Laurinburg Institute graduates Isaac Logan and Dr. Gerald Hassell provided vivid memories of their student days. Sara and John Stewart and Beacham McDougald shared photographs and information about the school. I am keenly aware that I am a white historian speaking for a black history so, whenever possible, I have quoted directly the voices of these and other original Institute associates.

I owe special thanks to Stephanie Frady, who acted as my research assistant and dogged detective in locating both published and unpublished materials. She also shouldered the tedious tasks of acquiring photographic permissions and securing interviews. Without her support, this work could not have been accomplished. My editor Gary Mitchem patiently answered my endless questions and cheerfully encouraged my work. I am grateful for his faith in this project and his persevering support.

Charles Jenkins gave me helpful information about the school and, more importantly, patiently listened to the stories I was discovering. Karen Jenkins provided food and a bed while I did research in the historical section of the Laurinburg public library. Craig Werner, Will and Celeste Pittman, Ina Hughs, Patricia and Martha Evans were my first readers and encouragers. Stephanie Wilder, along with Halbert Jones and Mary Ellen Bramble, helped edit the original manuscript. Kathleen Orozco offered advice. All of these friends supported me when I needed courage to keep going, but no one held me up more than my husband John Ellery. He endured two months of separation and many more months of isolation so that I could sequester myself and write. I believed that these stories should be told and he believed in me. Thank you all.

My own personal inspiration has been two black women, Vera Revels Campbell and Mable Ingram Ellerbee, who worked in our Laurinburg family home for over 30 years, and who taught me the valuable lesson of how to love, respect and honor people different from myself. My son, Blaise Ellery, daily inspires me with his dedication as a doctor to supporting all human beings both equally and fairly. It has been quite a journey through this historic pilgrimage, and I am grateful for the opportunity to shed light on so many stories that have lived in shadow for so long.

Preface

I grew up in the small farming and textile town of Laurinburg, North Carolina, in the post–World War II years and lived there until I went away to college. These were the years of "separate but equal" schools in the South, so I went to all white public schools. Lincoln Heights and Washington Park were the public black schools. I also knew that there was a private black school called the Laurinburg Institute. Their marching band was the highlight of every parade we had down Main Street. The white bands couldn't compete with the musical talent and showmanship of the high stepping Institute band. I also knew that Dizzy Gillespie had attended the Institute. He was by far the most famous person ever associated with Laurinburg.

Over the years, I met and heard about impressive people who attended the Institute. I became aware that the school has an outstanding national reputation, from California to New York City, primarily among black people. It even has an international recognition, with students coming from abroad including a former premier of Bermuda and basketball players from Europe, Russia and Africa. Yet, the white communities of Laurinburg and North Carolina in general hardly know a thing about the Laurinburg Institute.

I began to dig into the Institute's history, which is deep and long. In fact, the Laurinburg Normal and Industrial Institute is the oldest private black prep school in the United States. Founded in 1904 by Emmanuel and Tinny McDuffie at the request of Booker T. Washington, the Institute has been kept alive by four generations of McDuffies. Approximately fifty thousand students have attended the school, where they were prepared for success in life.

The history of the Laurinburg Institute is also the story of the conflicts and challenges faced in raising the black race out of poverty and ignorance. The Institute staff built the moral character and necessary strength within their students to confront the serious racism that they

The Laurinburg Institute marching band (1960) was the highlight of the Laurinburg Christmas parade down Main Street (Anzell Harrell Collection, courtesy of Chris Everett).

would face in order to fit in with the larger world. Some of the stories are small and some are great, but all of the stories within this history plot a continuous narrative about lifting the race. The cumulative effects of these accounts create an inspiring, even epic, history of struggle and triumph. It is my hope that another race, the white one, may now be cured of its indifference and take pride in the achievements of the Laurinburg Normal and Industrial Institute for the good of a more whole community. It is a story worth telling.

Introduction

For the white race it is almost impossible to comprehend what it took to lift blacks from the state of brutal slavery to their rightful place in the whole society. Indeed, we are still grappling with that problem today. Booker T. Washington has given us some idea of the magnitude of this problem in his biography *Up from Slavery*, which we draw upon in this account.

For over 250 years, the systematic destruction of the family unit during slavery created a devastating effect which no white culture has truly experienced. For most people, the family unit is the critical foundation of our futures, our destinies. Imagine what would occur without that firm foundation. There would be no inheritance, no land, no wealth, nothing. Not to mention, there would be no security, no confidence, no history at all except what could be told orally or in song. Add to that no education, no health, no stable community, and you can begin to imagine where millions of black people began after their release from slavery in 1865.

Starting from scratch has new meaning when you look at the beginnings of Booker T. Washington, and Emmanuel and Tinny McDuffie, the founders of the Laurinburg Institute. How far they came has to be measured against where they began. Emmanuel McDuffie, the son of "none," became the symbolic father of many. He did not flee to the relative safety of the North after the war; rather, he plunged deeper into the deeply divided and often dangerous South. He was determined to build a place for himself, his family, and his race, where they could stand and thrive.

Tinny, his wife, stood shoulder to shoulder with him and established that secure family unit so valuable to us all. All four generations of the McDuffie family have followed that example of relying upon an undivided family unit to provide strength and security for the next generation. Bishop McDuffie, the third generation and present (2024) head of the school, would also add a strong faith in God carried them through their many trials. This faithful cohesion has held the Laurinburg Institute together for 119 years.

When Walter P. Evans, a black Laurinburg merchant, contacted Booker T. Washington in 1902, he pleaded with him to send a teacher for the children in Scotland County which had no public school for blacks. Washington convinced the Snow Hill graduates Emmanuel and Tinny McDuffie to take the challenge of plunging into the leading white supremacist county in North Carolina. Evans nearly lost his life in the 1898 Democratic revolution, begun in Laurinburg, against the Republican-Populist parties, when more than 500 black voters were erased from the polls, many were beaten within inches of their lives and a some were murdered. It took enormous bravery and deep faith to walk into the lion's den of white supremacy.

In spite of the dangers, Emmanuel and Tinny McDuffie answered their call and carved out a place for themselves and others beginning with a hand-built log cabin, raised from trees which they felled on the drained swamp land deeded over to them in 1905 from the leader of the 1898 white supremacy movement. Five years later, the McDuffies contracted with the town of Laurinburg to educate all the black children in town for $700 per year. McDuffie hired seven teachers, who lived in his home, to teach over 400 local and boarding children.

The town of Laurinburg did not offer enough financial support to handle the expenses of so many students, whose numbers eventually rose to over a thousand. McDuffie and his staff depended on the kindness of Northern donors, who financed the school until 1953 when the first public black schools were built. The problem of a private black school bearing the burden of educating public black school children remained a controversy for half a century. It is well documented and discussed here from records in the North Carolina Archives.

Determined to be self-sufficient and prepare their students to lead productive, independent lives, the McDuffies, with the help of the Johnson brothers and other Snow Hill and Tuskegee graduates, created a curriculum designed to provide a basic academic foundation for the students as well as training in housekeeping, healthcare, industrial trades and agriculture. Many students acquired on-the-job training as they literally built the school from the bricks they made to the finished buildings and raised the crops and animals which fed them. The staff of the Institute shared improved agricultural techniques with the community farmers and hosted teacher training workshops.

McDuffie built Bigelow Hospital on the Institute campus in 1914. Dr. Nathaniel Jackson headed the hospital and provided care for the

Institute students and the whole black community for fifty-plus years. Female students acquired nursing skills and health care training by working at the hospital.

Associates of the Laurinburg Institute founded a local kindergarten, preparing children for the Institute. They created a library and provided classes beyond the Institute for adults. In addition, they founded a welfare system which provided food, clothing and transportation for elderly black citizens.

Responding to a call from the North Carolina State Department of Education in 1915, McDuffie shifted the focus of the Institute curriculum from agricultural and industrial training to training students destined for black colleges. Many of his students, including his own seven children, went on to black colleges and returned to the classroom as teachers and school administrators. The school population grew to over a thousand by the 1940s. The number of students served by the Laurinburg Institute during the first fifty years amounted to approximately 40,000 students.

As the school's reputation grew, more residential students came from as far away as New York and Bermuda. These boarding students added a broad perspective to classrooms filled with local kids, creating a sophistication not otherwise available to them. The excellent music and athletic programs especially enhanced that reputation. Shortie Hall founded a band program at the Institute that fostered many of the black public school band programs all across North Carolina. Students such as the now famed jazz musician Dizzy Gillespie and the NBA Hall of Famer Sam Jones added support and luster to the Institute's name. The emphasis on black history grounded students in their heritage and gave them pride. The dreaded public orations, required of all students, taught them how to be articulate and support their arguments while bolstering self-confidence.

From 1904 to 1953, Emmanuel McDuffie steered the Laurinburg Normal and Industrial Institute, keeping it afloat through thick and thin. The proud history of the school helped them to weather the next storms that hit the Institute in 1954. First, Emmanuel McDuffie died, forcing his son Frank McDuffie, Sr., to take over the school. Secondly, the Laurinburg and Scotland County school board finally built four new public schools for black students in 1952–1953, fifty years after they provided public schools for white students. Frank McDuffie had to reinvent the Institute as a strictly private school, which plunged from over a 1000 public pupils to a student body of 87 boarding students.

While the first fifty years of raising the race at the Laurinburg Institute were concerned with creating a space for black people to stand independently within their own community, the next seventy years were about integrating black people into the white community and, ultimately, into the community as a whole. Ironically, that shift was instigated by the establishment of separate public black schools in Laurinburg, the exact opposite of integration. Schools in Laurinburg remained segregated until 1966. The flagship institution, the University of North Carolina–Chapel Hill did not integrate its undergraduate school until 1954 under court order. Sports remained segregated, and those few black undergraduates who attended games were required to sit in separate sections from the white students.

Frank McDuffie, Sr., led the fight to integrate Division I college sports in the South and elsewhere. He rightly believed that the talent of black athletes could provide an opportunity for acceptance into an otherwise largely segregated society. He also knew that those talented sportsmen would have to be morally tough to endure what they would have to face. In addition, those athletes would have to meet academic standards, which were higher at that time in white schools, in order to play college ball. As in *The Wizard of Oz*, they would need a heart, a brain and courage as well as talent to make the grade.

Through his Harlem connection with Holcombe Rucker, Frank McDuffie was able to find the talent including Earl "The Goat" Manigault and Charlie Scott. Scott turned out to have the heart, brains, and courage to accept Frank McDuffie's challenge of being the first black basketball player on the University of North Carolina–Chapel Hill team and one of the first in the ACC. Charlie Davis was the second black player at Wake Forest University, and Chris Washburn joined the North Carolina State University team. All of them owed their success to the efforts of Frank and Sammie McDuffie. Frank coached them both athletically and emotionally, bolstering their self-confidence and courage. Sammie directed their academic studies and prepared them for their SATs. These targeted efforts on the part of the McDuffies were only the beginning.

Their son Frank "Bishop" McDuffie expanded the basketball program so that more than 60 Laurinburg Institute players joined Division I teams all over the country. He hired Coach Chris Chaney of basketball prep school fame, who led the Institute to the 2003 and 2005 national championships. Players came from as far away as Europe, Russia, Australia and Africa to study and train at the Institute. Many went on to play professional ball and even win places in the NBA Hall of Fame. Today Laurinburg Institute ranks sixth in the nation among high schools which have produced NBA players.

Besides creating a nationally respected basketball program, the administration and staff continued the school's tradition of character and confidence building. When integration became the law of the land, many black students found themselves trying to catch up academically to the white students, whose schools had received much more support than their schools. The black students often experienced discrimination and demeaning situations provoked by the privileged white kids. Poverty, single parent homes, drugs, addictions plagued many of them as well. Even if they came from good stable families, they often were assumed to be inferior. Some gave up and dropped out. Others found the support they needed at the Laurinburg Institute. Bishop's daughter Frances McDuffie, a Duke University graduate, joined her parents in teaching those fortunate students who found solid support at the Institute.

Emmanuel and Tinny McDuffie, Frank and Sammie McDuffie, Bishop and Cynthia McDuffie, and Frances McDuffie, along with their fellow staff members, created an environment which met students where they were and then raised them up to the standards necessary for a successful life. They can be rightly proud of the fact that since 1954 over 83 percent of their graduates have gone on to college or professional training. This book documents many of their success stories, but many more remain untold. It is my hope that someday more will be revealed about how vital the Laurinburg Institute and the McDuffie family have been in raising the black race in Laurinburg, in North Carolina, in the nation and even abroad. Their struggle has strengthened us all.

PART I

Slavery, Reconstruction and White Supremacy

1

Laurinburg, North Carolina
(1729–1865)

By 1729 settlers from the Highlands of Scotland began to arrive in the area. They came up the Cape Fear River from Wilmington, where legend has it, they found a painted sign saying, "The best land lies 100 miles west of here."[1]* From Fayetteville, the Lumber River carried those who could read to what later became known as Scotland County. The locals prided themselves on their literacy and boasted that their ability to read helped establish their settlements.

The life of the settlers revolved around self-sufficient farms for the most part. Many of the farmers owned slaves, but worked alongside them in the fields. I am told my own great-great grandfather owned slaves, in whose debt I stand today. The state of slavery was not always the patriarchic ideal whites prefer to believe. There are records in the Scotland County Memorial Library that list slave whippings, including the names of the slaves and the number of lashes, from 1823 to 1844.[2] Two excellent books document the history of this period. Joyce Gibson's *Scotland County Emerging 1750–1900* gives a detailed account of the settlement and history of the county while Nettie McCormick Henley's *The Home Place* records her life on a farm from 1874 to 1904. Numerous articles documenting first-hand accounts by the lawyer Maxcy John appear in the local newspaper *The Laurinburg Exchange,* founded in 1882.

Prior to 1840, Laurinburg amounted to little more than three houses owned by Duncan Wilkinson, John McLaurin and Hugh McLaurin, a few black cabins, the Presbyterian church, and McLaurin's general store and shop where whiskey was sold.[3] A blacksmith shop and a cotton gin completed the township.[4] Rockingham, the Richmond County seat, and Laurel Hill, where the post and stage coach stopped, were the larger towns in the area.

---

* See Notes at the back of the book, by chapter.

Schooling was a private affair established by families who shared teaching duties. The schedules of the schools revolved around the planting and harvesting seasons and usually amounted to no more than a few months at a time. The one room school houses taught the basics of reading, writing and arithmetic. There was no school for black children.

Laurinburg High School was established by the state in 1852 for both day and boarding white students. Duncan McLaurin was chairman of the board and suggested naming the school Laurinburgh by eliminating the Mc from his name and adding the burgh.[5] On the basis of the school, he got a post office built and designated the address as Laurinburgh, spelled as the Scottish city of Edinburgh. Later the name became Laurinburg.

Laurinburg grew beyond the scattered farms and public high school during the Civil War. The Wilmington, Charlotte and Rutherford Railroad (later the Carolina Central Railroad) was built before the war. The first train arrived in Laurinburg in 1861 although the track only continued to Rockingham due to the war.[6] Fearing attacks from the Union army on their shops in Wilmington, the railroad relocated the shops 100 miles inland to Laurinburg. The school was converted into apartments for railroad executives. The shops remained in Laurinburg until 1894, when they closed, and the Seaboard Air Railroad took over, running its track from New York City to Atlanta and moving its depot to Hamlet close by. The townsfolk refused to allow the shops to remain because they feared the rowdy, more transient shop factory workers would cause trouble.[7]

The shops brought both prosperity and rowdiness to the town. Main Street was lined with several dry goods stores, a boarding house, and a drugstore. Lawyer Maxcy John recalled that until 1889, "whiskey was sold here almost as freely as water.... Any person who wanted whiskey could get it by purchase at his grocer's, or he could make it to his heart's content."[8] Nettie Henley remembered:

> ... womenfolk generally thought of Main Street about the same way as the movies show Western frontier towns. The young sports would brag, "There are thirteen barrooms, and I had a drink in every one of them last Saturday." A lady hardly had the "durance" to go to town on Saturday afternoon, for all the hands came in from the farms, and white and colored men crowded along the dirt sidewalks, and the rough road down the middle was full of horse-and-mule-drawn buggies, farm wagons, and the Conestoga covered wagons of the up-the-country traders and mule-drivers.[9]

Moving the railroad shops to Laurinburg did not protect them from Sherman's army, which marched directly through Laurel Hill, four miles to the west of the town on March 6, 1865. The railroad shops and a gun manufacturing shop were destroyed. The devastation wreaked by Sherman's march took almost a decade from which to recover.

As Sherman approached the area, some slaves hoped to join the protection of his army and gain freedom. A deposition from Nathaniel McCormick, an eye witness to the following events, described the fate of one man who sought freedom. Willis Lytch, who was owned by Duncan McLaurin, the founder of Laurinburg, was "one of the few negroes who could read or write."[10] A group of male slaves, whom Lytch led, held a secret meeting on McLaurin property in order to determine how to flee. One black man, Dennis Murphy, was not allowed to attend the meeting and he reported them to the Home Guard. The Home Guard was made up of those men too old or too young to serve in the Confederate Army. They were told that the slaves had "plans to kill all the old white people and take their daughters for wives."[11] The group was arrested and court-martialed. Lytch was hanged from a pine tree on North Main Street and one man was gunned down when he tried to escape. Twenty-five slaves were hanged by the Richmond County Home Guard for trying to join General Sherman during his march through Laurinburg.[12]

2

Reconstruction and Republicans (1865–1898)

By 1877 Laurinburg became incorporated and a new white private school returned to the old school location under the leadership of W.G. Quakenbush in 1879. The newspaper *The Laurinburg Exchange* was founded in 1882 and continues until today. Six cotton mills were established along with a population of poor white factory workers who lived together in mill villages provided by the mill owners. Nettie Henley recalled that the farmers pitied the mill workers, many of whom were children, who always looked dirty and hungry.[1] Many blacks stayed on the farms where they had been slaves and worked as tenant farmers or sharecroppers.

When blacks were freed at the end of the war, they allied themselves naturally with the Republican Party, the party of Lincoln. Three of the four townships in the Laurinburg area had black majorities, which guaranteed Republican control from 1868 to 1898. This alliance opened opportunities for black men to hold public offices and serve on school boards. Forty-nine black men held public positions in Richmond County. Daniel M. Jackson was the first black man appointed to the board of education in the Williamson Township. The black merchant Walter P. Evans was the only Justice of the Peace in Laurinburg. The North Carolina legislature and governorship was controlled by the Republican Party with the cooperation of the Populist Party and black voters. They were called Fusionists.[2]

Prior to the Civil War, blacks did not have schools at all. Some freemen achieved the equivalent of a second grade education mainly through church affiliations. Blacks attended church with whites in Richmond County until the 1870–80s, although they were often physically

13

separated by a balcony where blacks were to sit. Gradually, the blacks formed their own churches, becoming completely separate by 1885.

After the war, the 1868 North Carolina constitution guaranteed free public education for all, but in 1869 the law designated separate schools for blacks and whites with a four month term for each. Richmond County reported to the State Public Instruction Department that there were four Negro schools with four teachers for 397 pupils.[3] By 1870–73 three black teachers, Norman Harlee, Hercules Steele and Stafford Calhoun, received second grade teacher certificates and taught 98 pupils in the Stewartsville section of Laurinburg. By 1874, there were 11 teachers for 756 black students while 22 teachers were hired for 515 white students.[4] In 1877 there were 11 black schools which were funded equally with the white schools.[5] Equal funding hides the fact that there were always many more black students than whites and many fewer teachers for blacks than whites.

Republicans and Democrats vied for the black vote primarily on concerns about the schools. Each party promised equal funding but neither party fully kept their promises, or only kept them if an election was imminent. Republicans offered petty public positions to black men and appointed a black man to the school board. Democrats, on the other hand, appointed black committee men to represent their schools, deal with parental complaints and handle teacher assignments, but they held on to the purse strings and did not allow a black on the school board. For an excellent discussion of the black and white school funding situation and the controversies leading up to the Democratic takeover in Richmond County see Gael Graham's article, "'The Lexington of White Supremacy': School and Local Politics in Late-Nineteenth-Century Laurinburg, North Carolina."[6]

3

Red Shirts, Democrats and White Supremacy (1898–1900)

As dissatisfaction with what the whites perceived as "black dominance" grew, violent actions against the blacks erupted. A black man named Duncan McPhater was lynched by a mob in Laurel Hill after an "election day disturbance ... incited ... by third party leaders" in Spring Hill when a white deputy was shot in 1892.[1] The lawyer and a white leader of the Democratic Party Maxcy John railed against blacks:

> There were Negro magistrates, some of whom could not write their names, one of whom, W.P. Evans of Laurinburg, was of the most unsavory reputation, and his conduct of the office even worse than his reputation had been.... This elevation of untrained and unprincipled Negroes to office and putting ignorant negroes on school boards and the county board of education, greatly inflamed the people, not only here in the county but throughout the State.[2]

Richmond County was solidly in the hands of the Republican Party. Democrats knew their only chance at taking control was to divide the county in two and create a new county. Starting in 1893 and again in 1895, the lower section of Richmond County applied to the North Carolina legislature for a separate county. The legislature and governorship were controlled by the Fusionists, which rejected the applications for separation.

The Democratic leaders organized for a full out fight in the 1898 statewide election. Maxcy John was elected chairman of the campaign. He reported, "Our people were determined to get rid of intolerable conditions facing them. Our local county government was in the hands of people without character for the most part, and even those who had any character were dominated by the rank and file of their supporters—incapable, ignorant and venal."[3] Taking their cues from their white neighbors across the border in South Carolina, the white men set the women to sewing red shirts and sashes to distinguish themselves from the opposition and to intimidate any who might oppose them. Laurinburg was chosen for the site of the statewide opening day of the 1898 Democratic campaign.

On May 10, 1898, more than 2,000 Red Shirts assembled, led on horseback by the Confederate officer Billie D. McLaurin. Charles B. Aycock and Locke Craig, who both became North Carolina governors, were invited to be the speakers and followed in carriages. The parade stretched a mile and a half long and marched through fifteen miles of the colored section and down Main Street in Laurinburg. Large banners with "WHITE SUPREMACY," "We want a white government," "48 Negroes in office," waved through the crowd. The rebel-yelling Red Shirts randomly fired guns, and "Little Zeb," the Confederate cannon fabricated in the railroad shops and still standing in Laurinburg, periodically blasted warnings to all who would vote Republican. Impressed by what they had witnessed as the "grim determination" of the Red Shirts in Laurinburg, Aycock and Craig reported back the next day to the Democratic state chairman Furnifold Simmons in Raleigh. Up until

Gun-toting Red Shirts posing at the Old Hundred polls in Richmond County on election day, November 8, 1898. More than 500 black citizens were stricken from the voter roles during the bloody Democratic takeover of North Carolina politics begun in Laurinburg, N.C. (courtesy of State Archives of North Carolina, Raleigh).

that time, they believed there was no hope of winning the 1898 election, but after their visit to Laurinburg, they knew they could win based on a platform of white supremacy.[4]

Blacks in Laurinburg, such as John E. McLean, a school committee man and poll holder, the Rev. D.M. Jackson, a school board member, and Walter P. Evans, a merchant and Justice of the Peace, steeled themselves for a fight, relying on their Republican allies for support. The black newspaper, *The Laurinburg Post*, edited by a teacher named Neal F. McEachin made a stand "to truly champion the cause of a prejudiced and oppressed people."[5] Their hopes were dashed by a reign of terror that began in mid–October and spread across the county until election day November 8, 1898. Indeed, the terror spread across the state, ending with the only coup d'état ever perpetuated in the United States, the bloody overthrow of the newly elected government in Wilmington, North Carolina.[6]

Republicans made only one attempt to campaign in the lower half of Richmond County. Their speeches were well attended by black voters but they were monitored by groups known as Red Shirts. Maxcy John reported that the Republican speaker "made statements inciting a crowd of colored youths in attendance in a manner suggesting they could make advances on white girls, the remarks being directed specifically towards the group of young colored men, some of whom were decided criminal in tendencies." Claiming that the white women of the county were filled with fear, three hundred Red Shirts on horseback arrived the next day to threaten the speaker, who denied the Red Shirt interpretations of his promises of "social rights and liberties." A member of the crowd shouted "Lynch him!" The leaders of the Red Shirts claimed to be preventing bloodshed by requesting that the speakers go back home. However, their parting words to the Rockingham Republicans promised otherwise: "That end of this road leads to safety (pointing towards Rockingham); but this end (pointing towards the Laurinburg center) for you now, leads to Hell."[7]

The Republican Governor G.H. Russell threatened to call in federal troops to maintain the peace. The Democrat Cameron Morrison, who later became governor, responded that "the county had enough ammunition to take on federal troops." Governor Russell took a train bound for Laurinburg, but the train was boarded by Red Shirts in Maxton, a few miles from Laurinburg, and the governor spent the rest of his trip hiding in the baggage compartment.[8]

The Red Shirts intimidated white Republicans with threats, but they visited "Hell" upon any black man who claimed his right to vote. Three black men were murdered during the campaign and many were severely beaten. These whippings were called "white capping" by the whites. Black men feared to sleep in their homes at night and hid out in the woods. Red Shirts broke down the door of the black land owner and farmer Murdock Shaw, who lived in Laurinburg, and threatened to harm his wife if he did not remove his name from the voter registration. Red Shirts met black men at the poll registration sites and threatened to "visit" them at home if they registered. A mob stormed the home of the merchant Walter Evans and demanded he come out. A doctor saved his life by saying Evans was too ill with typhoid fever to emerge, and the mob disbanded. Many of the white farmers, who depended on their black tenants, asked the black men to stay close to their white homes during the violence so that they could protect them.[9] At the same time, they asked their workers to take their names off the voter registration lists so that they would not be targeted by the Red Shirts, offering their tenants a "certificate of good character" to protect them from harm.[10]

A first-hand account written in a letter dated November 1, 1898, by W.H. Cooper recounts the terrible violence in grim terms:

> This is a big day for the Democrats. They commenced this morning about 4:00 by shooting a negro named Phil Dudley. The negro's house is riddled with bullets.... They then went to J.A. McBryde's place and whipped three negroes nearly to death. They then went over in [New Town] where the negroes live and broke down Murdock Shaw's door.... The negroes are scared nearly to death and I doubt very much if some of them will go to the polls next Tuesday. I did not go to the speaking today, but a party told me that Kitchin told the crowd to take the election if they could not get it otherwise.
>
> I look for some poor negro to get whipped again tonight. Every time they have a speaking down this way they always whip some negro before they adjourn. It looks like they don't intend to allow any of the negroes to vote at all. All the farmers are making the hands that stay on their places [take their] names off the books or promise that they will not vote....[11]

The *Richmond Times* and the *Washington Post* covered the shooting of Dudley. His wife said the mob arrived at 4:00 a.m. and demanded he come to the door. After dressing, he opened the door and someone in the crowd shouted, "He's got a gun! Shoot him." Ninety bullets later, his wife crawled from under the bed to find her husband shot dead.[12]

The combined intimidation of white Republicans and Populists with the reign of terror on blacks succeeded in suppressing the vote of 1898. In Laurinburg an estimated 500 black voters were removed from the polls, guaranteeing the Democrat win. Newspapers all over North Carolina, including the Raleigh *News and Observer* and the *Charlotte Daily Observer*, praised Laurinburg, calling it the "Lexington of White Supremacy" for firing the "first shot for white supremacy ... heard from Murphy to Manteo."[13]

The now infamous Wilmington massacre followed Laurinburg's lead. A special train was loaded with 150 Laurinburg men headed to the port city while the Confederate war hero Billie McLaurin sent word that five hundred Winchester rifles were available should they be needed.[14] At least ten blacks lost their lives in that revolt, the black newspaper was destroyed, and all blacks were removed from their newly elected offices.[15]

The leaders of Laurinburg moved quickly to apply once again for the separation of Scotland County from Richmond County. With a newly elected Democratic majority in the legislature, they succeeded in January 1899 to win approval of a new county. While Democrats congratulated themselves on a "bloodless" revolution for the whites, Scotland County emerged out of the bloodshed of countless, and often nameless, blacks.

Following the takeover of the North Carolina legislature, an amendment to the constitution was introduced and passed by a narrow statewide vote, which required a literacy test of any voter. This law essentially disenfranchised the majority of black voters. A "grandfather clause" was added that allowed all men registered before 1867 to vote. As a result, illiterate whites continued to vote.[16] Democrats thus secured their reign in North Carolina for a century to come.

Submitting to the violent repression of blacks in Scotland County, the respected leader of the black community in Laurinburg, Walter P. Evans, wrote an open letter to the *Laurinburg Exchange* in 1899 entitled "What the Best Negroes Will Do":

> If the negro will practice morality, industry, enterprise, economy, self-help, self-respect, race pride and business cooperation, with the same persistency and earnestness for the next ten years as he has the practice of politics for the last thirty years, I warrant you, the race question would be a back number. The Amendment will regulate itself and this great South of ours will be an earthly sanctuary: yea more, it will be truly the home of the brave, and the paradise of the negro. The colored men in Scotland county propose to try this new way. "W. P. Evans"[17]

The July 26, 1899, issue of the Raleigh *News and Observer* reprinted Evan's article and remarked on his good credentials, supported by Governor Russell and Senator Jeter Pritchard.

Blacks marked the tragedy of their defeat by staging a statewide gathering of 2,000 or more people on July 4, 1903. It was no accident that Laurinburg was chosen as the focal point of this gathering. So much pain and suffering among their race demanded a demonstration of solidarity. The *Charlotte Daily Observer* covered the event and pronounced it a peaceful gathering.[18]

4.

Walter Parsley Evans
(1865–1938)

As a spokesman for the black citizens of Laurinburg, Walter Evans played a major role. He was also instrumental in founding Laurinburg Normal and Industrial Institute. His story begins in Wilmington, North Carolina, where he was born, raised and educated. Evans was born on January 19, 1865, to a free-born black woman named Charlotte Mackey. His father Allen Evans earned his freedom by playing string music for large audiences in Wilmington. Evans was educated in public school and at the Gregory Institute, "which was then under the direction of Northern teachers who stood for thoroughness in their work above all things."[1] Before moving to Laurinburg, Evans worked as a deputy clerk in the office of the Registrar of Deeds in New Hanover County and as general delivery clerk for the Wilmington Post Office.[2]

Following his marriage to Josephine Meares in 1884, Evans moved to Laurinburg, where he and his wife opened a small grocery store in 1885. Evans believed that the way forward for the colored race was through progressive businesses that provided goods for the whole community and good jobs for educated black boys and girls. The small grocery grew into the Evans White Front Department Store, "one of the finest glass-front stores" on Main Street in the 1890s. Ever pushing towards more progressive, more modern businesses, Evans finally built a three story white pressed brick building in 1907 and installed the first elevator in town.[3]

Evans White Front Department Store provided 3,000 square feet of groceries, dry goods, men's clothing, fabrics for women and many other things, which were advertised frequently in the *Laurinburg Exchange*. Through smart marketing and enticing offers, Evans built a large clientele, both white and black, based on low prices and good service. His mail order shoe business became particularly successful. He also had a wood, brick, ice and coal yard business in addition to 200 acres of cotton farm land. In 1924, the local newspaper praised Evans' success reporting:

> By reason of his intelligent handling of the problems that came before him in the conduct of this small business, and by reason of his absolute fairness and honesty in dealing with his customers, he soon built up a countywide reputation as a merchant whose word could be depended upon. And this is one of the greatest assets any business man can have. ... He is the largest colored merchant in North Carolina, and he has always been sincerely interested in the educational and industrial progress of his race.[4]

Walter Parsley Evans (1921), was a prominent Laurinburg merchant who fought for the education rights of black children. He contacted Booker T. Washington in 1902 asking for a teacher to be sent, which initiated the foundation of the Laurinburg Institute. Photograph from *History of the American Negro: North Carolina Edition IV* (1921), 802.

Besides his mercantile businesses, Evans strove to improve the living conditions for the blacks in his community, who lived primarily in framed shanties with weatherboarding. He was instrumental in persuading the town to install water pipes in the colored section of town and built the "first plastered and wainscoted house for rent to colored people." Evans encouraged others to save their earnings and invest in property as he did. Subsequently, he built at least 36 new homes for rent to his community.[5]

During the period from 1868 to 1898, Walter Evans joined the Republican Party. He was appointed Justice of the Peace, a committeeman for the colored schools and a mail contractor. He ran for the office of Registrar of Deeds in the 1895 election, but met strong resistance from the Democrats and failed to win. The Raleigh *News and Observer* praised Evans as "one of the most intelligent men of his race in the

Evans White Front Store (left), on Main Street in Laurinburg, 1910 (courtesy of Durwood Barbour Collection of North Carolina Postcards, Wilson Special Collections Library, UNC–Chapel Hill, P0077).

county of Scotland. He is well educated, has been industrious, has accumulated a good estate, is educating his children, is a man of sobriety and the most prominent and influential man of his race in that section of North Carolina."[6] The Republican Governor Russell, Senator Pritchard, and Col. D.H. Dockery endorsed Evans for the post office position. Evans was an active member of the Presbyterian church, where he was an elder and a superintendent of the Sunday school. He was a member of the Masonic order and the Odd Fellows as well. Evans counted among his honors the invitations by Booker T. Washington to give a series of lectures at Tuskegee Institute on successful business practices and to address the National League of Colored Businessmen in Philadelphia.[7]

Sadly, Evans suffered the tragedy of losing his wife and business partner in a fire at his store in 1919. Josephine was standing on a ladder, stacking firecrackers for the Christmas holiday season when one exploded and started a chain reaction. Although some men grabbed a sheet and entreated her to jump into it, she was unable to release the ladder and collapsed, dying from her injuries a few days later.[8] Evans credited Josephine in large part for the success of his business: "She labored lovingly, constantly and faithfully in serving and conserving her husband's best business interests, and during all their married life she never caused her husband an unhappy moment."[9] Later in 1931, Evans married Annie D. Clark and had two children with her.[10] Annie was a student at the Laurinburg Institute and became the first black registered nurse at the Scotland County Memorial Hospital where she worked for twenty-five years.[11]

In spite of the respect and recognition Evans received from his own people and white Republicans, Democrats, especially Maxcy John, repeatedly defamed Walter Evans both in private letters and in the public newspaper. After John became the superintendent of the Richmond County schools in 1894, school funding decreased for blacks as it increased for whites. Walter Evans was dismissed as a school committeeman when he protested.

When John was appointed superintendent of schools in the newly separated Scotland County in 1899, he had all the black committeemen dismissed and replaced by white men. Enrollment in the 21 small schools for black children decreased from 87 percent to 65 percent, and the gap between spending for white students and black students widened from $1.47 to $6.67 per child. The black schools only offered elementary education. In general, white schools operated approximately two weeks longer per term than black schools.[12] By 1902, the situation for black children had worsened. The John–led school board reported[13]:

	White	Black
Teacher Pay	$2,793.96/ $25 per month	$1,659.07/ $19 per month
Building Cost	$517.39	$69.73
Kids Enrolled	1,168	1,968
Term Length	16 weeks	13 weeks
Teachers	28	18

A clear diminishment of educational opportunities for the black children of Scotland County was implemented by Maxcy John as he increased the benefits for white children. Walter Evans recognized this trend and protested. Maxcy John said that Evans was "an unmitigated nuisance in school matters" and "a determined and persistent negro and never lets up."[14] No doubt, Evans' own six children, Walter, William, Annie, Ruth, Robert and Charity, inspired him to keep fighting for the education of black children. Seeing his voice silenced concerning school issues, as it had been politically by the Red Shirt campaign, Walter Evans sought help at the state level and even beyond. He wrote a letter to Booker T. Washington.[15]

5

Booker T. Washington
(1856–1917)

Out of desperation to find a competent teacher for his children and other black children, on April 29, 1902, Walter Evans wrote a letter to Booker T. Washington, explaining his plight and begging him to send a teacher to Laurinburg. Washington was the president of the now famous Tuskegee Normal and Industrial Institute, which he founded in 1883 in Tuskegee, Alabama, at the request of a local black man and a local white man. Booker T. Washington gives his own account of his life and building the foundation of black education in the South in his marvelous autobiography *Up from Slavery*, originally published in 1900 and summarized in the following account.[1]

A slave in Virginia until he was seven years old, Washington moved to West Virginia with his mother to join his father after the war. As a child, his job was fanning the masters' dining room table. In West Virginia, he worked in the salt furnaces with his father and later in the mines. He worked as a house servant for the mine's owners as well.

At every step of his life, Washington learned something from his experience, which he records in his account, offering a template for others to follow. For instance, he first encountered numbers at the salt furnaces, where he learned that the number 18 was his father's barrel number. His passion for learning drove him to beg his mother for a book. An old alphabet spelling book opened his eyes as to how one can read by sounding out letters. A young black man, who could read, came to his community and taught him and other students by spending one night a week with individual families. Mrs. Viola Ruffner, the mine owner's wife, taught him the values of cleanliness, punctuality, honesty, and thoroughness on the job, which resulted in his pride for work well done. She sent him to school one hour a day in the winter months to continue his education.

Determined to get a thorough education, Washington made his way in 1872 to the Hampton Normal and Agricultural Institute in Virginia, where white teachers trained black students to be teachers for their own race. The founder of the school, General Samuel Armstrong, had served during the Civil War with the Union Army, where he learned about the promise of training black men:

> Two and a half years' service with Negro soldiers as lieutenant colonel and colonel of the Eighth and Ninth Regiments of the United States, Colored Troops convinced me that the freedmen had excellent qualities and capacities and deserved as good a chance as any people. Educational methods to meet their

Booker T. Washington (ca. 1905–1915), founder of Tuskegee Normal and Industrial Institute, sent two students in 1904 to found Laurinburg Institute. Portrait is by Harris & Ewing (courtesy Library of Congress).

> needs must include special practical training and take into account the forces of heredity and environment. A dream of Hampton School, nearly as it is, came to me a few times during the war—an industrial system, not only for the sake of self-support and intellectual labor, but also for the sake of character. And it seemed equally clear that the people of the country would support a wise work for the freedmen. I think so yet.[2]

After the war General Armstrong joined with the American Missionary Association to form the school in 1868. His philosophy, as stated in his diary, guided Washington, William Edwards, and Emmanuel McDuffie:

> The thing to be done was clear …: to train selected Negro youths who should go out and teach and lead their people, first by example, by getting land and homes; to give them not a dollar that they could earn for themselves; to teach respect for labor, to replace stupid drudgery with skilled

hands, and in this way to build up an industrial system for the sake not only of self-support and intelligent labor, but also for the sake of character.[3]

Washington's entry exam was cleaning a large hall. His thoroughness convinced the school head that he would be acceptable as a work/study student. Washington worked by day as the janitor of the school and, by night, he went to classes.

Upon graduation, Washington returned to his West Virginia community and started a school. Shortly afterward, General Armstrong invited Washington to return to Hampton and direct a night school for American Indians. Washington started this program from scratch and made a great success of it, so much so, that when the administration received a call from Tuskegee for a teacher, they immediately sent their most capable prodigy, Booker T. Washington.

Tuskegee Normal and Industrial Institute

Starting from scratch again in 1881, with an annual appropriation of $2,000 granted by the state legislature, Washington realized that his task was far greater than building a school and teaching students to read. He knew he had to teach a whole new way of life to children born out of slavery:

> ... we must do something besides teach them mere books. The students had come from homes where they had had no opportunities for lessons which would teach them how to care for their bodies.... We wanted to teach the students how to bathe; how to care for their teeth and clothing. We wanted to teach them what to eat, and how to eat it properly, and how to care for their rooms. Aside from this, we wanted to give them such a practical knowledge of some one industry, together with the spirit of industry, thrift, and economy, that they would be sure of knowing how to make a living after they had left us. We wanted to teach them to study actual things instead of mere books alone.[4]

Washington acknowledged that blacks believed that, if they learned to read, they would not be required to do hard labor. He often repeated his dismay with black men who learned to read just a little and suddenly felt "the call" to preach, thereby avoiding hard work. Washington rolled up his sleeves and went to work clearing fields and planting crops "because we wanted something to eat."[5]

Washington taught by example the dignity of labor and the values of independence and self-reliance. He built up credit by taking small loans and faithfully paying them off. He created a student-run brick manufacturing business that trained students for future jobs and provided the materials to build the many buildings for Tuskegee Institute. As each new need arose, he found solutions which allowed for career training and provisions for the school, and fulfilled commercial needs in the wider community. The manufacture of bricks, furniture, and mattresses, along with produce from the farm, served to provide a steady flow of income for the support of students. This industrious self-sufficiency also cemented good relations with both black and white citizens, who purchased the surpluses and augmented their own wealth.

Perhaps because of his experiences as a slave and his early associations with white Southerners, Washington, respected white concerns about political and social equality. He himself had concerns with black legislators, who could neither read nor write, and feared that they could be led down the wrong paths by wily white politicians. Washington believed that "back of the ballot [black men] must have property, industry, skill, economy, intelligence, and character," and they must take into consideration the values and needs of their local communities.[6]

In his now controversial speech at the Atlanta International Exposition on September 18, 1895, Washington stated, "In all things that are purely social we can be as separate as the fingers, yet one as the hand in all things essential to mutual progress.... Social equality is the extremest folly."[7] The Atlanta crowd gave him a standing ovation with these remarks. However, Washington, always stated his full support of equal justice for his race under the law and sought to bring blacks to equality through education and industry rather than through "outside or artificial forcing."[8]

Raising the Race by Raising Funds

Just as he built Tuskegee Institute from the ground up, Washington also built strong relationships with patrons, who, over time, came to trust him to use their funds wisely. He made repeated visits to philanthropists, who often would donate a mere $2.00 on his first visit, and who, when seeing the value of their investments grow in real results, would contribute as much as $50,000 in later visits. Washington recognized:

> ... very few persons have any idea of the large number of applications for help that rich people are constantly being flooded with.... I have usually proceeded on the principle that persons who possess sense enough to earn money have the sense enough to know how to give it away, and that the mere making known of the facts regarding Tuskegee, and especially the

facts regarding the work of graduates, has been more effective than out-
right begging.[9]

Among the many donors to Tuskegee were Andrew Carnegie, Col-
lis Huntington, Paul Sachs, William Baldwin, the Peabody and John
F. Slater Funds, and, most importantly, Anna T. Jeanes and Julius
Rosenwald.

The estate of the Boston Quaker Anna T. Jeanes left Tuskegee a
million dollars for the support of black teachers in 1908. Julius Rosenwald became the president of Sears, Roebuck and Company in 1909 and
a trustee of Tuskegee Institute in 1911. With the Jeanes' grant, Washington and his staff set up a project at Tuskegee in 1910 to support their
graduates in teaching black students all across the South.

From Washington's close friendship and trust, Rosenwald established the Rosenwald Fund in 1917, which granted matching funds to
locals to build small black schools all over the rural South. Over 800
brick schools were built in North Carolina alone, 14 in Scotland County
from 1918 to 1925. A thorough account of this remarkable project can be
found in Thomas W. Hanchett's "The Rosenwald Schools and Black Education in North Carolina," 1988.[10]

Booker T. Washington also created another strong relationship
with Walter P. Evans, whose 1902 letter acquainted him with the dire
situation in Scotland County. Washington began to search for a black
student who would make the difficult commitment to found a school
for black students in Laurinburg, North Carolina. He travelled to Snow
Hill, Alabama, where the Tuskegee graduate William J. Edwards had
established the Snow Hill Normal and Industrial Institute for black
children in 1893.

Calling the students together, Washington asked for a volunteer
to step forward to take on the challenge of journeying to Laurinburg
and setting up a school. According to Bishop McDuffie, the grandson
of Emmanuel and Tinny McDuffie, the group of students stepped back,
leaving Emmanuel and Tinny standing there. Washington thanked
them for volunteering and asked them seriously to consider his challenge. He knew it would take courage and strength to make the journey
through Klan infested territory, but he had faith that his prodigies were
well prepared to fulfill the promise that was invested in them, just as he
fulfilled the faith that his Hampton Institute mentors had in him.[11]

6

Emmanuel Montee
and Tinny Ethridge McDuffie
(1881–1983)

The story of Emmanuel and Tinny McDuffie covers more than a century. The following account was taken from "Sketch of My Life" by Emmanuel McDuffie, published by William Edwards in *Twenty-Five Years in the Black Belt* in 1918.[1] Emmanuel was born in Snow Hill, Wilcox County, Alabama, on December 24, 1883, to Emanuel and Emma McDuffie. He never knew his father, who died six months prior to his birth. McDuffie recalled that he was known among the children in his neighborhood as "the son of 'none,'" since he never had the support or guidance of a father, as the other children had. His mother was left with seven children to raise on her own. She died when he was 10 years old, at which time, his old grandmother, known as Aunt Polly, assumed the care of the children. She owned a small farm and was admired as a "great farmer" because she raised forty to fifty bushels of corn and four or five bales of cotton each year. Emmanuel was put to work plowing with an ox in the fields. Life was little more than the struggle to put food on the table and clothes on their backs. His grandmother passed away when he turned 15, leaving all the children to "shift for themselves." It was then that Emmanuel set his sights on getting an education.

Snow Hill Normal and Industrial Institute

After graduating from Tuskegee Institute, McDuffie's cousin William J. Edwards founded Snow Hill Normal and Industrial Institute in 1893. He formed a strong relationship with the philanthropist Anna T.

Jeanes, who helped support his efforts in establishing his school, and, later, Edwards introduced Jeanes to Booker Washington. With her help, Washington created the first widespread effort to educate black Southerners.

Edwards allowed McDuffie to enter the school as a work study student, going to school at night for two and half hours and working during the whole day. McDuffie had an eye-opening experience as his education proceeded:

> Until I entered Snow Hill Institute, I had a very vague idea about life as it pertained to the Negro. In fact, up until that time, I was of the opinion that the Negro had no business being anything; but after entering the school and being surrounded by a different atmosphere and seeing what had already been accomplished by Mr. Edwards, I soon realized that the Negro had as much right to life and liberty as any other man.[2]

Emmanuel Montee McDuffie (1918), a graduate of Snow Hill Normal and Industrial Institute in Alabama, accepted the challenge of Booker T. Washington to travel to Laurinburg, North Carolina, and found Laurinburg Institute in 1904. Portrait is from *History of the American Negro: North Carolina Edition IV*, 1921, 179.

McDuffie describes the many difficulties he faced at Snow Hill including finding "sufficient clothing." All he had was what he wore and that outfit eventually was patched beyond repair. His teachers were "extremely hard against dirt and filth." His situation became alarming because he was required to clean his clothes once a week. Although he cleaned them in the spring at night, they often did not dry by morning and he was forced to wear wet underclothes for days, which proved painful and caused medical problems for years to come. McDuffie suffered until the principal gave him an ill-fitting second hand suit and another set of underwear. In spite of his many trials and tribulations, McDuffie persevered because "I was willing to make any sacrifice to obtain" an education and "be prepared to be of service to my people."

McDuffie relates that Edwards was a shining example for him to follow. Edwards was a strong advocate for the Christian mission of discipleship and service. Constantly repeating the Tuskegee motto and, later, the Laurinburg Institute motto "Deeds, Not Words," he believed that in "losing their lives for others, they have saved their own." Christ was his model when he said in his address at the Tuskegee twentieth anniversary celebration in 1903:

> The work of Jesus Christ and his disciples was not on the transfigured mountain, but at the foot among the masses.... We must go down to the foot of the mountain among the masses. We must go out into the rural districts for there it is that the people are a hungry and thirsty crowd, and there it is that the harvest is great, but the laborers are few, and there it is that the work of the world must be done.... Speaking the word would not atone; hearing it would not redeem; and seeing it would not save. The word had to be made flesh and blood in the person of Jesus Christ, the Son of God, and then come down on earth and live, move, and dwell among us.... Education, in order to be real, must be applied; in order to be effective, it must be digested and assimilated. It must become a part of your flesh and blood; it must transform you into a new creature and then go out and move, live and dwell among us.[3]

William J. Edwards (1918), the founder of Snow Hill Institute, inspired Emmanuel and Tinny McDuffie to found Laurinburg Institute and offered them a template as to how they should proceed. Portrait is from *Twenty-Five Years in the Black Belt* (1918), frontispiece (courtesy of www.docsouth.unc.edu).

Through his experience at Snow Hill Institute and the mentoring of

Edwards, McDuffie transformed into that new creature through adversity and suffering to confidence and purpose. When the call came, he was prepared to go.

Edwards offered his graduating students a blueprint for their future lives as they set out on their mission to found schools all over the South:

> It is expedient that you go away. To be successful as a teacher, you must fix your mind upon three things: The building of a suitable schoolhouse, arousing in the people a spirit that will make them support your efforts and the planting of yourself in that community. Select a suitable field in which to work and then make up your mind to stay there. I believe the best place for you is in the rural districts. Go there and take a three months school as a nucleus and add one month, then two and so on until you have a six or seven months school. You must be economical in living. Year by year, manage to buy land and build you a neat and comfortable home. You can't do much in the way of getting people to buy land so long as you haven't any. You cannot do much towards having people forsake the one room log cabin so long as you live in one. You must teach by example as well as by percept.[4]

Emmanuel McDuffie followed his mentor's wise words and earned the respect of every person he encountered through hard work and determination to succeed. In times of discouraging struggle, he often repeated to himself the poetic mantra: "The bud may have its bitter taste but sweet will be the flower." He realized "he could not dream himself into a noble character" without "rolling up sleeves and putting shoulder to the wheel." The *Laurinburg Exchange* characterized McDuffie's importance to the community in 1932 thusly:

> Having no church, society nor organization of any kind upon which to rely for support, building an institution of this kind, has been a constant burden and struggle upon the principal and founder since its inception. Many times the work would have failed had it not been for the strong determination and abiding faith of its principal who was willing and able to stoop down and lift himself up by his own boot-straps. Mr. McDuffie has done more, for in working out his own success, he has pointed the way by which any boy of vision and energy can make a place for himself. Such men are the greatest asset to the race. While laying the foundation and building their own success, they become examples and benefactors of other struggling youths whom they help up from places of poverty and obscurity to positions of large service and usefulness.[5]

Other accounts of Emmanuel McDuffie support this high praise, and more. McDuffie met Tinny Ethridge at Snow Hill Institute, where she was also a student. Tinny was born May 11, 1881, in Wilcox County, Alabama. They became engaged and, after Booker T. Washington made his plea for volunteers, Emmanuel and Tinny were married in 1904 and began the journey of their lives to Laurinburg, North Carolina.

Making the decision to go to Laurinburg was not an easy one. Tinny was pregnant with their first child. They had to leave behind all the support of family and friends. The journey to Laurinburg meant traveling through racially dangerous territory controlled by the Klu Klux Klan. They had no money and no knowledge of what they would encounter when they arrived. The family account says they travelled by train in a freight or baggage car because they were not allowed to sit in the white passenger cars. They prayed that their car would not be side-lined, as many were, so that they could reach their destination in North Carolina. What normally took a day of travel in those days, took them a week.[6] In any case, they arrived with five cents in their pockets and hope in their hearts.

PART II

The Laurinburg Institute
Emmanuel M. McDuffie
(1904–1953)

7

Laying the Foundation
(1904–1917)

The McDuffies arrived in Laurinburg on September 15, 1904. They had a hard time winning the confidence of the local black community because "the people had been so often deceived and hoodwinked by political demagogues and supposed race leaders, that they had no confidence in anyone."[1] The trauma of the Red Shirt campaign was still painfully vivid in the people's minds and they did not know whom to trust.

In spite of the unwelcoming nature of their arrival, the McDuffies set up a school in an old public school building. They had seven students and fifteen cents in cash. Through working with the people "on the streets and in the churches," the McDuffies gradually won their confidence and slowly increased the school's enrollment. When they outgrew their surroundings, they came up with a bold plan.

It took courage to approach the County Sheriff Billie D. McLaurin, the same Confederate war hero who led the Red Shirt parade in the infamous overthrow of the Republican Party in the 1898 election. The white and black communities had been split apart violently. Nonetheless, Emmanuel and Tinny McDuffie marched up to the front door of the sheriff's home, a brave thing to do, since blacks were expected to go to the back doors of white people's houses. When McLaurin opened the door, he seemed astonished to see two young black people standing there, but he did not say a word. Emmanuel explained that he and his wife had been sent to Laurinburg by Booker T. Washington and William J. Edwards, at the request of Walter Evans, in order to found a school for black children. He wondered if Captain McLaurin might be able to help them find a place to build a school. McLaurin still did not speak a word. Thinking that the sheriff was deaf, the couple stepped up closer to the man and shouted their request again. McLaurin remained silent and backed away. Tinny took the hand of Emmanuel and quietly said, "Let's

Tinny and Emmanuel McDuffie (ca. 1950), founders of the Laurinburg Institute, host a graduation luncheon on the lawn of Laurinburg Institute (courtesy of Frances McDuffie).

go." As they walked away, Tinny whispered to Emmanuel, "I sho hope he doesn't brutalize us for this."[2]

Sometime later, Sheriff McLaurin showed up at the McDuffie's lodging. He called Emmanuel out and told him to get into his truck. Emmanuel was afraid that some harm would come to him since McLaurin didn't explain why, but he was also too afraid to say no, so he got in the truck. McLaurin drove him to a marshy piece of land just north of Main Street, across the railroad tracks. After he got out of the truck, McLaurin pointed to the marsh and said, "This oughta be good enough for you niggers."[3]

When Emmanuel brought Tinny to look at the site, she "broke into tears" and said, "It's nothing but a swamp.... I hope the mosquitoes don't eat us up." Emmanuel looked on the bright side and said, "But look ... it's full of trees. We will have plenty of wood to build our school."[4] Emmanuel and Tinny cleared and drained the swamp with the help of their black neighbors. They built a crude log cabin from the trees felled on the land and proceeded to set up their school.

As the school grew, Billie McLaurin donated four lots over to the Laurinburg Normal and Industrial Institute in 1905, 1907, 1912 and 1917. Enlisting the help of a white man, even the help of *the* white man who led the Red Shirt march, turned out to be a smart move on the McDuffie's part. They appealed to Billie McLaurin's humanity in accomplishing a good deed, and, perhaps, they offered him the opportunity for atonement for the violence that he and others had unleashed on the black community. McLaurin became a supporter of the McDuffies and, in doing so, began healing the wounds of the whole community. Today, fourth generation Judge Frances McDuffie reflected: "It was remarkable that the white citizens of Laurinburg allowed them to be there. They took great pride in everyday citizens."[5]

The primary employment of the black citizens of Laurinburg was tenant farming or sharecropping. The blacks lived on white farms, just as they had done under slavery, and worked for white men who offered them little more than a shack to live in and food for their tables. The children of blacks worked alongside their parents in the fields. What little schooling they got revolved around the planting and harvesting seasons. Taking children out of school was common during these periods. Frank McDuffie explained: "Since their absence from school was a decided economic advantage to landlords, they were frequently excused from school attendance through the influence of large landowners. ... It is ironic that the Negro child's chance to learn was constrained by an economy whose prosperity he helped to produce."[6]

As late as 1919 the minutes of the Laurinburg School Board reported: "The attendance officer was allowed to give permits for up to two months of school absence if the student was harvesting cotton."[7] McDuffie needed the support of the white landowners in order to provide students for his school at all. He was able to convince a few landlords that "the school's program would make Negroes more economically useful to them. Some ... even encouraged their favorite tenants to send at least one of their children to the Laurinburg Institute during the school's early years."[8]

One such tenant, James Pollard, was "encouraged to send his youngest son, E.J., to the Laurinburg Institute."[9] His grandfather, a landowner, paid for his schooling and, upon graduation around 1910, willed him a small business. His business grew and he opened a restaurant for colored people in town. Eventually Pollard himself owned three tenant farms. Pollard said: "I encourage all of the families who tend my farms to send their children to school.... Education offers the only hope for colored people to break away from this disgraceful system of sharecropping."[10]

Early Days at the Institute

Emmanuel McDuffie continued to improve his own education by attending Tuskegee Institute in 1905. A publication, entitled *Industrial work of Tuskegee graduates and former students during the year 1910*, reported that McDuffie had established the Laurinburg Institute in September 1904 and, by 1910, the school had 305 students and 10 teachers, 7 of which graduated from Snow Hill Institute.[11] The first teachers hired were Miss Lilian Smith, who arrived in 1904 and Hamilton Johnson, who came in 1906 and later became the treasurer of the school.[12] Because the Institute was a private school, students paid a $2 monthly tuition, when they were able, or joined the school as a work study student. Initially, because most families had little money to spare, many parents paid in goods such as eggs, a hog, and produce. Boarding students paid a $12 monthly fee plus tuition. They stayed with local families in their homes. As needs arose for the school, Tinny McDuffie and Lillian Smith canvased both the black and the white communities asking for donations to be sold at suppers or fairs. Mrs. McDuffie reported that they "did not apply to a single white family who failed to donate something. In various ways the white families exemplified their interest in the Institute."[13]

The McDuffies were aware that the success of his school depended more upon the black community support than the white community. They understood the necessity of raising the economic base of the black citizens of Scotland County through the support and encouragement of the school so that the Institute could reap the rewards of their efforts through tuition-paying students. Tinny McDuffie, who was known for her memorable recitations of prominent black orators, quoted Booker T. Washington in reference to the importance of self-reliant independence[14]:

> One farm bought, one house built, one home sweetly and intelligently kept, one man who is the largest tax payer or has the largest bank account, one school or church maintained, one factory running successfully, one truck garden profitably cultivated, one patient cured by a Negro doctor, one sermon well preached, one office well filled, one life cleanly lived—these will tell more in our favor than all the abstract eloquence that can be summoned to plead our cause.[15]

For that purpose, the McDuffies, the staff and the students organized "societies" in the black communities which would meet monthly to discuss the needs of the community. McDuffie encouraged thrift and savings in order to buy homes and to secure farm land. He showed the people how they could get off the crippling tenant credit system through low interest loans from the Negro Farmers' Conference and the Workers' Conference.[16] The societies created a system of cooperation to aid each other in the purchase of supplies and to support each other in times of illness or death. The organization of the black community produced excellent results. McDuffie recalled that upon his arrival, "there were not more than thirty-five acres of land owned by the Negroes in this area."[17] By 1910, he could report: "Where there was ignorance and indifference, now there is a fair measure of thrift and intelligence. The people are buying homes and property, and in many ways showing signs of aspiration for a better and more useful life."[18]

As the student population quickly grew, McDuffie sought the support of five large foundations: the Peabody Educational Fund, the John F. Slater Fund, the General Education Board, the Anna T. Jeanes Fund, and the Julius Rosenwald Fund. All of these foundations contributed to the establishment of the Institute, and they will be discussed further in the following chapter. However, by far the largest contributor to the Institute in the early days, was Anna Jeanes, who had supported the

The Laurinburg Institute boys' dormitory Edwards Hall (1914) was named for William Edwards, the mentor of the McDuffies at Snow Hill Institute. The original wooden building was funded by Northern donors and built in 1906. It housed boarding students and teachers, and was updated to brick in 1914 (courtesy of Durwood Barbour Collection of North Carolina Postcards, Wilson Special Collections Library, UNC–Chapel Hill, P0077; 8-64).

Snow Hill and Tuskegee schools beforehand.[19] She explained, "Others have given to large schools; if I could I should like to help the little country schools."[20]

With the funds raised by McDuffie and his staff, the first building was constructed in 1906 and, in 1914, converted to brick. It was dedicated to McDuffie's Snow Hill mentor William Edwards. Edwards Hall doubled as classrooms for students and as the residence of the teachers. Eventually, Edwards Hall became the classroom building for first through third grades and the upper floors became dormitory rooms for boarding young men. At the same time, a wooden chapel was built called Friendly Chapel. Although the McDuffie family deeply believed in the Christian faith, the school always remained strictly undenominational, never falling under the control of any particular church. Nonetheless, students were required to attend chapel services both morning and evening. Religious education, for the McDuffies, was the foundation of the character building they so vigorously sought to instill in their students.

By 1909 McDuffie had raised enough funds to build a large classroom building which would accommodate the growing student body and provide a large auditorium which would serve the community as well. Moore Hall included eight classrooms, an administration office, a

Moore Academic Hall, Laurinburg Institute (1909) contained the academic classrooms, a library and a 1000 seat auditorium (courtesy of Durwood Barbour Collection of North Carolina Postcards, Wilson Special Collections Library, UNC–Chapel Hill, P0077; 8-65).

library and an auditorium which seated a thousand. Initially the Institute followed the normal school courses of reading, writing and arithmetic, and the first graduating class in 1910 consisted of three students (one from South Carolina, one from Ohio and one one from Fayetteville, North Carolina). All of them became teachers.[21]

Booker T. Washington's Speech

In November of 1910 Booker T. Washington made a trip to Laurinburg in order to inspect the new school and encourage his disciples Emmanuel and Tinny McDuffie. While there, Washington made a speech at the ball field to a large audience of both black and white citizens. The lawyer Maxcy John introduced Washington. A reporter from the *Laurinburg Exchange* enthusiastically reviewed the speech which made the cover of the newspaper on November 10, 1910.

Washington's approach was to soften racial tensions by candy coating past relations. He praised the black people saying that "the negro … is the only race of men on earth which has ever looked the white man in the face and lived" and that he was here "under a special invitation: in fact, he was sent for" and that "the South is the best place for the colored man on the face of the earth."[22] He claimed that the South was misunderstood and that lynching "existed more in the imagination than anywhere else." He even went on to say that "the southern white man is the negro's best friend" since the whites had "civilized and christianized" blacks who came from "a state of barbarism and absolute savagery."

Washington appealed to blacks to settle down and, through honest and reliable labor, establish themselves as productive members of society. He encouraged thrift and savings in order to build a better future. He said,

> … never come to town without bringing something to sell.… The white folks don't draw the color line on your chickens and eggs.… The soil draws no color line, the rain draws none, the sun draws none, except in favor of the negro, and with the friendship and help of the white man, with a reputation of reliable and honest service, with something saved each year, with clean habits, the negro's prosperity and progress and happiness are assured here in the South.

Washington also pointed out that the white man has a responsibility to help the black man. In a sly attempt at irony, he noted that the white man gives "the black child more credit for having more sense than he really has" when he provides only four months of school for the black child and eight months for white children. Washington pleaded for better schools and teachers, longer terms and better pay for educators.

The reporter called Washington's address "remarkable" and "nothing less than wonderful." He ended by complimenting the black leaders of Laurinburg who brought Washington to town: "they did as well for their big man as we could have done for one of our distinguished men...." A banquet was prepared at the Laurinburg Institute to celebrate the momentous occasion. When Booker T. Washington passed away in 1915, Walter Evans suspended his business for an hour in the morning to honor the great man and published a tribute to him saying, "God made one Moses, one Joshua and one Booker T. Washington."[23]

Industrial Training

By 1910, the Institute shifted from the very basic courses required for education to industrial courses needed for life. Parents objected to this shift in direction because they "believed that the aim of education was to free their children from manual labor."[24] McDuffie explained:

> ... we had a task in the plan of co-ordinating mental and physical labor. Such an idea is full of objections and handicaps, and it is admitted that

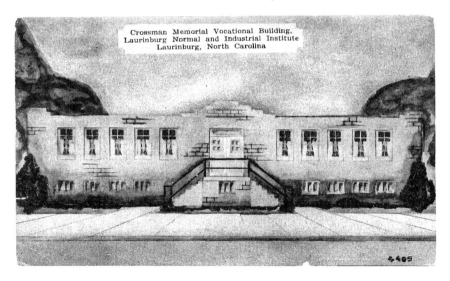

Crossman Memorial Vocational Building, Laurinburg Institute (ca. 1910), was the site of the initial vocational classes in sewing, cooking, housekeeping, laundering, farming, wheelwrighting and blacksmithing (author's collection).

such organization involves friction, daily embarrassment, and apparent disadvantages of educational progress, ... [however] at Laurinburg Institute the ironing board, the dust pan, the frying pan, the hammer, the saw, the brace, the bit, the plow, became the allies of the crayon, the blackboard, the map, and the book from the beginning, but the first Industrial class was in 1912.[25]

Providing a foundation for skilled labor and agricultural progress was entirely necessary for the well-being of the community at large. It was also critical for the running of the school.

Courses were offered in sewing, cooking, housekeeping, laundering, farming, wheelwrighting and blacksmithing. Eventually, auto mechanics, brick masonry, plastering and printing press programs were added as opportunities for jobs developed beyond farming and housekeeping. These programs not only prepared students to earn a living but they also benefited the school, which depended upon the income derived from the students' labor and provided food for the students' and staff's meals. The boys were required to work on the school farm one weekday per week plus all day Saturday. They also participated in the construction of various school buildings. Girls maintained the school with kitchen, laundry and housekeeping duties.

The teachers came from some of the best black schools in the South and included graduates from Tuskegee Institute, Shaw University, Snow Hill Institute, Fisk University, Claflin University and Benedict College. McDuffie's brother-in-law and fellow Snow Hill graduate, I. Ellis Johnson joined the faculty in 1912 and remained until 1953. Because of a technicality concerning state qualifications in 1932, Johnson assumed the title of Principal while McDuffie became the president, remaining in full control of the Institute.[26] I. Ellis Johnson's brother, Hamilton H. Johnson became the Treasurer of the school. Tinny McDuffie, who was also a Snow Hill graduate, was chief cook and bottle washer for the school. She supervised the maintenance, food, laundry and care of the boarding students in particular, as well as providing for her own large family. Six of her seven children taught at the Institute after graduating from college. Her sister Amanda Johnson prepared lunches for the public school children who joined the Institute around 1910.

The Laurinburg Graded School District Makes a Deal with the Institute

The General Statutes of North Carolina as early as 1868, and repeated until 1943, stated "the children of the white race and the children of the colored race shall be taught in separate public schools; but there shall be no discrimination in favor of, or to the prejudice of either race."[27] The North Carolina legislature created the Laurinburg Graded School District in 1909, which included all of Scotland County and specified the responsibilities of education for both white and black children. At that time a $30,000 bond issue provided the funds to build Central School, the first public school in Scotland County for white students. It offered grades one through 11. The black citizens were promised a third of the bond issue to build a public school for their children. Instead, the school board made an agreement with Emmanuel McDuffie to educate all the black students in the community. In 1901 there were 21 small black public schools in the county but these schools only offered elementary education through the second grade.[28]

The Laurinburg Institute was granted $700 per year for the support of teacher salaries for all high school black students in Scotland County and many local kids as well, grades kindergarten through eighth grade.[29] The 1910 census showed that blacks made up over 55 percent of the Scotland County population. This investiture by the school board in the Institute showed that they recognized the good work that McDuffie was doing in raising his race through education, but the small amount of financial support, which was entirely unequal with the white support, reflected badly on the board. They failed their fellow black citizens and further burdened McDuffie with the responsibility of raising funds to provide the best education he could. The unusual deal between the public local school board and the privately owned Laurinburg Institute proved to be a great bone of contention between the black community and the white community for years to come.

The Ninth Annual Report of the Principal and Treasurer (1914)

By the year 1914, Emmanuel McDuffie could report substantial accomplishments of the school in his annual report which follows. Claiming that "Negroes outnumber the whites three to one" in the county, McDuffie listed 14 teachers for 474 public and boarding students from North and South Carolina, Georgia, Virginia, and Kentucky. McDuffie noted that all his teachers were required to do community service.

Religious services were held morning and evening in the chapel by the Rev. Larkin King, a Snow Hill graduate who joined the staff in 1912. A YMCA program was offered for boys and a Missionary Society for girls. The students ran a Sunday night program called Christian Endeavors, which became a tradition at the school lasting more than a hundred years.

Graduating students were mostly teachers but all students graduated with a "knowledge of some trade so as to make an intelligent living with their hands."[30] McDuffie compared the earning capacity of his students to uneducated blacks in the community by saying that, before graduating from the Institute, they could earn "50c a day and 3 pounds of meat and a peck of meal per week" while, after graduation, they were earning "almost $45.00 per month."[31] The trade courses offered paying jobs for students as well.

A print shop, supervised by the Rev. Larkin King, was established on campus, which served both the needs of the Institute as well as the public. It employed 14 boys and offered work year round. The shop printed monthly *The Eastern Searchlight*, which informed donors about the Institute's accomplishments and needs, as well as the bi-weekly *Community Guide,* which served the local black community.

Oak and sycamore trees were planted and an orchard of fruit trees. The boys' dormitory Edwards Hall was recovered in brick. All the other buildings were painted.

The income for the year 1913 to 1914 was $10,433.64. The Laurinburg School Board gave $700 for teacher salaries, but the school had to raise the remaining $2,300 in order to meet its salary costs. Other income included $1,730.10 for tuition and $922.65 from industry such as printing and agricultural sales. Donors made up the majority of funds with $6,360.35. These donors were listed meticulously by name and amount they donated. Many donations were small, between $1 and $5, though a few ranged up to $250. In my review of the donors, I could find no prominent white person from Laurinburg on the list. Most of the funds were raised by thousands of letters to Northern potential donors. Donors also gave clothes, shoes and books for the needy children.

Bigelow Memorial Hospital and Dr. Nathan E. Jackson

Perhaps the most impressive accomplishment of the Institute in 1914 was the building of a hospital, which served both the Institute staff and students and also members of the black community. Bigelow Memorial Hospital, a two-story wooden building, was constructed on the Laurinburg Institute campus in memory of Caroline T. Bigelow of Brookline, Massachusetts.[32] In order to care for the health of the black community, McDuffie raised $2,000 to build the Bigelow Memorial Hospital. The students and parents provided the labor to build the hospital, which proved their support of the project and saved money for the school.[33]

McDuffie brought the first black doctor to Laurinburg, hiring Dr. Nathaniel E. Jackson to serve the community as well as care for the Institute students. The hospital, "modernly equipped with [an] operating room" and a registered nurse, offered opportunities for the female students of the Institute to study nursing under Dr. Jackson and his staff. A three year curriculum was added for nurse training.[34] White local physicians contributed "both service and influence to make the hospital succeed," especially, Dr. D.M. Prince was "a substantial promoter" of the medical facility.[35] The Institute also hired a dentist and created a pharmacy to serve the students and the wider black community. Walter Evans provided "up-to-date" office spaces off campus on Main Street for the doctor and dentist as well.[36]

Dr. Jackson directed the hospital for more than fifty years beginning shortly after his graduation from Leanard Medical College in

Dr. Nathaniel E. Jackson (ca. 1950–1960), was the director of Bigelow Hospital, built in 1914 on the Laurinburg Institute campus, which served all the black community as well as students. Portrait is from *Heritage of Scotland County North Carolina—2003*, 290 (courtesy of Fannie Jackson Gilmore and Sara Stewart).

Raleigh in 1907 and postgraduate work at Howard University in Washington, D.C., and in Philadelphia. He specialized in obstetrics and gynecology, but being the only black physician and surgeon in the area, Jackson treated everyone in the community and beyond. He was a consultant at the Leroy-Perry Hospital in Fayetteville and a member of the staff at the Scotland County and Hamlet Hospitals.[37]

Jackson provided a clinic for pre-school children who had physical handicaps. His daughter Fannie Jackson Gilmore reported he "visited practically every

African-American home in Laurinburg, often without compensation for his services."[38] She recalled that he was rarely paid in cash but with produce—eggs, chickens and pork. "A patient would call and cry to my dad that the hog had died. My father would ask if his part of the hog died, too."[39]

Jackson loved tennis and had a tennis court in his back yard. His daughters recalled that the whole community would come over on Wednesday afternoons when the stores closed at 1 o'clock to play tennis. His sons, Nathaniel and Franklyn, were champion tennis players, along with Emmanuel "Mac" McDuffie, who won many trophies in Northern tournaments. His daughters, Marcelle Jackson Bethea and Fannie Jackson Gilmore, taught school at the segregated Laurinburg public schools after 1953, and, later, at the integrated schools for over 40 years.[40]

A Newspaper Reporter's View of the 1914 Institute Graduation Ceremony

A reporter from the *Laurinburg Exchange* offered this review of the 1914 commencement proceedings, where he learned that the Institute "gives a thorough English education" as well as a "moral, religious and industrial" one.[41] McDuffie himself read the Harvard Classics and encouraged his students to do likewise.[42] The reporter was amazed at the "musical numbers, in which those taking part exhibited more than ordinary ability," and he was also impressed with the four orations given on the subject of "Some Results of Industrial Education among the Colored People of the South." He noted that "These orations were far above the ordinary and the speakers in their selection of language, delivery and collection of subject matter reflected the great credit upon Prof. McDuffie and his teachers, and we venture the assertion that there are not fifty white people in Laurinburg who know just what a work is being done in McDuffie's school."[43]

Following the lead of Booker T. Washington and William J. Edwards, the McDuffies designed their school so that the students would not only learn basic academic skills but also acquire "industrial" skills. These skills answered the practical needs of their own community and prepared them for jobs within the larger community controlled by whites. Reflecting the example of Tuskegee, McDuffie joined training with labor to build and support the school itself. Very little cash was available among self-subsistence farmers so the school accepted farm goods or labor in exchange for education.

In the early years, the Laurinburg Institute offered classes in subjects that would train women to find jobs as cooks and housekeepers and men to find employment as farm workers. Later on, automobile mechanics, brick masonry and plastering were added to the industrial training program. The *Laurinburg Exchange* reporter was impressed not only with the academic demonstrations of the students but also with the handicrafts exhibited at the 1914 commencement. Besides examples of printing, blacksmithing, and sewing, he noted particularly "a variety of articles, such as baskets, hats and numerous fancy receptacles woven out of pine straw."[44] I well remember the handmade pine straw baskets we had in our home.

Leading by Example and Supporting Local Farmers

The McDuffies owned their own home and led by example for productive citizens to own property and contribute to the tax base. They also sought to improve "the moral tone" of the black community by sending their students out into the community and "reaching the masses" to live the "sober side of life" and "awakening the dormant energies of the Negro for good."[45] Emmanuel McDuffie was far more than a teacher. He was a visionary, sparked by the missionary zeal of William Edwards and Booker T. Washington, to reach far beyond the mere classroom to enlighten the wider black community, preparing them for an independent future.

The Jeanes Foundation supported the school's establishment as well as the Institute's extension work, which included training farmers to improve their crops, spreading to 3,000 or more persons in the community. Besides teaching within the school, McDuffie reached out to the black community, particularly the black farmers, to teach them better agricultural practices, such as rotating crops and improving the quality of the soil. In the early years, McDuffie would ride horseback out into the country where he would meet with the farmers and encourage them to practice good agricultural methods. Having been a student at Tuskegee, where George Washington Carver founded the Farmers' Institute in the early 1900s, McDuffie learned about crop rotation and other beneficial methods to improve animal husbandry. Shortie Hall, a Laurinburg Institute faculty member, described Mr. McDuffie's dedication to the black community and the respect he earned from them in return:

> ... he never for a moment forgot his people and his relation to them. If he found a destitute family, he could, and often did, seek to relieve their

distress immediately. He had included in the Laurinburg Institute budget a small fund for that very purpose.

There is a story about McDuffy [*sic*] and President Hoover's visit to North Carolina. It appears that the President wanted to hunt rabbit in the area. A "colored" man in the neighborhood was said to have good hunting dogs, and a Secret Service agent was sent to the man's house to ask to borrow the dogs. The Negro firmly denied the request. The Secret Service man protested, "Don't you understand it's the President of the United States who is asking for your dogs?" The Negro was still firm. "He can't have 'em. Can't nobody have 'em. Not even Mr. 'Manuel McDuffy hisself can have 'em."[46]

McDuffie organized a farmers' conference, which was attended by hundreds of men, women and children. Through practical demonstrations, the farmers learned new techniques to improve their crops. McDuffie inspired the attendees with "the new truth and the new light ... pointing them on to a better way."[47] By 1917 McDuffie could report that "now, both white and black have taken the deepest interest in the work and we now have the absolute confidence of all the people."[48]

Besides McDuffie's close association with Booker T. Washington and Tuskegee Institute, he also maintained close ties with William Edwards and Snow Hill Institute. Donald Stone, a descendant of Edwards, recalled that the Laurinburg Institute "was Snow Hill's proudest accomplishment. The bond between Snow Hill and Laurinburg was especially deep."[49] William Edwards, the founder of Snow Hill and mentor to the McDuffies, visited the Institute on a number of occasions and even sent his son Wendell to finish school at Laurinburg Institute. The first permanent building, the boys' dormitory and grammar school building, was named for Edwards. He made the commencement address at the Institute in 1932.

Edwards founded the Black Belt Improvement League in 1925. Emmanuel McDuffie was appointed to the Board of Directors. With the motto, "Back to the farm," the league supported land acquisition by black farmers by creating a $25,000 fund, which was loaned out to applicants for the purchase of homes and farms. The league also encouraged the beautification of homes and offered prizes for best farm, garden and poultry farm. The health of communities was promoted by erecting Y.M.C.A.s wherever possible. The league sought out the best markets for agricultural products and promoted friendly relations among the races.[50] McDuffie served on the board until the league was disbanded in 1941.

*The Colored Civic League
and the Rev. Larkin L. King*

Proof of the McDuffies' impact on the local black community was borne out by the founding of the Colored Civic League by associates of the Laurinburg Institute in 1915. The Rev. Larkin L. King directed the program. King had been friends with McDuffie and Johnson at the Snow Hill Institute in Alabama. McDuffie encouraged him to come to Laurinburg in 1912. King taught printing classes at the Laurinburg Institute and served as the chaplain of the school.[51] Many of the original Institute postcards and *The Eastern Searchlight* publications, which so eloquently publicized the school, were produced in King's printing classes.

The objective of the Colored Civic League was to support the youth and encourage them to "stay at home, and uplift their fellows, to beautify their homes, encourage the education of the young and the dignity of labor, to teach the young people to have what they make, to be polite and self-reliant, and to become Christians and Sunday school workers."[52] They also promoted good sanitary conditions and the health of their community.

By 1927 the Colored Civic League had six small buildings which included the Hallowell-Wellington Kindergarten, named for two women from Massachusetts who donated the funds to build the school. The kindergarten provided care for up to 120 pupils aged 3 to 6 years old. The kindergarten was operated as a non-profit and charged ten cents a week for care and meals per child. Transportation was a problem for the children so the Reverend King bought an old hearse from the McDougald Funeral Home and refurbished it with benches for the kids to use and also to provide bus service for others in need.[53]

A Miss McLean remembered teaching there in the 1940s. She said the children were divided into two groups, the beginners and those that were preparing for first grade. Materials for class were printed in-house by the Reverend King's students. She taught Bible lessons, music, the alphabet, the numbers 1–100, recognizing colors and even beginning reading. The children also learned to share because of "the very limited number of toys" and to take turns on the slide and swings.[54] Graduation day was a big event for the families of the children, who dressed in caps and gowns as they marched for their diplomas.

The Civic League also sponsored a welfare department which supported those in need with clothes and food. Sewing classes were offered to teach girls to make their own clothes. Additional classes in printing, typewriting, music, and Bible training were taught. They also maintained the only public library in the area available to blacks with more than 8,000 books and open six days a week.

Teachers' Institute

In the summer of 1915 the North Carolina State Department of Education provided summer Teachers' Institutes for the improvement of instruction in the schools. The Scotland County Teachers' Institute for black teachers was conducted at the Laurinburg Institute. The two week program was attended by 32 black teachers, six more than attended the white program. The black teachers were eager to learn new skills that would improve their instruction techniques. Prof. Levister of Shaw University in Raleigh directed the program.[55] Encouraged by the attention given to his school by the State, McDuffie wrote to Nathan C. Newbold, the white General Education Board Agent for black education in North Carolina, asking him to come visit the Institute in the fall of 1915. Stating plainly, "I need you to help me," McDuffie expressed his determination to bring his secondary school up to the highest standard the state required.[56] He emphasized the industrial aspect of the school and described the positive impact of the school on the black community. Newbold responded that "our greatest need is ... well-trained teachers for white and colored schools. If you can organize a teacher-training course in your school, I feel quite sure it will be of great assistance to your people in that section of the State."[57]

Agent Newbold visited the faculty at Laurinburg Institute in December 1915 and encouraged them to shift away from farming and commercial job training to a stronger academic program which would prepare students to go on to college and to enter the teaching, medical and law professions. After a statewide survey, Newbold reported that there was a need for 325 teachers in the North Carolina black public school system and only 130 teachers expected to be graduating from teacher-training programs.[58] Laurinburg Institute, then, gradually strengthened its academic program so that it would better prepare students to go on to college and, in turn, strengthen the North Carolina public education system with well-educated teachers.

8

Raising Funds from the North for Southern Black Children

The Jeanes Foundation originally funded the establishment of the Institute. Around 1910, the town of Laurinburg provided only $700 for the education of 400 or more local students. Boarding students usually paid in goods or labor since there was little cash available to their families. Some income came from the produce and industrial goods produced by those students at the Institute. Following the example of Booker T. Washington, McDuffie turned to the North in order to raise funds for Southern black children.

McDuffie created a newsletter, which was printed in the Laurinburg Institute print shop run by Chaplain Larkin King. It was called *The Eastern Searchlight* with the motto, "A Light Shining in Darkness." This newsletter was directed mostly to Northern philanthropists who bought subscriptions and provided financial support for the Institute. The four page monthly newsletter contained photographs of the school and illustrated student activities. An account of accomplishments would be given as well as pleas for funds to support particular needs of the school, such as prize money for excellent student achievements, salaries for teachers, physical plant maintenance and new buildings.

The Eastern Searchlight appealed to donors through human interest stories such as the following 1949 account by the Institute graduate Nancy Green, who writes from Howard University:

> I have worked hard since being here, and I don't mean to let up because you and the teachers there taught us that keeping everlastingly at it would bring success. However, it has been hard going to stay here. One time I was just about to give up college, but…. I received a Searchlight and I remembered how I use[d] to hold them and help prepare them for mailing. The little paper inspired me when I read of what the former graduates of Laurinburg

are contribut-
ing to the world.
It made me real-
ize that I too have
a goal to reach and
if they have done
it, I can do it.... I
will never let you
and Laurinburg
Institute down....
I am working hard
because I came
here for a purpose
and I am willing
to make any sacri-
fice in order to ful-
fill it.[1]

Green echoes the
same firm resolve
that McDuffie
declared when he
attended Snow Hill
Institute. It makes
one realize just
how much one can
accomplish if you
change just one life
for good. That good
ripples out to the
broader world and
multiplies from gen-
eration to genera-
tion. McDuffie had

THE EASTERN SEARCHLIGHT

A LIGHT SHINING IN DARKNESS

VOL. 19   LAURINBURG, N. C.   APRIL 1949   NO. 10

ANNUAL PRIZE FUND

Due to lack of money and hard trials we have had this term, our students are wondering will friends be able to give anything toward prizes this year. Many of them have already requested t h a t we write for information regarding this fund and we are taking space to invite attention of friends to this article.

Will not someone give one of the following prizes? Two $5.00 prizes for the printing department. One $5.00 for the best student in agriculture.

One $5.00 prize for the most efficient waitress in the dining room.

One $10.00 prize f o r Home Economics.

One $10.00 prize for the best all around Bible student.

One $10.00 prize for the best essay on Health Conservation.

Fifty dollars will provide for all the prizes named above.

We will thank any friend who will turn a listening ear to this item of our needs.

GENERAL EXPENSES
$3,000 WILL COMPLETE FUND AND CLOSE SCHOOL FREE OF DEBT

Dear Readers:

I hope you will not class me as burdensome f o r bringing this matter to your attention again, but the end of t h e term is near at hand and I believe the friends of the school and readers of this little paper will do as much to help close the year free of debt now as they have done in former years, so I am sending this reminder that you may know just how close we have come to our goal.

I am trying to complete a fund of $15,000 for salaries and general expenses and if I c a n secure $3,000 the school will again close free of debt just as it has done during its 44 years of existence. One friend has given $150.00 and will give $100.00 more if I can secure the remaining sum. As most of our readers helped with these items last term, I am hoping that each one may be able to do as much for the work again just now. The least amount, even one dollar will be helpful and the same will be highly appreciated.

The Eastern Searchlight (April 1949), was a monthly publication of Laurinburg Institute to inform donors and supporters about the needs and accomplishments of the school for many decades (courtesy of the Scotland County Memorial Library, Special Collections, Laurinburg, N.C.).

his eye on the future where the seeds he planted became as spreading grass covering a vast field.

Besides the newsletter, Director Emmanuel McDuffie, Dean I. Ellis Johnson, Amanda Johnson and Treasurer Hamilton Johnson wrote countless letters, some handwritten and some typed, for nearly 40-plus years. The letters from "the Black Belt of North Carolina" were formulated and repeated the same messages with slight adjustments relative to the latest disaster or the latest need. M.H. Harding, Director of The National Information Bureau, made inquiries in 1931 with the State Division of Negro Education:

Mr. McDuffie, for a number of years, has been basing his appeals to givers on what he states to be terrible crises such as fire, pestilence, etc., and more recently on the run on the First National Bank and the Scotland County Savings Bank in which "the funds of the School went down in the crash." He talks about the "tragedy of having to hear 600 boys and girls crying because they must be put out of school this term."[2]

Harding goes on to say that the amount of money requested varies and is usually connected to teacher salaries, half of which public officials will pay, but McDuffie claims he must raise the rest.[3]

Letters were sent as far away as Alaska, where both the *Seaward Daily Journal* and the *Juneau Empire* published articles about how "hard hit" the school had been as a result of the closures of two banks, where the Institute had deposited its money.[4] The Johnson brothers' letters emphasized the "great burden" that McDuffie carried and they appealed for financial support to "save his health and prolong his life."[5]

These emotional appeals were effective. By 1917 the Laurinburg Institute had 14 teachers and around four hundred local students as well as boarding students from North Carolina, Virginia, South Carolina, and Georgia. The residential students initially were boarded in local homes. When the number of boarding students grew beyond the local capacity, McDuffie's vigorous financial campaign raised enough funds to build dormitories, a hospital and both academic and industrial buildings so that by 1917, McDuffie could boast, "counting land, livestock, five large and three small buildings, [the Institute] has a property valuation of $30,000 all free of debt."[6] Emmanuel McDuffie was included in the 1921 edition of *History of American Negro,* where the editor offered this praise: "His work at Laurinburg has been of such character as to commend it not only to the colored people but also to the best white people, including bankers and State and County officers, from whom he bears words of hearty commendation."[7]

Emily Howland was one of the northern donors who substantially supported the Institute. She was a Quaker abolitionist and philanthropist from Sherwood, New York, who both taught blacks and served as director of the black refugee Camp Todd in Arlington, Virginia, during the Civil War.[8] A postcard addressed to Emily Howland from the Laurinburg Institute and illustrating the original Emily Howland Hall and girls' dormitory establishes their connection at least as early as 1912. The note on the card read: "This is only a token of appreciation for the many good things which you have done for us. May God continue to bless you. ... From your girls of The Laurinburg N & I Institute."[9] The original wooden building succumbed to fire in 1923, when the students were all in chapel. It was later replaced by a brick building simply called

Howland Hall. The McDuffie family and female teachers lived on the second floor with a parlor for the girls and teachers, the girls on the upper floors, and the first floor housed the cafeteria, laundry and kitchen.

Emily Howland (ca. 1897), was one of the first large donors to the Laurinburg Institute. As a Quaker, she served as director of the black refugee Camp Todd in Arlington, Virginia, during the Civil War. The girls' dormitory Howland Hall was funded by her in 1912. Portrait is from *American Women: Fifteen Hundred Biographies with Over 1,400 Portraits*, 1897.

Other large benefactors included B.N. Duke, who gave $25,000. The gift was made on condition that the school raise a matching amount in order to found an endowment in 1925.[10] He later added an additional $25,000 to the fund.

Small, as well as large, donations were solicited all over the country. The female students of Wellesley College in Massachusetts wrote articles in their college newspaper praising the faculty of Laurinburg Institute for their accomplishments and encouraging their own students to contribute to the school Service Fund. Jessie Benson wrote that the "sum will go to help educate another useful citizen for our country, perhaps a girl your own age. Give and Laurinburg Institute will thank you!"[11] The Wellesley girls gave $140 to the Institute in 1943. Vassar girls also contributed to Laurinburg Institute in 1940. The school newspaper reported that Miss Helen Sandison, a faculty member of the English Department, had

> ... checked carefully on the rating and record of Laurinburg, and was so impressed with what she found that she consented to represent it.... [The Institute has] an A-rating in North Carolina, and educating nearly 1000

Howland Hall, girls' dormitory at the Laurinburg Institute (ca. 1925), original wooden building ca. 1912 (courtesy of Durwood Barbour Collection of North Carolina Postcards, Wilson Special Collections Library, UNC–Chapel Hill, P0077; 8-62).

students a year. Thirty-five teachers work in good buildings, some of them brick.

And yet, the total annual budget (1939) is a meager $34,000, the full teaching budget only $19,000—for those thirty-five teachers! The figure tells how far every dollar must go. The chief needs are for salaries, upkeep and essential extension of plant, and aid to boys and girls who have not clothes or books to get them through the school year.[12]

Funds were also raised locally by both white and black citizens through fairs and festivals. Local people would donate goods, such as a dozen eggs or a side of hog, and the other citizens would purchase the donated items. This method often was used to raise funds for immediate needs such as sports equipment and band instruments. Mrs. Amanda McDuffie (perhaps Johnson) was a "devoted helper" in these endeavors, leading the charge in "securing funds to meet the payments on the property."[13]

Boarding students paid $12 per month for room and board plus $2 for monthly tuition. Emmanuel McDuffie always believed in providing a musical education as well as an academic education for his students. On their admission forms, boarding students were asked what trade they wished to pursue, "Do you intend to become a teacher?" and "Will you study instrumental music?"[14] McDuffie realized that students could earn a living by any of these methods. The school also received support from the trade and music training programs.

By the 1930s the Laurinburg Institute band became an orchestra, which played at large functions for hire, or a smaller swing band, which travelled the surrounding counties playing for dances for both white and black folk. Shortie Hall, the band director, and the student trumpeter Dizzy Gillespie played for these gatherings. The bands were in high demand and produced a regular source of income for the school. During the war, the officers at the Laurinburg-Maxton Airbase often hired Hall to play for their parties.

The Laurinburg Institute also became well-known for its choral program, which won many state competitions under the direction of Frank McDuffie. Emmanuel McDuffie said, "I may send singers north and elsewhere … in order to obtain the necessary funds to continue our expansion...."[15] William Maize confirmed that the Institute chorus "has touched both the hearts and pocket-books of great numbers of listeners."[16]

The faculty member Shortie Hall recalled that funds were so short that even the faculty were required to contribute a fixed amount to the school fund each payday. His monthly salary was $80. Hall and his friend J.T. Speller, who eventually became the principal of I. Ellis Johnson School and East Laurinburg Elementary School, resented having their wages garnished, calling the practice "robbery" because "no one ever told them what the money was used for."[17] However, Hall knew that McDuffie often came to the assistance of needy folks in the wider community.

9

Educating the Public
Within a Private Institution

Booker T. Washington originally had emphasized the industrial element of his schools because he wanted his students to aid him in constructing the school itself and, furthermore, he wanted to provide them with the knowledge they needed to learn a craft that would support them after graduation. The opportunity for a college education was almost impossible for a black man at that time especially in the South. Washington gradually built a college level program at Tuskegee Normal and Industrial Institute and, by 1912, he no longer was urging his graduates to found industrial schools but to concentrate on founding normal schools, which would provide teachers for a public education system.[1]

Although educators such as Booker T. Washington and William DuBois were advocating for an education system which would lift blacks away from their traditional slave roles as agricultural workers and house servants, other men supported maintaining those roles through black training schools. In 1917 the U.S. Bureau of Education, with the support of the private Phelps-Stokes Fund, hired Thomas Jesse Jones, a "specialist in the education of racial groups," to conduct a national survey and create a report concerning the education of black people. The two volume result, *Negro Education,* described the abysmal conditions of black educational systems nationwide, but "accepted racial segregation and emphasized the need for … a different kind of instruction and curriculum in black schools."[2] For reasons as varied as lack of intelligence and the need for hard labor, Jones advocated for black vocational training schools with little or no opportunities for academic education which might lead to more professional careers and a better life beyond the fields and servitude. This study founded a decades long official policy for the inferior education of blacks.

Emmanuel McDuffie walked a tightrope between the "industrial"

Ninth grade public school children (1937), with private students together at the Laurinburg Institute (courtesy of Myrtle Ware and John and Sara Stewart, *Images of America: Scotland County,* 2001).

training school and the "normal" academic school. His Snow Hill mentor William Edwards was a strong advocate for solid academics, and, with the encouragement of the director of the Division of Negro Education Nathan C. Newbold, McDuffie began to move in the direction of stronger academics to supply the teachers so badly needed. A brief overview of North Carolina's education system for blacks follows, as well as a discussion of the unique role Laurinburg Institute played as a private school educating public school children.

Funding a North Carolina State Black Public Education System

The Southern Education Board and the General Education Board (GEB) were founded at the turn of the century by Southern leaders and Northern funding. Rockefeller backed the GEB. These organizations worked to establish mostly white schools across the South.[3] As stated,

Laurinburg voted for a bond issue that would build the first white graded public school, Central School, in 1909. The black community understood that the $30,000 bond would include a $10,000 black school as well. This promise was not fulfilled.[4]

The George Peabody Fund and the John F. Slater Fund supported the establishment of black colleges and preparatory schools. In North Carolina, church denominations founded four black colleges. The Presbyterians founded Barber-Scotia College in Concord and Biddle Institute (later Johnson C. Smith University) in Charlotte. The Episcopalians built St. Augustine College in Raleigh and the African Methodist Episcopal Zion Church established Livingstone College in Salisbury.[5]

The Anna T. Jeanes Fund supported black teacher training and salaries while the Rosenwald Fund provided matching funds for building black schools. The North Carolina State Division of Negro Education Director Nathan Newbold recognized early on that these philanthropies would be important sources to aid him in building a firm foundation for the black public education system. He contacted Booker T. Washington's supporter and head of Sears, Roebuck and Company Julius Rosenwald in 1915, before his fund was set up in 1917, and asked him to build a school for blacks in Chowan County, which he did.[6]

Agent Nathan C. Newbold became the director of the North Carolina Division of Negro Education in 1921. He created five positions on his staff to handle the Rosenwald funding including the white W.F. Credle, Supervisor of the Rosenwald Fund, and the black G.E. Davis, Supervisor of Rosenwald Buildings. These three men and the white W.A. Robinson, Supervisor of Teacher-Training and High Schools, formed close relationships with Emmanuel McDuffie. They often lodged at the Laurinburg Institute and even wrote letters under the Institute letterhead.

Over a period of time from 1918 to 1930, these men, with the support of the Rosenwald Fund, built 14 small brick school houses for black students in Scotland County. These schools offered grades one through eight. One of the stipulations of the Rosenwald Fund was that matching funds must be raised by both the white and the black communities. This requirement offered an opportunity for a meeting of the minds of the often opposing races. It also offered whites the chance to do good for the blacks and create a more harmonious environment where trust could begin. These critically important programs, founded by Rosenwald and Jeanes, ended up funding over 800 small black schools in North Carolina, more than in any other state in the South.

McDuffie earned the trust of Newbold, Credle, Robinson and Davis. While overseeing the building of Rosenwald schools in Scotland County and inspecting the Laurinburg Institute in 1924, George Davis wrote to Newbold: "May I say I am impressed very favorably with all I saw—the very excellent buildings, and the fine group of teachers. I am confident Mr. McDuffie is doing a very fine grade of work.... Mr. McDuffie is quite anxious to come up to our state requirements and I am sure he will."[7] Davis gave the commencement address at the Institute in May of that year.[8]

In 1920, the city of Laurinburg floated bonds for $150,000 to build a white public high school, which was completed in 1923.[9] As it had done in the past, the Laurinburg School Board offered the Institute $2,000 per year in exchange for educating the Laurinburg black children including elementary, intermediate and all county high school levels. The funds offered were hardly sufficient for 600-plus local students, in addition to the boarding students from outside the region. Nonetheless, the State of North Carolina accredited Laurinburg Institute in June 1924 and provided some funds for teachers' salaries.[10]

Not only did McDuffie establish mutually respectful relationships with the State but he also earned the respect of white people in Laurinburg. Maxcy John wrote the following glowing report to Newbold in a 1927 letter:

> [McDuffie] is a quiet, capable man, says enough but is never very talkative. He knows the races and understands the necessity for contacts that must be without friction. He has no admiration for the subservient hambone member of the race only as his services and honesty entitle him to respect; but he believes in respect to all men who are worthy of it, be they white or black. He believes that the colored race is necessary to the success of the white race, and the white race in the south and the colored race must live together in peace and harmony, if the colored race is to achieve its highest ends. He believes in work for the laboring man and tries to make the boys and girls see that the most of them must go to work and work hard at difficult and often dirty work if they are to succeed; and that they must be reliable in their dealings with all, and especially in their relations to their work.
>
> The principal has no illusions. He understands the racial industrial and political situation and the relation of the race to it and the white race in regards thereto, as fully as did Booker T. Washington. Professor McDuffie is an asset to any southern community, or would be if he were living [in] it.[11]

One can read between the lines here the white refrain that the black man should "know his place" and that that place is as a laborer for the white man. Through the encouragement of Newbold and Washington, Emmanuel McDuffie began to shift his attention to the academic training of his students, which would prepare them for the newly established black colleges and for work beyond hard labor. This move did not please everyone.

Newbold received many inquiries from Northern philanthropists asking for information about the Laurinburg Institute. The donors complained of being flooded with requests for support from McDuffie, and they needed confirmation that the Institute was trying legitimately to fill the need for education of black children because the State and the local board of education were not meeting the need. Newbold responded that "for a number of years we did everything we could to aid in having the [Laurinburg Institute] high school standardized," and he wrote many letters recommending the school after visiting the Institute on a number of occasions.[12]

He also recognized the great burden that McDuffie was under and knew that the school did not meet state standards. As an example from 1926 to 1927, Newbold related that the Institute had 11 teachers for 788 students, which was about half of the number of teachers per student needed.[13] He told one potential donor that the Laurinburg Institute was "the last of the schools that is existing only on the principle of begging for support," and that it was humiliating for the town of Laurinburg, which "is one of the wealthiest communities in North Carolina," not to provide a public school for black children. In fact, "the influential white people [of Laurinburg] … seemly have taken the attitude that it is all right for the community to have its Negro children educated by the white people from outside the state; in fact they seem quite content to have this arrangement, and even lend their assistance to the principal in pulling money out of other people's pockets."[14] Newbold repeatedly told donors that the shameful situation in Laurinburg was due to the lack of white support for black education where "to this day it has no public school whatever for Negroes" and that McDuffie, in spite of his "secretiveness" in providing verifiable information on the financial and administrative affairs of the Institute, was dutifully fulfilling his obligations to educate black children as best he could.[15]

Controversy Over the Lack of a Public Black School, 1926–1927

The white community built Central School in 1909, offering $700 to the McDuffies to educate all black high school and many lower grade students. By 1920, the Laurinburg Graded Schools were allowed to offer bonds for $150,000 in order to build the Laurinburg High School, again another white school.[16] No funds were allocated for a public black school yet again. A growing dissatisfaction with this state of affairs among the black community began to boil over into appeals to the State for help.

The following table, showing white and black educational expenditures and facilities in Scotland County from 1905 to 1930, was collated by Roger McGirt for his master's thesis at UNC from the superintendents' biennial reports to the State[17]:

	1905	1910	1915	1920	1925	1930
Enrolled						
White	765	1761	2154	1720	2120	2279
Black	1761	2369	3186	2982	3320	3258
Attendance						
White	445	1257	1759	1185	1679	1839
Black	794	1539	2735	2110	2203	2265
Number of Schools						
White	24	23	24	21	16	6
Black	19	22	22	23	27	30
Term Length in Days						
White	84	111	143	137.6	171	171
Black	81	100	102.9	111.2	129	120
Teachers						
White	27	34	49	60	71	76
Black	21	29	40	49	56	69

By 1930, Scotland County ranked 43rd in the state for white schools and 65th for black students. Besides the fact that white students received more teachers than blacks for considerably less enrollment, which always had been the case, two facts appear outstanding. As the white schools consolidated from 24 down to 6 campuses, they were supplied with 19 school buses by 1930. Black students had no buses at all.[18] Many attended small one-teacher schools around the county until the eighth grade and, then, dropped out due to lack of transportation to the Institute high school. The other outstanding fact shows that, at first, school terms for both whites and blacks were almost equal, but by 1915 through 1930, there was increasingly a considerable difference, from 41 to 51 days, between whites' time in school and blacks' school time. This drastic cut in school time for black students also put heavy burdens on the teachers who did not receive pay for those cut days and often had to take jobs outside school to make up the difference.

In his assessment of these facts, Roger McGirt stated that the "problem of educating the ... negroes of the county is a serious one. ... buildings are inadequate and the equipment is poor."[19] He viewed the most serious problem for the blacks was the "poor attendance" of the "tenant classes," which caused "many over age pupils" who were trying to catch up due to their lack of attendance. Scotland County ranked 100th or last in the state for black attendance. McGirt advocated for a full time welfare or truant officer who would encourage students to return to school. Black citizens such as Walter Evans also pressed the State to do something for the black students.

Walter Evans made numerous attempts to encourage the Scotland County school board to provide a public school for black children. When he learned in 1927 that $12,000 had been allocated by the State to Scotland County for the "Equalization of the State public school[s]," Evans appealed to white Dr. W.E. Shaw, who was "an exponent of the people's rights in law, equity, education and even medicine" and a member of the Scotland County school board. The letter, which Evans copied to Newbold, reflects Evans' frustrations after thirty years of unheeded pleas. His own words deserve to be repeated here:

> We do not clamor for your mayoralities, nor your sheriffalities, nor your town commissioners or your county commissioners, or county offices or mixed school houses, thereby peacefully surrendering all our citizens' rights to any and all political affiliations; because of all this we do feel that you should be diligent in seeing that we are instantly clothed in our fullest educational rights....
>
> As a businessman I attach much importance to economy in all phases of private as well as public life. But my people cannot understand why one set of tax paying citizen's application for necessary school building should be tabled on the grounds of economy or insufficient funds; when the other set at the same time enjoy the expenditures of possibly $300,000 for school building and equipment and my set still remain jammed in a rented building and constantly paying taxes for graded school building. We sincerely pray that your board come to the relief of this struggling humble mass of Colored Citizens and give us a promise and hope now, realizing that black humanity is but the same as white humanity and that hope deferred maketh any human heart sick.
>
> The progress of the times carry with it civic and town pride in the black man's breast as well as the white man's and we when comparing our school facilities with those of other schools elsewhere and find ourselves at the foot of the ladder without a town owned graded school building, the winter of our discontent sets in upon us and a chilly fog engulfs us because the Negroes' school houses and his churches are the social lungs through which 13 million Negroes breathe and have their warmth and their hope....
>
> In most other races, it would seem that Slavery has produced resentment, bitterness and hatred that frequently expresses itself in violent rebellion, but not so with the Negro; Slavery produces in him patience, hope, tenderness, good will—strange as it may seem—and a profound trust in God. I, for

one, am proud to belong to a race in whom trial and difficulty and suffering can produce such noble fruits of the spirit.

> Yours very truly,
> W.P. Evans[20]

Maxcy John wrote to N.C. Newbold in response to the request made by Evans to provide a public school for black students in 1927. John said that Evans was "rotten ... the bastard son of a mulatto and a jew ... a jew who is known for his slickness above other jews.... He should be the most competent man of his race here and is all of that; and he is at the same time the trickiest and most damaging factor among his race here."[21] This claim is contested by Evans's own family members, who have stated that his father was a slave, who earned his freedom through a musical career. Through his ill-advised statement, John exposes not only his prejudices toward blacks, but also towards Jews.

John continued to play the sexually immoral card, as he had done during the Red Shirt campaign, by accusing Evans of intimidating the black female teachers, who boarded at his home prior to 1895, and demanding "the highest sacrifice a woman can make," which they refused. He went on to say Evans "has separated more negro men from their wives than any other negro" in the county. Further, John claimed that Evans had demanded a kickback from the fees of the black physician and the black dentist for his "influence." Publicly John called Evans corrupt in his performance as a court magistrate.[22]

Walter P. Evans enlisted the help of the Rev. J.C. Nelson of the Zion Methodist Church who also wrote Newbold complaining of the lack of state and local support for a black public high school. Maxcy John and the Rev. Larkin L. King, President of the Colored Civic League and Chaplain of the Laurinburg Institute, countered their argument and supported McDuffie's school. King wrote that Evans led a band of misfits who "filled their places on the chain-gang, work-house, and the courts."[23]

Newbold believed the town of Laurinburg had an obligation to provide public facilities for black school children and to appoint a responsible board to oversee its management. Even if the Institute could cover the high school requirements, a separate elementary school was needed. When Newbold suggested he come to Laurinburg to meet with the divided communities in a conference setting, John responded in 1927:

> ... there is not any situation demanding your attention or a meeting on it. Mass meetings are never marked with great wisdom unless one strong character dominates. A negro mass meeting to consider schools,—not for me, if you please. Any sort of meeting here now for negroes would only

get the shiftless and worthless and the agitators, and the diligent ones would not come if the weather permits gathering of crops at that time. At night they would be so tired they would not come unless spectacular display were expected of something more than a mere sane sober get together conference.[24]

John exposes his white supremacy intent in this revealing comment. His support for McDuffie and the Laurinburg Institute hides his lack of support for a public black school, characterizing those who support a public school as shiftless, worthless agitators. Hoping to shame John and his fellow white leaders, Newbold pointed out that no other responsible community in North Carolina is "practically farming-out its school for one race of its citizens" and that "you are not going to have the peace, content, and happiness of your colored population until the community assumes its responsibility and provides a public colored school." He offered help with funds to construct a building. Newbold regretted the fact that the white citizens of Laurinburg "want to evade their legal duties … and have foreign people pay their bills," and he stated that: "This is really a very painful situation to us because we are very proud of our State and all of its communities."[25]

N.C. State Report of School Situation for Negroes in Laurinburg in 1926

During the summer of 1926, Newbold sent W.A. Robinson, the white State Supervisor of Teacher Training and High Schools, to Laurinburg to investigate the complaints of the black leaders and to speak with both white and black citizens concerning the matter of a black public high school, or the lack thereof. Robinson's report was both thorough, fair and somewhat damning of the white community.[26]

After interviewing the leaders of both the black and white communities, Robinson stated that "the education of the Negro children is farmed out to a private institution" and that this distribution is the basis of the complaints of black citizens, who "express very great dissatisfaction." One problem cited was the location of the new black housing development called Washington Park in the southeast part of town, where half the blacks lived. It was far from the Institute in the northern Newtown, and there was little transportation for the students. The housing developer Jasper T. Gibson, who was on the school board and in favor of building a public black school, donated land for a public school but none was provided. Robinson noted complaints of "immoral conduct," inadequate training for teachers, over-crowded classrooms, and the lack of any opportunity to express dissatisfactions by the parents in an appropriate setting.

State public school funds were allotted according to student attendance, but the mere $2,000 handed out by the all-white Laurinburg school board "would not pay for more than 3 normal school teachers or properly certified high school teachers." Parents accused McDuffie of inapproachability, saying he was only responsible to the board. The board, however, seemed little interested in the Institute other than doling out the annual check. Walter Evans had repeatedly asked the board to oversee affairs at the Institute or to provide a public alternative. The trustees of the Institute lived out of town, many as far away as Boston, and did not meet in a place accessible to local parents. In fact, the black members of the trustee board were described as "very ignorant Negroes ... who were dummy members of the board."

Parents resented the fact that McDuffie raised thousands of dollars from Northern philanthropists for the support of mostly local children who, by right, should be offered free public education. They did not wish "to be objects of charity." By 1924 the Institute had 479 students, only 47 were from out of the county.[27] McDuffie was accused of making "fictitious claims" such as teaching trades when "not one trade is being taught" at that time and "even the hospital cannot turn out nurses."

When funds are short and poverty is ever present, it is not surprising that many in the black community distrusted McDuffie, who closely held exclusive access to all funding, which, to be fair, he raised through tireless toil. How much of the funding went into the school and how much went into the pocket of McDuffie cannot be determined. Certainly McDuffie and his family spent their lives in service to the education of black children, but because there was no trustworthy oversight and because McDuffie did not share information concerning the financial status of the school, suspicion ruled the day. There have always been questions concerning who owns what and what part is public and what part is private. The original deeds from Billie McLaurin list the Laurinburg Normal and Industrial Institute as the rightful owner of the property. But, of course, McDuffie and his descendants are the owners of the Institute, which always has remained a private institution even until today.

The confusion of these ownership issues goes back to the failure of the white community to provide adequate public schooling for black children in Laurinburg. Maxcy John, in writing to support McDuffie and to provide an excuse for the school board's behavior, mentioned in his letter to Newbold that the board distributed the amount of taxes that the black community paid to the Institute for the support of local black children. Newbold was enraged by this dodge. He immediately tore into John saying: "This, as you know, is illegal in North Carolina." He then proceeded to recount the laws and the actions of the State Supreme Court which specifically forbade dividing school taxes between races. Newbold continued:

> However, even if the community should undertake to do this, that is, give the Negroes for school purposes only the taxes which they pay, then in all fairness such a community should give them a pro rata share of all corporation taxes, such as railroads, telephones, telegraphs, electric lights, and the like; also the actual amounts they pay as fines, forfeitures, and penalties. Certainly the Negroes use the public utilities I have referred to, although they may not own stock in them, but they would certainly have an equity in such properties. It is suggested that if a careful investigation should be made covering all these points, it would be found that the Negroes are actually contributing to the support of the white schools.[28]

Newbold campaigned for 35 years to provide public black education facilities in Laurinburg. He wrote Davis in 1927 asking him for help assessing the situation in Laurinburg, stating:

> I can see no good reason why it should be necessary for people outside North Carolina to be solicited to provide funds to educate the colored children of any community, especially those in the elementary grades. As you know, this is what is being done at Laurinburg because the public school authorities are not providing anything like adequate support for the large number of local colored children who attend, or should attend, the McDuffie School.[29]

Newbold succeeded only in establishing small rural schools in Scotland County through the Rosenwald Fund. Robinson suggested, and Newbold agreed, that the black citizens might be satisfied if a public elementary school was built in Washington Park and the Institute continued providing a high school education. Neither of these suggestions came to be until 1953 when the first public black schools in Laurinburg opened. Robinson summed up his report by saying that most of the black citizens wanted change and that:

> The biggest handicap in the way of a change is the cheapness to the School Board of the present arrangement. Whether such an arrangement is legally permissible is doubtful. It is hardly carrying out the moral responsibility of the School Board to a large part of its citizenry.[30]

Pressured by the State to provide public education for black children, the Laurinburg and Scotland County school board tried to negotiate taking over the existing property of the Institute through sale or rent and to assume control of the school, but the McDuffies refused to relinquish their ownership. The local white community seemed pleased to offer minimal support for the education of overwhelming numbers of black students. They also understood that the McDuffies were doing an excellent job with the ability to raise funds from the North for public school children. Nonetheless, the local white school board turned a blind eye to the many needs of black students. The State, however, under Newbold, did offer more support as is clear from the financial list of support for the Institute supplied by white Superintendent A.B. Gibson for over a thousand local black children's education in March 1948[31]:

> **Local:** $7,783 for upkeep, vocational education, and library books
> **State:** $42,195 for teacher and principal salaries, $1,087 for books, janitors, library supplies and utilities
> **Veterans Administration:** $16,000 for the support of 172 veterans for vocational training in brick masonry, farming and auto mechanics

While the white schools had 19 buses to transport its students to high school by 1930, the only black high school in the county, Laurinburg Institute, had none. The health instructor, Esther Carlson, badgered the state education department until, in 1935, it supplied one bus for all of the black children in Scotland County.[32] By the late 1940s, a few more buses were supplied. It is no wonder that so many black children never progressed beyond eighth grade in Scotland County.

10

Marshaling On

*Buildings, Teachers,
Programs and Students
(1918–1953)*

In spite of the lack of adequate local financial support, McDuffie managed to build several permanent buildings for the expanding student population, with private funding that he raised himself. The unpublished Ph.D. dissertation *An Interpretative History of Laurinburg Normal and Industrial Institute, Laurinburg, North Carolina* (1948), by William Maize for Rutgers University, provided much of the material presented in this chapter.[1] He made extensive interviews with Institute faculty and staff, which have been a valuable source. Between 1919 and 1933 the campus grew to include a teachers building, the Anna L. Woods Cottage (1919); a sewing and home economics building, Shaw Hall (1923); a middle school for fourth through seventh grades, McKenzie Hall (1928); and, finally, a gymnasium, the Maxwell Building (1933), and a brick church, Friendly Church (1933). Four cottages were rented to married faculty members. Many smaller wooden buildings housed the farming and industrial equipment. Acres of productive fields and animal husbandry farms provided for all the needs of the school. Athletic fields and a tennis court completed the 26 acre Laurinburg Institute virtual village. As great an accomplishment as creating this village was, McDuffie remained focused on people rather than things, as he said:

> It has never been our end to acquire houses, land, and industries; these we have used as a means of enabling us to accomplish our end, which was and still is to seek and to save that which has been lost. For forty-three years, then, we have been here, seeking lost boys, lost girls, lost men, and lost women.[2]

By 1932, there were 27 teachers instructing 684 students in 11 grades. All teachers were college graduates from such schools such as Fisk, Spellman, Tuskegee, Shaw, Hampton, Atlanta, North Carolina A&T, St. Augustine, South Carolina State, Fayetteville State, and Winston-Salem State. Some had graduate degrees from the University of Chicago, University of Pittsburgh, and Manhattan College.[3]

Seven McDuffie children graduated from college and six returned to teach at the Institute.[4] Some of them married Institute graduates or graduates of the colleges they attended. Many of their partners became teachers at Laurinburg Institute as well. After graduating from Atlanta College and Juilliard, Verdelle, known as "Dibba," taught piano and English. She also was the church organist. Musa attended Hampton University and married Charles Butler, who was killed in Korea as a soldier in the U.S. Army. She taught home economics and also played piano for Institute events. Iva attended South Carolina State and married Judson Melton. She was in charge of the library, which grew to over 9,000 volumes by the 1940s. Iva taught English while Judson taught math and science. Emmanuel, known as Mac, attended Tuskegee University and Hampton University, and was an athletic coach and a tennis champion. Reginald attended Tuskegee Institute and North Carolina Agricultural & Technical State University. He taught history after serving in North Africa in World War II. Reginald married Joy Jackson, who was hired to teach math and physics after she graduated with honors from Fisk University.

McDuffie Family (ca. 1940), from left to right, Emmanuel McDuffie, Tinny McDuffie, Verdelle "Dibba" McDuffie Efferson, Musa McDuffie Butler, J.C. Melton, Iva McDuffie Melton, Reginald McDuffie. All seven of the McDuffie children went to college, six of whom returned to teach at the Institute along with their spouses (courtesy of Shirley McDuffie McCoy).

Frank McDuffie also attended North Carolina A&T State University where he met and later married Sammie Sellers. Frank received a master's degree in history at the University of Pittsburgh and an honorary doctorate degree from North Carolina A&T State University. He taught history, choir, physical education and coached basketball. Sammie taught home economics, math and science. Frank became the headmaster of the Laurinburg Institute when his father died in 1954 and founded one of the finest basketball programs in the nation.

Emmanuel and Tinny's seventh child Gwendolyn attended Gramblin University and received a doctorate from there as well. She later became chair of a department at the university. One can see why some called the Institute an organization of nepotism.[5] It was indeed a family business and remains so today. Yet, through the diligence of the McDuffies to educate their own children, they passed their own good fortune on to thousands of other children over a 119 year period, generation after generation. Other teachers found their way to Laurinburg Institute in unexpected ways.

James T. Speller: How an Engineer Becomes a Teacher and a Principal

By the early 1930s, the pool of available black teachers was considerably increased. In fact, many fine professionals, who could not find work in their fields in the white world, turned to teaching to make a living. Although this blockage was a great disappointment for the professional graduates, it provided an avenue for schools like the Institute to acquire excellent faculty members and teachers. Just such an example is J.T. Speller. As a boy, Speller was fascinated by "horseless carriages" and his father promised him one if he would work and save up for one.[6] Instead, being a very bright young man, Speller used his savings to attend the high school branch of North Carolina A&T College at age 13. He often would have to sleep in parks and doorways at night, but he did well in school. Speller stayed on for college and graduated with the first group of electrical engineering students. He was president and valedictorian of his 1933 class.

In spite of his accomplishments, Speller was unable to find work as an electrical engineer because he was black. He stayed on at A&T as band director for three years. Speller later reflected: "The future of the white college graduate is considerably brighter than that of the Negro college graduate. White educators can sell their talents to a much broader labor market. They are even hired in our own Negro communities."[7]

When World War II occurred, he became a civil engineer with the Air Force and designed airfields, including one at Seymour Johnson Airbase in Goldsboro, North Carolina. Still, it was difficult for him to find work in civilian life. He and his wife travelled to Laurinburg for a visit and learned about the Laurinburg Institute. Mr. McDuffie offered him a job teaching, which he accepted because the school was "almost college-like."[8]

Speller arrived the year after Shortie Hall, the new Institute band director and the inspiration of the musician Dizzy Gillespie. They had met when Hall's Tuskegee band came to play at a North Carolina A&T football game in 1929. Speller never forgot the amazing performance which brought the crowd to its feet in a standing ovation. Both men had faced the frustration of being limited to the black community in spite of their hard work and amazing talents. They became close friends, sharing many evenings together in stimulating conversation. They even performed together for the band students. Speller played clarinet while Hall blew his trumpet.[9]

Hoping to supplement his income and practice his skills as an electrical expert, Speller applied for a North Carolina electrical contracting license but was denied access by the local white inspector. Speller says the inspector "out-tricked himself" and he was able to pass his licensing board. His license is number 225 out of thousands in North Carolina today.[10]

Speller taught at the Institute for almost 17 years and, then, taught at the new public school in Laurinburg, Lincoln Heights in the 1950s. He became principal of I. Ellis Johnson, the former Lincoln Heights when Mr. Johnson retired, and became principal of East Laurinburg Elementary School until his retirement in 1977. Although he never fulfilled his dream of a permanent job as an electrical engineer, he did go on to inspire many young people in their search for a better, more fulfilling life.

Coach Ivory Smith and Isabelle Smith: Poetry, Football and Farmer Training

Ivory and Isabelle Smith, who were originally employed by McDuffie in 1932 and taught the student musician Dizzy Gillespie, were among the significant teachers at the Institute for twenty years. Ivory had been a great football player on "a championship team that had whipped ass among the southern colored colleges in 1925" at Tuskegee Institute.[11] He coached and taught vocational training in agriculture. His goal

Isabelle T. Smith and Ivory H. Smith (1952) taught at the Institute from 1932 to 1954. Isabelle wrote a column for the Institute community newspaper and taught English. Ivory coached football and directed the veterans programs and the agricultural program, which also interacted with the local farming community. They wrote poetry and published *Life Lines: A Collection of Inspiring Poetry and Prose* (1952), from which these portraits and the opening poem derive.

as a teacher was to "bring half croppers (those who did not own their land and had to share half their crop) to full land ownership."[12] Dizzy Gillespie described Ivory Smith, his football coach, in this manner: "Mr. Smith left me with a very funny attitude, feeling both love and fear for him. He reminded me of a tenacious bulldog, but at the same time he acted warm and kind."[13] Gillespie offers further insight into Coach Smith in a later chapter.

Ivory Smith ran the farm vocational program and oversaw all of the extension work among community members, including the local chapter of the New Farmers of America and the Veterans Farmer Training Program. The ten-page outline of his duties and objectives in the 1940s would be overwhelming for most men, but Smith relished his challenges, just as his boss McDuffie faced his insurmountable difficulties, with faith and courage.[14] Smith directed students in the construction and repair of all the Institute farm equipment from hog and poultry feeders to fertilizer and mowing machines. During World War II, the New Farmers ran a stamp and bond drive, collected 46,000 pounds of scrap metal, raised funds for the Red Cross and ran a group of 240 persons for food war production.

Under community improvement, Smith supervised the repair and building of 27 small family homes in Laurinburg, helped in the reduction of tenancy by the sale of land to farmers and established written contracts between tenant farmers and the land owners so that obligations and responsibilities would be clearly understood. The Institute offered prizes for the best farm animals and produce and the best beautification of homes and gardens. Health improvement was encouraged in the community through diet, sanitation, and regular doctor and dentist check-ups at low prices. Immunizations were encouraged for children.

Evening classes were offered to the community, including crop and soil improvement, forestry demonstrations, and health organization. Smith planned to create a community store so that citizens could benefit from the co-operative management of merchandise and food. Publication of all these plans were printed and distributed to all community members so that they could be well informed and participate in these freely offered programs. A publication called *The Mirror* continued to inform the public of up-coming events such as the annual farmers picnic. Ivory and Isabelle Smith contributed a regular column to the publication.

Demonstrations of the effectiveness of these community improvement efforts by the Institute staff and students were borne out by visits of William Maize to local black-owned farms in the area. Smith informed him that, starting from about 35 acres of land owned by blacks in Scotland County in 1904, blacks now owned 162 farms in 1945. Farmers such as Joshua Newton, Peter Newton and James Wall credited the Institute with helping them establish their well over 100-acre farms, which produced tobacco, cotton, watermelon, cantaloupe, cows, pigs, poultry and eggs. Peter Newton said, "I am a proud parent of Laurinburg Institute. Professor Smith has guided us well."[15]

The soft side of Ivory Smith was encouraged by Isabelle Smith, who taught sixth and seventh grade English and who collaborated with Ivory in writing poetry. She had attended Snow Hill, Hampton and Tuskegee Institutes. After listening on the radio to a sermon by Dr. Hugh Fulton of the local Presbyterian Church, they wrote a poem together. Later, they published a book of inspirational stories by others along with their own poems called *Life Lines: A Collection of Inspiring Poetry and Prose* (1952), the sales of which were intended to fund the building of a community center in north Laurinburg.[16] In order to support their fund-raising project, the Smiths developed relationships with the white leaders of the town, including J.F. McNair, Hervey Evans, Edwin Morgan, and Z.V. Pate. One of their poems, "The Fervent Prayer of Black America," opens this book. William Maize, Dean of Florida A.&M. College, wrote the foreword for the book and the master's thesis on the history of Laurinburg Institute from 1904 to 1948, which contributed to this text. Maize characterized the Smiths' efforts: "The education and advancement of their race has always, as it should be, been their primary desire in life."[17]

One memory of Isabelle Smith persists in the mind of Dr. Frances McDuffie Foster. The daughter of Frank and Sammie McDuffie, Fran was a pupil in Isabelle's sixth grade class. Each morning Isabelle would open the class with a story that had a life lesson in it. Fran, now in her 80s and still practicing medicine, said, "I have never forgotten that story."[18] The story went something like this. A man was crossing a mountain with his donkey loaded with goods for delivery. Suddenly the donkey stopped and refused to move. The man beat the donkey and couldn't move him. Eventually the donkey proceeded up the mountain. A bit up the road, the donkey stopped again. In spite of beating him harder, the donkey refused to budge. After a while, the donkey continued on its own up the hill. Once again, for the third time, the donkey came to a halt receiving another beating. At last the donkey arrived in town on the other side of the mountain. In time, the man learned that there had been a robbery on the trail up ahead of where the donkey stopped the first time. The second time, the donkey had saved him from an avalanche and the third, the donkey had avoided a truck accident.

The moral of the story was "be careful how you beat your donkey, catastrophe could be waiting ahead. ... There could be a reason for a frustrating blockage. Reflect and accept God's will. It seems obstacles are there for a reason."[19] Frances Foster often found comfort and hope in Isabelle's story when she faced adversity throughout her long career as a doctor.

In 1953 the Smiths moved to the first public black school Lincoln Heights, along with I. Ellis and Amanda Johnson. The superintendent of the county schools L.M. Peele summed up the invaluable service of Ivory Smith: "I am proud of this man and delighted in showing and telling others what he has done. He is an asset to the county, state and the country. In the next 50 years Scotland County hopes to be able to point to another of his race who will have done as well as he has."[20]

Student Relations

Emmanuel McDuffie always kept his focus on his students and their needs. He explained: "The primary function of Laurinburg Normal and Industrial Institute is to prepare young men and women of the Negro race for those walks of life which will put them in the most useful relation to their race and country."[21] The school programs evolved over time to meet those useful needs. Time was needed as well to train and hire black teachers who could fully prepare students at the levels required. Initially in 1904, the goal was to prepare them to teach basic reading, writing and arithmetic to elementary students. The 1910 census listed 10 teachers who could both read and write, mostly graduates of Snow Hill Institute. Then in 1910, the Institute added courses which would support housekeeping for women and farming for men, most of whom worked for white people in the area. By the late 1910s and early 1920s, brick masonry, plastering, printing, nursing and auto mechanics were added to the curriculum to create a system of independent employment and better pay.

As the state of North Carolina cried out for help for accredited teachers in 1915, the Institute added a full academic curriculum which would prepare the students "so that they can attend the five state colleges for Negroes, and the eight church and private colleges for Negroes in North Carolina, and colleges and universities elsewhere in the country."[22] Trained black college-educated teachers, including the McDuffie children, were more available at that time. The State of North Carolina accredited the Laurinburg Institute in 1924. Eleven grades, offering such non–locally needed courses as French and Latin, fully prepared students for college work and the world beyond. A twelfth grade was added in 1945. After the war, the Veterans Administration provided funds for 172 men to take half-day classes in brick masonry, auto mechanics and vocational farming.[23]

Teaching methods at the Institute seemed far ahead of most schools, black or white, at the time. "Direct teaching and learning instead of 'hearing lessons'" were encouraged so that students could see how to apply his newly acquired knowledge.[24] Rote learning, such as memorizing long lists of states and capitals, was discouraged. Individual instruction was often necessary as students were not always matched with the appropriate age-related class. Some were older and, due to the demands of crop harvesting and truancy, behind in their course work. For this reason, Fridays were devoted to individualized remedial work.[25]

Course work was not the only objective of the administration. McDuffie put great emphasis on character building in his school.

Maize listed the qualities that the school sought to eliminate: "shift-lessness, indolence, improvidence, extravagance, untidiness, dishon-esty, untruthfulness, business unreliability, lack of initiative, suspicion of his own race, and ignorance,"[26] and recognized the need for charac-ter building because:

> The administration at Laurinburg has been deeply conscious of the fact that we live in a complex democracy. For this reason the school has attempted very earnestly to provide for innumerable situations so that the young people may learn to cooperate, to have and to use the finest social spirit, and to help youth accumulate right ideals and a comprehensive good will.[27]

Good manners, cleanliness, self-control, self-motivating initiative, responsibility and respect for others were qualities McDuffie and his staff worked hard to develop in their students. McDuffie said, "…we have tried to teach *them* and not subjects."[28]

Athletic, musical, and religious programs often encouraged the good characteristics the school wished to imbue because students wanted to be part of those activities more than challenging classroom activities. Football, baseball and basketball were offered as well as ten-nis. Chorus and band were popular and highly successful, as seen in the following chapters. Christian Endeavors, a student-run weekly chapel program, along with YMCA programs for boys and girls, encouraged active participation and Christian values. Students also participated in clubs such as the McLauren Literary Society (1909) and the Young Men's Debating Club (1911) as well as the Negro History Club, Art Club, Boy Scouts and Girl Scouts. Every student was required to join at least one club, which met once a week. Leroy McLeod was the first art instructor at the Institute in the early 1980s. After seeing McLeod's art work, Frank McDuffie told him "you're gifted," and gave him a job, which boosted McLeod's low self-esteem. According to McLeod, the Laurinburg Institute was a "vital asset" to the area, which gave students a "chance to excell, a legacy all by itself."[29]

Northern Students Go South and Southern Students Go North

Meanwhile, the Laurinburg Institute grew with the combined help of the state, local funding and relentless fund raising. Originally board-ing students came from the surrounding states such as South Carolina, Virginia, and Georgia. As the Institute's reputation spread among black folks, students came from as far away as New York City by 1919. Daniel Pollitt explained:

> ... in World War I a number of blacks in the South went north to work in the defense plants ... the same thing happened in World War II. ... The husband would get the job, send for the wife, send for the kids and then if he was laid off, he would send them back. So Laurinburg Academy became the school for a lot of northern kids who would go home during bad times, but it also became, in the process, sort of a prestigious prep school for northern kids who would go south to this prestigious prep school.[30]

The unstable conditions of the economy often shifted so that the women and children would have to return home to their families in Laurinburg while the father stayed on to work. This circular movement, from south to north and north to south, helped to spread the reputation of the Laurinburg Institute. By the 1940s, boarding students included 195 pupils from North and South Carolina, Georgia, Alabama, Arkansas, Missouri, Texas, Ohio, Michigan, Washington, D.C., Maryland, New York, New Jersey, Connecticut, and Pennsylvania.[31] It also created a more sophisticated environment for local students beyond the borders of the tiny farming town of Laurinburg. The combination of "Country," the name northern students gave the local kids, and kids from big urban cities made for a vibrant mix. The North Carolina boarding student Isaac Logan related his impressions of the northern students:

> Well, culturally they seemed to be a little more sophisticated in the way they carried themselves and dressed and often referred to some of us being "Country," in a friendly way, but not putting us down. My memories from the Institute that are unique and interesting were the students that attended who were from NY, NJ, IL. They sang all of the latest R&B "Black Music" out of Detroit. They often talked about them gathering together on a street corner under the street light singing DOO WOP songs like they were on stage.... There were these five guys that love to sing. They were the Doo-Wop group. This group of guys sang outside while waiting for the doors to open at the cafeteria for breakfast, lunch, or dinner; winter, spring, or fall. Also, they sang at the Dance Hops we had to compete with the Girls' group; the Malloy Sisters, Ernestine, Doris and Anna Rose. They were really good and I enjoyed them all.[32]

Two Inspirational Stories: Henrietta Davis and Willie Freeman Parker

While many stories of early Laurinburg Institute students have been lost, two shining examples have been preserved. Both began in

Laurinburg in 1916 when Henrietta Davis and Willie Freeman Parker were born. In 2019, at the age of 103, Henrietta Davis was the oldest living alumnus of the Laurinburg Institute. Davis began school at the age of seven and attended the Institute until 1927, when her family moved to Raleigh. The Institute honored her achievements in 2016 by entering her into the Laurinburg Institute Hall of Fame as a Legacy Alumni. Andre Mack, a Laurinburg Institute graduate and reporter for the *Laurinburg Exchange,* interviewed Davis who recalled "her love of reading developed at Laurinburg Institute. She remembers always doing her best at work, including, picking cotton."[33]

Such determination, which may be ascribed to the inspiration of her early Institute training, can be demonstrated by Davis's unrelenting drive to achieve the best education possible. Perseverance is the quality that most characterizes Henrietta Davis. She completed high school in 1945 at age 29. While working a full time job with the Division of Employment Security in Boston, Massachusetts, Davis enrolled in Northeastern University. By taking one course per year for 21 years, Davis earned her college degree in recreational studies in 1978. The university honored her with a named brick in their Walk of Fame. The Laurinburg Institute can be proud of providing the foundation for Henrietta Davis's remarkable education. She stands as a shining light for others to follow.

A fellow classmate of Henrietta Davis, Willie Freeman Parker was also a shining example. Parker, too, was born in Laurinburg in 1916. Unlike Davis, she graduated from Laurinburg Institute and, later, Shaw University. She, then, returned home to teach math at the Institute. There she made her indelible mark on her students. When she passed on at age 101, in 2018, Lawrence Jackson III had this to say about her influence on his father's life:

> He always told me she failed him because he played around. He was smart enough to pass the class, but he didn't do what he was supposed to do, and she failed him.... She helped him get on the right track. She pushed him so that he went on to NYU. She wouldn't let him off the hook, and he taught school as well because of her.[34]

Parker inspired many in her family to become educators. She raised funds to send her adopted brother Charles Freeman, Sr., to college. Upon graduation, he taught school at Pate Gardner Elementary School and at Job Core. His son became a teacher as well. Charles Freeman, Jr., recalled that "education was paramount to her. If you did not get an education it was a loss.... There was no going to the field for the girls. They were going to school."[35]

Parker continued her own education earning a M.A. and Ph.D. from Oral Roberts University, where she served on the board of trustees. She taught school in New York, after leaving the Institute, and Portsmouth, Virginia, where she remained until her retirement in 1979. One of her Portsmouth students, the Rev. R.I. Addison, visited Parker each summer in Laurinburg for 20 years because she inspired him to teach:

> She had a great impact on me because I was eventually employed in the school system. I didn't want anything to do with that school house. That was not my intent.... I had retired from the Air Force, and then I worked for a newspaper firm as a manager. I lost a job to downsizing. I applied for a job teaching English and stayed there 25 years, and her influence led me to apply with the school system.[36]

The Laurinburg Institute responded to Agent Newbold's 1915 request for training students to educate others by implementing a new curriculum aimed at college preparation. The lives of Henrietta Davis and Willie Freeman Parker are proof that the Institute succeeded far beyond the immediate needs of the state, reaching far into the future and across state lines.

A Tribute to Emmanuel McDuffie and Laurinburg Institute

When William Maize began his investigation of the Laurinburg Institute for his master's thesis at Rutgers University in 1947, he expected to find a simple school. He learned, however, that the Laurinburg Institute was much more than that. He also came to understand that the accomplishments of the Institute all boiled down to the inspired faith and mission of one man, Emmanuel McDuffie. Maize offers this explanation:

> An institution may rest on either of two foundations—on a plan, or on a man. Laurinburg was founded on a man. Dr. McDuffie saw his vision and was obedient to it. He began just where he was and with what he had. He set his will to his task, as though daring to repeat the saying: "Because I live, ye shall live also." Then his work grew as nature grew. It is not built from without but from within. Laurinburg Normal and Industrial Institute's security is not in its educational scheme, but in its personal tradition. Teachers and students throughout its history have walked by faith in McDuffie.
> It should be realized ... that Laurinburg Institute is essentially a spiritual enterprise, conceived as a form of missionary service, perpetuated as a school of character, and maintained by a long series of self-sacrificing teachers, who through the routine of their work have communicated the

spirit of their consecration and have sanctified themselves for others' sakes.

Within the body of instruction there is an institutional soul, a spiritual tradition, which gives to the work a peculiar character, and the influence of which one feels about him like the gentle air of springtime. Fidelity, conscientiousness, loyalty, cheerfulness, and sacrifice meet one on every hand. Religion is healthy-minded and generous. Work and prayer are daily companions. The visitor finds himself observing in a corner of the world the way in which the entire world ought to be directed and controlled—a great spiritual penetrating and illuminating daily life, lifting work into worship, and showing its faith in its works. Not until the soul of Laurinburg Institute has been discerned through the form of its industrial life and through its contributions to racial progress and national life is the Institute seen as it really is.

No life is whole that is not holy, and no life is holy that is not whole. That is the daily confession in worship and in work of Laurinburg Institute's educational creed.[37]

11

Phillmore "Shortie" Hall

A Teacher's Point of View
(1934–1945)

Phillmore "Shortie" Hall recorded the following selection of stories with Johnny Hodge, Jr., who wrote them down in 1977, for his Ph.D. dissertation at the American University in Washington, D.C.[1] Hodge also interviewed Frank McDuffie, Jr., in 1976, and many Institute faculty and students provided him with written memories of their experiences at the school. More than ninety pages document Hall's ten years as a faculty member at the Laurinburg Institute from 1934 to 1945. His detailed memories give us a vivid view of the day-to-day occurrences in the classroom and dormitories as well as significant events. Shortie Hall was not only a faculty member, teaching seventh grade, but he was also the Dean of Boys, living in Edwards Hall with the boys, and he taught and conducted the band, significantly influencing the foundation of black school bands across North Carolina and other places. Furthermore, Hall developed the talents of the now famous jazz trumpeter Dizzy Gillespie, who offers his own story of the Institute in Chapter 12.

Phillmore "Shortie" Hall was orphaned by the age of nine.[2] He taught himself to play the organ his father owned and earned nickels and dimes playing jazz wherever he could. Eventually he was taken in by a white family to work in their small grocery store in Indianapolis, Indiana. Phillmore was only five feet tall so, even as a child, he was called Shortie. His job delivering food to the local music academy gave him the opportunity to hear classical music performed. The students and staff invited him to play jazz for them as well. His white employers, who treated him as family and shared their meals with him, gave him Booker T. Washington's autobiography *Up from Slavery,* which inspired him to save what he earned from small jobs so that he could attend Tuskegee Institute. He arrived at the school at age 14 and got a job for 30 cents a day, blowing his bugle for taps, reveille and meal times. The director of the Tuskegee band Capt. Frank Drye, a former bandmaster in the 10th Cavalry, encouraged Hall to join the school band and, through rigorous training, Hall became the master of many instruments. He eventually became the director of the Tuskegee Institute band himself. The author Ralph Ellison, who was a student member of Shortie's band, said this about his teacher:

Phillmore "Shortie" Hall (ca. 1950s) was Dean of Boys, taught seventh grade, and established the Institute band and orchestra (1934–1945). Dizzy Gillespie recognized him as his mentor. Hall played a significant role in inspiring black public school bands across the state. (courtesy North Carolina Bandmasters Association 2002 Hall of Fame).

> Shorty Hall was hardly five feet tall, ... but he could blow the hell off a big-bore symphonic trumpet. ... He played all the difficult variations and triple tonguing. ... He had the facility of Al Hurt. So there is a direct line leading from Capt. Drye, the ex-cavalry bandmaster, through Shorty Hall to Dizzy.[3]

Emmanuel McDuffie first heard Hall's band perform at Tuskegee, when his two sons, Emmanuel (called Mac) and Reginald, attended there.

Hall went on to live the professional life as a musician, traveling all across the country with a variety of orchestras and smaller jazz groups, including recording with The Black Birds of Paradise and performing with the Speed Webb band for another ten years. He played in such well-known venues as the Cotton Club in New York City. The economic crash in 1929, leading to the disastrous Depression, led to many performance cancellations. Hall began to tire of life on the road and wanted to settle down just as McDuffie was looking for a band leader.

From the earliest days of the Institute, Emmanuel McDuffie had organized his curriculum around three student career objectives, which were plainly stated on the 1910 Institute admissions form: learning a trade, teaching or becoming a musician. Vocational training had been the objective of most schools for blacks, which was confirmed by the

1917 U.S. Bureau of Education's study *Negro Education* by Thomas Jesse Jones. Yet, McDuffie had another vision for black students, who were offered a firm English education and musical training. By 1934, no other known black secondary school in North Carolina offered instrumental training.[4] Verdelle "Dibba" McDuffie, who had attended Juilliard, taught piano, and Raymond Barnes, a graduate of Tuskegee, helped a few students to form a band. Because Hall could play almost any instrument, he was the perfect candidate for the job. Through their Tuskegee connection, McDuffie offered Hall not one but three jobs as a teacher, Dean of Boys and band leader. Hall accepted, arriving on campus in the midst of the Depression in 1934.

When the Institute student Walter Carlson came to pick him up after his arrival, Hall asked him to drive around the town before going to the Institute so he could get a sense of the community. Hall's first impression of the living conditions of the Laurinburg black community was dire. The heartbreaking description of what he saw follows:

> ... the boy passed small frame "shotgun" farm houses ... a rickety and forlorn chimney jut from the tin roofs that were badly in need of repair. The houses were propped up by bricks at the corners, and small children and dogs played underneath them with the rats. ... The barefeet of the sharecropper and his family had beaten the yard bare. No tree, no bush, no flower bloomed there. A pigpen reeked at its door, and down the hill was the open well where filth was certain to drain into it. Lean, mangy hounds strode about with flies biting at their open sores; the flies had flown straight from the place in the tall weeds that served as an outhouse. Phillmore thought to himself, "My God, how could anyone who lived such as this keep well or be ambitious?" ...
>
> The sharecropper's imprisonment was not only confined to the land; it must have extended to an enslavement of his mind. The system appeared to be a good teacher. It taught the cropper to mind the soil, use the fence rails for firewood, to make no repairs and to practice no economy or self-help through gardening or animal husbandry. With the cotton and peanut rows running to his front door, he could hardly have instituted this practice, even if the system had not robbed him of his will.[5]

Arriving at the Institute, Hall had a different impression. Healthy food crops were in the fields surrounding the school, the grounds were manicured and inviting, and the buildings were impressive. Three large brick buildings housed both the classrooms and the boarding students. Smaller wooden buildings housed animal husbandry and agricultural supplies, a hospital with a doctor, pharmacist and a dentist on staff, a library, gymnasium and community activity center, a virtually self-sufficient, self-contained, vibrant village. A football field and tennis courts completed the picture.

Hall described his first impression of President Emmanuel McDuffie as "a tall, powerful looking man inclined to be swift in his actions. He had a manner that won him friends and a mind that earned him respect."[6] Hall wondered why a school would need both a president and a principal? He discovered that, when the state certified the school in 1932, McDuffie did not qualify for the title of principal so I. Ellis Johnson assumed that title, while, at the insistence of both white and black citizens, McDuffie acquired the title of president. As president, he maintained complete control of the school and made all final decisions concerning finances, faculty and students.

In their initial meeting, Hall recalled that McDuffie spoke "with pride about his school" and "stressed the value of community service."[7] McDuffie's philosophy of duty and service to the less fortunate, which was so well ingrained by his own mentor William Edwards, guided his every move. Hall explained how this philosophy was instilled into the Institute students' hearts as well:

> The students who came to the school were continually reminded that the educational plant was not solely for their individual enrichment, but to lead the race forward. During their time spent in the classroom, the shop, the laundry or the kitchen, they were subject to the gentle yet constant pressure of duty. The students were the trustees of knowledge and had an administrative duty to spread that knowledge among the less fortunate who could not go to school; they were to help others of the race toward a happier and more healthful way of life.[8]

Hall also learned that the student body varied greatly—from children of local sharecroppers, some of whom were the first in their families to attend any school at all, to urban kids from families of professional teachers, doctors and lawyers. Some pupils had been expelled from school or had low academic averages. A few kids, even, had served time in juvenile reform schools. The student body represented every walk of life, but each member was expected to support every other member regardless of class differentiation or background. The faculty was there to serve each and every member where they began and to guide them forward with hope and encouragement to a better life.

As Hall and McDuffie toured the Institute campus, Hall learned that Edwards Hall was the early childhood learning center with kindergarten through grade three on the lower floor and with the boarding boys' dormitory upstairs. McKenzie Hall housed grades four through eight on the lower floor and boarding girls lived on the second floor. Moore Hall contained grades nine through twelve along with the industrial and mechanical arts shops. Hall was told that, as far as the North Carolina Department of Education was concerned, his salary was for teaching the seventh grade. His other two jobs, band director and Dean of Boys, were funded by the Institute's general fund. His total salary was $80 per month.

The first challenge Hall faced was motivating the boarding boys to clean up and maintain the dormitory where Hall also lived. He found it in a complete state of uncleanliness and disorder.

> To show the pupils that dignity lay in cleanliness, he himself shouldered the mop, the pail, the rags and the paint brush. If there were those who grumbled they could do no less than follow. Soon the boy's dormitory no longer looked dingy and dark—it was spotless. The floors shone all the time and the walls were clean with fresh paint. Some boys even had the girls in home economics to make new drapes for them. Young artists hung their paintings on the wall and boys in the industrial arts department made frames for the paintings. Other boys made bookshelves, small cabinets, and desks to go in their rooms. Moreover, all beds were made army style.... The young men held their first open house in December of 1934 to show off their newly decorated rooms. From then on, Edward Hall was a clean place in which to live. If anyone dared to make it anything less than perfectly clean, then that person had his peers, not the Dean, to deal with.[9]

As the Dean of Boys, Hall had the responsibility of managing all seventh through twelfth grade boys. This job required both sternness and sympathy. Hall "did not joke and tease with his students" but he was "kind and most of all fair."[10] He often counseled and comforted the homesick boys living far from home, offering them good advice about how to make good decisions. He also disciplined them when they misbehaved.

One such student, Elijah Campbell, was a particular challenge. Elijah was an eighteen-year-old brick mason when he arrived on campus. When his teacher demanded his trowel, Elijah refused and the teacher called him a "black bastard."[11] Elijah pulled a knife, which resulted in his being sent to Hall for punishment. Rather than expel the student, as so often happened in public schools, Hall explained that he had "acted unwisely and rude" and asked Elijah to apologize to his teacher.[12] The young man refused, believing the teacher owed him an apology. Hall sent him to the hospital where he was tasked to clean floors on his knees all day and night. The next day, Elijah still refused to apologize. This standoff went on for three days and three nights until Elijah caved and begged his teacher's pardon. Patience was required to break students of a lifetime of bad habits. Never giving up on a student was both the administration's policy and Hall's philosophy. That kind of long term commitment in the face of angry stubbornness served many students well. Elijah went on to graduate, go to college and become a principal of an elementary school.

During weekdays, Hall taught 49 seventh graders the subjects of English, spelling, mathematics, history, health and physical education. Managing so many pupils would be a challenge for any teacher, but Hall had additional problems other than numbers. Some students were so much older and bigger than their classmates and, sometimes, even their teachers such as small Shortie, that they presented unique challenges, particularly concerning disrespect and disruptions in the classroom. Hall had one particular girl named "Big Rose" who was 16 years old and who continually disrupted his lessons. One day when Hall entered the classroom, he noticed that trash had been thrown all around the room. When he commented that he didn't know "why certain people seemed to enjoy working in a dirty room," Rose defiantly confronted him, reporting that she had trashed the room.[13] Sensing her anger, Hall asked her to leave the room and calm herself. Rose refused, challenging Hall to try and make her. He approached her desk and quietly repeated his request. Rose slapped him hard across the face. Instinctively Hall "dealt the girl a stunning blow to the jaw that sent her sprawling across several rows of desks," and announced, "Now... You will all keep this room as clean as if it were my house."[14] After that dramatic event, no student challenged his authority.

Hall quickly learned that his students were not prepared for seventh grade level instruction. Although he had appropriate text books for the seventh grade, his students could not understand them. Hall estimated that their abilities ranged between third and sixth grades. He also learned that the teaching methods he had been taught at Tuskegee would not work for these students, who "could not even understand the language in which their teacher's courses had been coached."[15] Further problematic for him was the fact that many students were far older than the age-appropriate classes he had expected.

As Roger McGirt reported earlier in 1930, the challenges of matching age-appropriate students with class levels was an endemic problem in black Laurinburg schools because of the constant absences caused by labor demands on tenant farms. The following assessment of Institute parents' occupations as late as 1948 clearly shows how dependent families were on their children's labor. Parents listed their occupations as mechanics, teachers, ministers, and other occupations (76), farm owners (52), and work on other people's farms (562).[16] The overwhelming number of farm hands who worked for other people, mostly white people, vividly illustrates the dire situation facing blacks in education. The approximately fifty day difference between black school terms and white school terms also added to the impossibility of achieving grade levels, which white kids reached without difficulty.

Shortie Hall accepted the challenges these problems presented and determined to meet his students where they were. He borrowed books from the elementary teachers and assigned them based on the individual abilities of his pupils. Hall firmly demanded that his students demonstrate their commitment to learning even though they often could not answer his questions correctly. He himself would openly admit, "I don't know, but I'll find out."[17] Hall did not tolerate whining and excuses, but promised to support any student who tried hard. He encouraged his students to be the best that they could be and recognized that motivation was everything: "You can't teach people anything. ... You can only bring out those God-given talents that are within them."[18] When the students got discouraged, Hall repeatedly reminded them: "It would be better for one thousand to be ready when the doors opened for Negroes than none to be ready when opportunity knocked."[19]

Because Hall insisted that he teach each student according to his abilities, whether that was second grade level or seventh, he found himself in hot water with Emmanual McDuffie. When the president found out about Hall's teaching methods, he called him into the office and confronted him. According to Hall, McDuffie "made clear ... that the faculty was to follow his orders without question or protest."[20] Always trying keep the school up to State standards, McDuffie had required that his faculty teach to the Iowa Standardized Test and he knew that Hall was not teaching the material required at grade level for the test. When McDuffie questioned him about his methods, Hall responded: "I ... know what I am doing, Mr. McDuffy. ... I do not believe that the success of our children depends on their passing this test, Mr. McDuffy. Those tests were not made for our children, Mr. McDuffy. Someday, people will realize this."[21]

Although they disagreed about teaching to the test, they respected each other's opinions, so McDuffie allowed Hall to continue teaching on an individualized basis. In fact, many Institute teachers did just that because of the lack of any consistency in the education of black children due to absences and age differences. The Institute teachers prided themselves on meeting the students where they were and molding them into productive, responsible, "tax-paying citizens."

One thing Hall and McDuffie agreed upon was the importance of creating an excellent musical program. Frank McDuffie conducted the choir, which sang on the local radio station WEWO on Sunday mornings and competed in statewide competitions. Verdelle "Dibba" McDuffie taught classical piano and music theory. Prior to Hall's arrival, the Tuskegee graduate Raymond Barnes had taught band and math, but neither subject suited him well. Perhaps he was not up to the many challenges he faced. On the other hand, Shortie Hall thrived when given a challenge.

Hall's first challenge in creating a band program was to acquire instruments because few students could afford them and there was no money in the budget to purchase them. Initially, he and the administration appealed to the community for help, and they raised funds through fairs and school activities. With the money they raised, Hall went to an instrument dealer in Fayetteville and arranged to purchase "used instruments on a long-term, low-payment plan."[22]

Secondly, Hall needed to persuade students to enroll in what had been a very low-functioning band class. Many students had no musical training, and those who did could not read music. Shortie Hall showed off his talents by playing his trumpet in chapel and class. He would interchange classical European tunes such as the "Fantasy on the Carnival of Venice" by Paganini with jazz numbers such as Louie Armstrong's "Didn't He Ramble."[23] The students were impressed by "the man who could 'blow his horn just like Louie Armstrong'" and, soon, they were begging to join his band.[24] He started with fifteen students, who included the only two musicians who could play, Norman Powe and John "Dizzy" Birks Gillespie. They met after class in his seventh grade classroom, which doubled as the band room and office.

Just as Hall had had to make adjustments for his unprepared pupils while teaching his academic courses, he also had to find ways to instruct his band members so that they would have a positive and encouraging experience with music. He found that the usual school band books were "befuddling" to the novice: "Most of them taught too much too soon. The students were expected to read music, count, hold the instrument a particular way and breathe correctly within a short time. Little time was provided for the student to get a 'feel' for his instrument on his own."[25] Shortie Hall's philosophy of teaching musical instruments to novice students was very much as he had learned to play, the natural way. Teach them how to care for the instrument, how to assemble and disassemble them, keep them clean and in good repair. Hall also taught the history of the instruments including the African origin of the banjo, a popular instrument in minstrel bands at the time. Then, give a child the instrument and let him experiment with the sounds they can make. Hall said: "Watch a child. ... Don't coach him at first, let him alone. If the child is allowed to produce a sound on his own, he is much more inspired by this tone than he is by the one that the director has forced him to make. Forcing a child to try to produce tones that are too difficult for him, will only discourage that youngster."[26]

Hall emphasized alternate fingering and breathing techniques for the horn players. Discouraging them from breathing through their noses, Hall kept a clothespin in his pocket and threatened to pinch their noses if he caught them breathing incorrectly. He also believed that the director should ask the student to "play" his instrument rather than "blow" it: "As soon as the director says 'blow,' the students will inevitably fill their diaphragms with air, puff out their jaws and blow like they are trying to puff up a balloon. Once a student acquires an improper way of tone production on, for example, a cup mouthpiece, the band director will have uncalled for problems later."[27] Ironically, one student, who had learned to play by "puffing out his jaws," was Dizzy Gillespie, whom Hall "used to get after," but later Hall had to admit "he can do anything he wants to now."[28]

Once the student had a feel for his instrument and knew how to care for it, Hall taught them how to listen, what he called "ear training." They learned "to recognize intervals, i.e., major thirds, minor thirds, perfect fifths, augmented fourths, and major, minor and chromatic scales."[29] Once the band understood major triads, the students could tune themselves by listening carefully and adjusting their tones to others.

Hall himself was an expert listener. He credited his unusual ability to zero-in on out-of-tune sounds to his partial loss of hearing during a severe illness before arriving at the Institute. His friend, fellow teacher and former band leader, J.T. Speller reflected upon Hall's many talents thusly:

> Shortie was one of the best trumpet players that I ever heard perform. There were few musicians of our race, or any other race for that matter, who were so innately talented. But more importantly, he was an excellent teacher. He knew band instruments and what to expect from the instruments. He could shut off all the instruments but the one he was listening to, and from his director's stand he could tell each student what notes they were missing and how to produce that tone correctly.[30]

Soon the students formed a true ensemble under Hall's instruction. They became so well-rehearsed that practices attracted the local farmers and community members, who came by after work for a little relaxation and entertainment. After practice, Hall and his musicians would join other faculty and students getting out of athletic and choral practices at the Campus Inn for a snack and lively conversations. It was there that Dizzy Gillespie introduced Hall to his future wife Lucy Lee McLeod.

It didn't take long for word to get around that the Laurinburg band was great entertainment. The enrollment of musical boarding students grew quickly. They were invited to play at many of the black North Carolina colleges and they won many trophies at "every Negro Music Festival" and at the State Choral Music Festivals.[31] The greatest honor, however, for the band was being invited to play at the 1938 World's Fair in New York City. The New Farmers of America, an organization begun by George Washington Carver at Tuskegee Institute, was looking for a black band to represent them at the fair. The English teacher Isabelle Smith let Hall know that a review board was coming to assess the band's quality, among many other bands. The excitement among the students was overwhelming. They played two John Phillip Sousa marches and "one very difficult overture" for the judges, who were so impressed that they eventually chose the Laurinburg Institute band to be their representatives at the World's Fair.[32]

Twenty members of the New Farmers organization volunteered to drive the forty band performers to New York City, where they stayed at a hotel in Harlem. It was the first time many kids had left Scotland County and some were overwhelmed. Earnest Terry was in shock and could not perform. When Hall asked him what was the matter, Terry asked, "Are we in another country, Mr. Hall?" Hall responded, "For many of us, son, yes, this is another country."[33] On the way home, they stopped in Philadelphia to tour historic sites as well. Their musical education brought them much more than classroom experiences. It opened their eyes to a wider world of opportunity.

In spite of Hall's success as a band leader and his three jobs at the Institute, he could not make enough money to support his growing family so he played with a traveling minstrel show in the summertime. He could earn in one week what he earned in a month at the Institute. When the Laurinburg-Maxton Army Airbase opened during the war, he took a job as the superintendent of Domestic Services, working seven nights a week. On the weekends, white bands would play for the officers, but when the officer in charge, Colonel C.J. Baynes, discovered that Hall was a jazz performer, he would ask the bands to let Hall play one tune with them. Soon, the bands asked him to play full time with them and they paid him for his services. Baynes offered a sterling recommendation for Hall when he later decided to take a job in Durham.[34]

Although Hall could make more income playing on the road, he missed his family, and he found great satisfaction in educating young men and women. Hall was a powerful advocate for musical education in the South. In his 1938 speech at Tuskegee Institute entitled "A Need for Music in Secondary Schools," Hall encouraged the college graduates: "Our children need men and women dedicated to the task of bringing instrumental music into our high schools. Your task will not be an easy one; you will have little to work with. But you must be ready when doors open in this field of study for our race."[35] In 1938, there were only two band programs in black public high schools in all of North Carolina, one in Raleigh at Washington High School and one in Asheville at Stephen Lee High School. In contrast, over 5,600 white high school musicians took part in state contests in that year.[36]

Many credit Shortie Hall as the founding inspiration of many band programs throughout the state as his own students proliferated. For instance, Walter Carlson became the band director at North Carolina A&T State College in Greensboro, North Carolina, and Marvin Davenport directed the Johnson C. Smith University band in Charlotte. The first degrees in music were offered in the early 1940s at North Carolina College in Durham and at A&T in Greensboro.[37]

During the war at the request of black citizens, North Carolina Governor J. Melville Broughton created the Negro Navy Band. Hall was asked to provide recommendations for the band and he submitted four names, including Walter Carlson. The Navy Band played more than a thousand performances statewide for parades and war bond rallies as well as concerts. Out of the 26 band members who remained in North Carolina, 20 founded band programs in black public schools.[38]

When Shortie Hall decided to accept a position as band director of Hillside High School in Durham, North Carolina, in 1945, Emmanuel McDuffie declared that it was "impossible to fill his place" at the Institute.[39] Perhaps the testimony of one of his students, Dr. Marion Thorpe, who became Chancellor of Elizabeth City State University in Elizabeth City, North Carolina, offers the best summery of Hall's impact on students' visions of themselves:

> One of the most interesting things about the teaching and advisement of Mr. Hall was his proven ability to motivate students who knew almost nothing about music to excel as instrumentalists. His procedures provided for personal, friendly relationships with his students while demanding excellence in performance and consistency in discipline. Young performers were led to feel good about themselves and their accomplishments.[40]

The jazz trumpeter Dizzy Gillespie, whose account follows, made this acknowledgment of Shortie Hall as well:

> I owe a great debt of gratitude to Maestro Hall. He was one of the great pioneers of our music. ... [He was] a great influence on my early days when I was down South behind the cotton curtain. He's turned out more musicians than you can shake a valve at. I never did call him Shorty. I had too much respect, but that's his professional name. We should get rid of the

Shorty anyway. One day, we're going to get rid of the Dizzy, too. ... Just call me Dr. Gillespie.[41]

When Shorty Hall passed away in 1984, his last wish was fulfilled, to be buried in his Hillside High band uniform.[42] Hall was inducted into the North Carolina Bandmasters Association Hall of Fame in 2002.

12

Dizzy Gillespie Offers a Student's Account of the Institute (1933–1935)

In his autobiography *To Be, or Not ... to Bop* (1979), written with Al Fraser, Dizzy Gillespie described his experience as a boarding student at Laurinburg Institute from 1933 to 1935.[1] Documented sources of teachers and students from the period of 1904 to 1954 are few, so it is especially important to present Gillespie's story. He offers a personal account of what it was like to be a student at the Institute.

John Birks, as he was known at Laurinburg Institute, was born in 1917 in Cheraw, South Carolina, about 20 miles from Laurinburg. He graduated from the intermediate public school there. His father had been a bass player and inspired his two sons to play piano, trumpet and trombone. Explaining his natural inclination to rebel, Dizzy recalled that "my father ... used to whip me every Sunday when I was a kid. Can you imagine that? It was a regular event, something you could count on."[2] Dizzy's father died when he was ten years old, but in junior high, Dizzy played in the school band. The school provided him with "old raggedy instruments" because his family could not afford to buy him one. Although his band teacher could not read music, Dizzy learned to read through a distant cousin who taught a friend who taught him.[3] He developed a reputation among local musicians who allowed him to play with them at dances and juke joints.

After he finished middle school, he went to work at the only job available to a young black boy, digging ditches on a WPA road gang. This experience taught him two lessons, which he never forgot. First, seeing the illiteracy of his fellow gang members who could only sign their names with Xs, he knew he wanted a better education, and second, he learned that he was "too small and lazy for a life of hard labor."[4] Determined to crawl up out of the hole of his family's poverty, Gillespie had the good fortune of good neighbor, Catherine McKay, who was student nurse and band booster at Laurinburg Institute.

McKay knew that the Institute band was going to lose a trumpeter and a trombonist when they went away to college in the fall. The Institute band and orchestra were part of the income sources for the school. Students, who often had no money for tuition, traded playing in the band for board and tuition. The school got paid for the band and orchestra performances, which had become quite popu-

Jazz musician Dizzy Gillespie (1947) attended Laurinburg Institute (1933–35), and was a strong supporter of the school. This portrait by William Gottlieb was made in New York City (courtesy of Library of Congress).

lar in the region. McKay talked up Dizzy and his brother as potential replacements for the graduating players. McDuffie agreed to give them a try.

When McKay told Dizzy about the opportunity, he was skeptical because he had no money, no clothes and no instrument. McKay's response was "You've got lips, don't you?" Dizzy agreed: "I went to Laurinburg Technical Institute strictly on my lips. They gave me food, tuition, room, books, and everything else I needed, free."[5] With a towel, toothbrush and a change of underwear, John Birks arrived on campus.

Gillespie was one of hundreds of boys and girls who came to Laurinburg with nothing and left with a bright future ahead of them. This quality of the school cannot be more emphasized. Unlike many white private schools, where students pay their way and many are academically better prepared, Laurinburg Institute is unique in that they took students where they were—often poor, illiterate and hopeless—and built character, self-reliance, literacy and skills to face a challenging world. Gillespie remembers that "Laurinburg seemed like a complete little town" with "classrooms in McKenzie Hall, dorms, ... a large football field and outside basketball courts, a hospital, ... an administration building ... [and] some of the healthiest-looking crops I'd ever seen.... [T]o a hungry boy like me, the thought of all that food growing around made the place very attractive."[6]

Gillespie learned very quickly that the administration did not tolerate bad behavior and complaining. The philosophy of self-reliance was central to the teachings of the Institute. When Gillespie found that he was being devoured by bedbugs, which were called chinches in the South, he let out a scream that brought the dorm headmaster running. Gillespie was told to air out his mattress in the sunlight which would kill the bugs. He also learned to put kerosene in sardine cans and place them under the bed legs to keep the bugs from crawling up. "What about the eggs?" he asked. The headmaster told him to stop complaining. He could learn to live with the bedbugs or he could do something about it.

The next day he skipped classes, went to the shop and made himself a new straw-stuffed mattress. Soon the whole boarding population made themselves new mattresses. Gillespie remembered that lesson well:

> At Laurinburg they placed great stress on self-reliance in the Booker T. Washington tradition and on lighting candles rather than cursing the dark. It didn't pay to complain or to ask too many questions about shortcomings around there unless you were ready to do some work to change things. I learned you can get a great sense of pride from solving your own practical problems, and I know that I slept better and chinch-free on the mattress I made with my own two hands.[7]

Gillespie also learned lessons from the agriculture program where he was taught that good crops come from good soil management and crop rotation. In winter you plant clover to add nutrients to the soil, and in spring, you harvest healthy food to eat. "That's the key to raising good crops and a lesson about living a rewarding life. Plant on your own personal richness your gifts or talents."[8]

Music and English were Gillespie's special talents. Many of the other subjects he ignored. Rather, he threw himself night and day into studying music, often practicing 24 hours a day, alternating between the trumpet and the piano. He learned about Western harmonic musical theory and studied classical music and piano his first year with Verdelle "Dibba" McDuffie, the eldest child of Emmanuel and Tinny. She had attended Atlanta College and Juilliard for piano training. A saxophonist named Mr. Barnes led the band as well. The Tuskegee graduate

The Laurinburg Institute band (1934), with Dizzy Gillespie (second row far left), helped raise funds for the school (Anzell Harrell Collection, courtesy of Chris Everett).

and band director Phillmore "Shortie" Hall took over the band the second year. Hall had had a professional career as a trumpet player, playing with bands all over the country including the Cotton Club in New York City. A master of many instruments, Hall had his hands full learning the job and trying to teach students to read music. Hall enlisted Gillespie's help with the less well trained students and pretty much left Dizzy alone to work on his own musical ideas. For Gillespie, this freedom was a real boon. He appreciated the "quiet and serenity of being in the country," which gave him the opportunity to greatly expand his musical ideas and he "developed a very serious attitude about music."[9]

Shortie Hall, who was also Dean of Boys and headmaster of the boy's dormitory, remembered these incidents relative to Dizzy's seriousness:

He clowned all the time, that's why the kids nicknamed him Dizzy. He was very serious, however, about his music. Sometimes in the wee hours of the morning around 2:00 a.m. or 3:00 a.m., Dizzy would knock softly on my door there in the boy's dormitory. He and his roommate Benny Pool would be arguing over something that I had taught during band rehearsal that day. The two boys were so interested in what they were learning that I never hesitated to welcome them to my quarters at any hour. There we'd sit while I explained the lesson all over again.[10]

I tried to teach Dizzy to master the horn, to put his personality into the trumpet. I was always doing some little things myself, like I put some things from the overtures like the "1812" into "Tiger Rag," or passages from "The Poet and Peasant Overture" into a break on "Dinah." ... I like to hear Diz play that piece ["A Night in Tunisia"] with all the embellishments. He makes a know-nothing piece sound like an opera. Diz is just as great a master playing trumpet as Einstein is in science.[11]

When Dizzy saw that the football players got more food on their table than other students, he joined the team. His coach Ivory Smith, another Tuskegee graduate and champion player, tried to discourage Dizzy, because he was small and unable to stand up to a charge. Smith stripped off the good equipment Dizzy had put on for practice, piece by piece and gave it to other, larger players. Dizzy said: "Every time that he took back a piece of equipment, I'd imagine three more pork chops piled up on my plate at dinner."[12] By making the winning touchdown during his first game, Dizzy proved himself worthy of those extra pork chops. Later, however, his music teacher Hall pointed out to him that, if he lost his teeth against the junior college-level footballers who played the Laurinburg Institute team, he would not be able to pursue a professional career as a trumpeter. Dizzy never played in a game thereafter except as a band member.

Gillespie offered a number of stories about his relationship with Emmanuel McDuffie, his son Mac McDuffie, and McDuffie's nephew Isaac Johnson. He considered them part of the negro elite in their community. The young men Mac and Isaac would slip into the girls dorm after hours, but when Dizzy attempted to take over their territory with a midnight rendezvous, they reported him to McDuffie and he got a whipping. Shortie Hall remembered that "Diz used to be into devilment all the time. Every time I turned around I had to go see Mr. McDuffy about Diz. I remember one time he climbed in the girls' dormitory. Sometimes he'd be shut out of the cafeteria [as punishment] five days a week."[13]

Gillespie was impressed with Emmanuel McDuffie and, later, his son Frank McDuffie, who took over the school in 1954 after Emmanuel's death. He describes the hierarchy in black society at the time as (1) the undertaker, (2) the doctor, (3) the lawyer and (4) the schoolteacher, but the principal was on a level with the undertaker. Dizzy recognized McDuffie as "a powerful man" because "whenever I saw white people speak to him, they talked with respect." He knew the story of McDuffie's journey to Laurinburg and his starting "this school for poor black kids on pure balls and guts ... he was doing a fantastic job for the people in this area."[14]

McDuffie "ran Laurinburg like a family." I. Ellis Johnson, his brother-in-law, who married Tinny's sister, was dean of the school, and Johnson's brother was treasurer of the Institute. Dizzy said, "It was nepotism if I ever saw it." After McDuffie's seven children graduated from Laurinburg Institute, they all went on to college and came back. Gillespie had great admiration for Mr. McDuffie. Once, when Dizzy corrected Tom Blue, the bass drum player who couldn't read music and who was 100 pounds heavier than Dizzy, Tom came at him enraged. Dizzy pulled a knife to defend himself. When he was called to the principal's office, McDuffie asked if he had pulled a knife. When Dizzy answered yes, McDuffie asked why? Dizzy responded: "Look at him and look at me.[15] ... he could have hit me in my mouth and ruined my embouchure. Mr. McDuffy, I plan to go into music as a career, and I wouldn't be able to play." McDuffie believed him and didn't whip him. Dizzy said, "he was a very understanding man." He went on to characterize McDuffie: "Mr. McDuffy was such a tremendous fellow and stood for such great ideals; I wanted to be around a man of his stature. With all the deprivation, and as hard as we had it down South, he managed to uplift us and instill in us a sense of dignity."[16]

The campus of the Laurinburg Institute was a haven for the black students who longed for respect and dignity. Outside the campus, it was another story. Gillespie frequently travelled with the small elite Laurinburg Institute band to entertain both white and black folks. Shortie Hall recalled an amusing incident when the group was performing at a South Carolina night club and a fight broke out. When the police arrived, they told the band to play "The Star Spangled Banner," which forced the pugnacious fellows to come to attention.[17]

A young white man from Laurinburg was their booking agent and would often travel with them. Once after a gig in Cheraw, Dizzy was asked to drive because the others, including the white guy, were too inebriated to do so. He had never driven before and must have seemed erratic. Two policemen spotted him late at night near the Pee Dee River and nearly ran Dizzy into the river. Dizzy swerved and hit the police car, choosing being arrested over drowning in the river. The policemen thought they were running moonshine. Dizzy was arrested and put in jail. However, one of the policemen had known Dizzy's father and believed his story that they were musicians coming back from a gig. He was released.

Another frightening incident happened to Gillespie on his way home between Gibson and Cheraw. He was hitchhiking alone and he stopped at a store to get something to eat. When he came out, a white man "pulled a gun and said, 'Nigger, do you know how to dance?'" He shot three rounds at Gillespie's feet, which "made me so mad that I did a little buck dance for him.... You'd stop somewhere and get ripped off, and nobody'd ever find out what happened. I often thought about leaving the South, but there was no place better to go."[18]

Dizzy's mother moved to Philadelphia in 1933 during the depression to find work. He was upset because she had moved so far away and felt compelled to follow her. At the same time he was nearing graduation and wanted his degree. Gillespie went to Shortie Hall, his mentor and friend, for advice. Hoping to relieve his fears of moving to a strange place and his disappointment at not graduating, Hall "expressed his faith in John Burke Gillespie: 'You are one of God's chosen people, John. You have a gift—your music. Use your talent and it will multiply; bury your talent and it will decay.'"[19] Gillespie did leave the South in 1935 and ran away from his summer farming job at the Institute. He had failed physics and needed to pass in order to graduate. Years later in 1946, he was touring with Ella Fitzgerald and stopped at the Institute to perform. Emmanuel McDuffie presented him with his diploma and a football letter and Dizzy recalled: "I was very proud of that—after thirteen years, finally taking the step up from being a South Carolina high-school dropout. Mr. McDuffy said he always knew I was gonna amount to something."[20]

The city of Laurinburg presented Gillespie with the Key to the City in 1967, at long last recognizing the treasure that they had when Gillespie was there. At the event, someone reminded Gillespie of a song he liked to sing and play when he was at the Institute, "Goin' to Heaven on a Mule." Dizzy said he "used the philosophy behind it to build my act. The 'mule' is my background in black folk culture and 'heaven' is where I'm at."[21]

Dizzy Gillespie became a great advocate for the school. He and Frank McDuffie dreamed of building a jazz center on the Laurinburg Institute campus called "The John Birks 'Dizzy' Gillespie Center for Cultural Change and Jazz Hall of Fame."[22] Raising the 2.5 million dollars needed for the project proved too difficult. Nonetheless, Gillespie spread the word among well-off blacks that the Institute was a great place to send their kids. He also donated substantially to the Institute.[23]

13

Significant Others

Ray, Moncur, Jones, Covington,
Swan, Johnson, and Collins

Eddie Riley Ray: Record Producer,
First Black Executive at Capitol Records

The strong music program at the Laurinburg Institute also produced other important musicians and music producers. Coming from the Blue Ridge Mountains in 1942, when he was 16, Ray attended the Laurinburg Institute because "it was one of the best and one of the few

Eddie Riley Ray (ca. 1960), was a Laurinburg Institute graduate and was one of the first black executives in the record industry (courtesy of N.C. Music Hall of Fame, Concord, N.C.).

boarding high schools in the country for African American kids. A lot of very important people graduated from that school. Dizzy Gillespie graduated a few years before I did!"[1]

Eddie Ray worked for Decca Records and became the first black executive for Capitol Records in 1964. He produced Ricky Nelson, Fats Domino, and Pink Floyd, among others, and wrote "Hearts of Stone," which made it to the top of the 1954 R&B pop charts nationwide. Ray gave Mike Curb, who became president of MGM Records, his first break in the record business at Capital Records. Curb subsequently hired Ray as his senior vice president at MGM Records. In 1981 President Ronald Reagan appointed Ray to the U.S. Copyright Royalty Tribunal, where he served for eight years. Ray has been a significant contributor to the North Carolina Music Hall of Fame.[2]

Grachan Moncur III: Jazz Musician

Grachan Moncur III may also have heard about the Institute because of Dizzy Gillespie. He came from a family of jazz musicians in Newark, New Jersey. Moncur, who was known as "Butch" at the school, attended Laurinburg Institute for four years beginning in 1952. Unlike many students, his family paid tuition so that he could attend. He met his wife there and his grandson Bruce Moncur also attended the school in the 1990s. Moncur is one of the few living graduates who knew all four generations of the McDuffies. He fondly remembers that "everyone

Grachan Moncur III (1952), played football for the Laurinburg Institute, and he was also a band leader. He played jazz trombone with Art Blakely and Jackie McLean, when they performed at the Laurinburg Institute, and recorded with them on the Blue Note record label in the 1960s. He played with Miles Davis, Herbie Hancock, Sonny Rollins, and Ray Charles (Anzell Harrell Collection, courtesy of Chris Everett).

called [Emmanuel McDuffie] Mr. Chubbs." Another vivid memory of his Institute years was when his best friend Willie Harris saved his trombone from disaster. A fire started in his dorm and Willie grabbed his horn and dashed out of the building just before it collapsed.[3]

As a leader in the Institute band, Moncur sat in with the professional jazz musicians Art Blakey and Jackie McLean when they visited the Institute. Out of this opportunity, he recorded four albums with McLean for Blue Note in the 1960s, including *One Step Beyond* and *Destination.... Out!*, which showcased pieces composed mostly by Moncur. He played with many great musicians including Miles Davis, Herbie Hancock, Sonny Rollins, and Ray Charles. Moncur has recorded nine albums in the lead and 42 albums as a side man. Since 1977 he carried on the free jazz tradition by teaching others.[4]

Sam Jones: Ten Times NBA Champion and Naismith Hall of Famer

The basketball program, under Emmanuel's son Frank McDuffie, produced athletes who won several first place championships in the Conference of Independent Schools Athletic Association.[5] Among those

players was Sam Jones, who was from a poor section of Laurinburg called Blood Field. Jones's father was a brick mason who helped to build the Institute's first gymnasium. Fran McDuffie Foster remembered that Sam lived with them on campus one summer. He was so skinny that Frank, her

Laurinburg native Sam Jones (1969), put the Institute on NBA radar. He played for the Boston Celtics, winning ten NBA championships, and was elected to the NBA Hall of Fame (public domain).

father and Sam's coach, insisted that he "drink a quart of milk every day."[6] According to Bishop McDuffie, Jones developed his "set shot" on account of the cold in the wintertime. Jones would back up to the pot belly stove in the old gym so he could warm his backside. When he felt the heat, he would "shoot the ball, judging the distance by the heat through the rafters, off from the backboard, nothing but net."[7] Upon graduation, Frank McDuffie encouraged Sam to enroll at the all-black North Carolina College (now North Carolina Central University) in Durham in 1952. The three-time Basketball Hall of Famer John McLendon was coaching there at the time. Jones remained a big supporter of the Institute, even attending graduations as late as 2005. He led the way for many black athletes to attend college and, then, on into professional basketball.

Breaking the color barrier was not easy. The Boston Celtics Coach Red Auerbach came to North Carolina looking for talent among the white national champion Tar Heels at the University of North Carolina–Chapel Hill. He heard that "the best player in the state was actually playing for Hall of Fame coach John McLendon."[8] Sam Jones later recalled that "[Bill] Russell and I are the most successful players in winning championships in the NBA. Yet he [Auerbach] never saw us play a game because they had no scouts.... The coaches called other coaches to see how other players were playing. They took their word for it."[9] McLendon convinced Auerbach that Jones had the talent he was looking

Sam Jones's Laurinburg Institute graduation (1952), including from left to right, Wesley Bennett, David Thompson, Sam Jones, Margaret Gee, Jimmy Hardy and Arthur Kibler (Anzell Harrell Collection, courtesy of Chris Everett).

for so the Celtics chose Jones in the first round of the 1957 draft sight unseen. Coach Auerbach showed courage in 1964 when he broke the unwritten rule that at least one player on the basketball floor must be white. Sam Jones was among those five black players including Bill Russell, Tom "Satch" Sanders, K.C. Jones and Willie Naulls.

Jones played for the Boston Celtics for 12 years. He was known as "The Shooter" and "Mr. Clutch," propelling the Celtics to the most dominant position in the NBA. Jones led the team to ten national championships from 1957 to 1969, the most of any player except his teammate Bill Russell. A team statement characterized him as "one of the most talented, versatile, and clutch shooters for the most successful and dominant teams in NBA history.... His scoring ability was so prolific, and his form so pure, that he earned the simple nickname, 'The Shooter.'"[10] The Celtics retired his team No. 24 in 1969 by which time Jones held 11 Celtics records including his achievement as the only player in team history to score more than 50 points in a game. Jones was the second draftee into the Naismith Memorial Basketball Hall of Fame in 1984 and the first black draftee into the North Carolina Sports Hall of Fame. He played on the NBA 25th Anniversary All-Time team, the 50th Anniversary All-Time team, and the 75th Anniversary All-Time team. After retiring as a player, Jones shared his skills as a coach at Federal City College, North Carolina Central and the New Orleans Jazz.[11]

Sam Jones became a beacon for the many young men who followed him to the Laurinburg Institute, where they learned not only basketball skills, but also enough academic skills to get into college and to continue on into professional ball. Jones sent Jimmy Walker from his Roxbury neighborhood in Boston to the Institute. Walker also became a professional basketball player. Years later in 1994, Jones came to the aid of the financially struggling private school. He proudly declared: "It was a school where you came a boy, but left a man."[12]

When Sam Jones passed away in December 2021, LeVelle Moton posted this tribute on the Facebook *Laurinburg Institute* page. It shows how one positive action can lead to a much brighter future for many.

> Without Sam Jones, the "Culture" connected with basketball wouldn't exist. Let me explain. I was born in Boston (Roxbury). In the 60's, Black Celtics players were only allowed to live in Roxbury. There was a kid that Sam took a liking to with an array of talent in Roxbury. Sam sent the kid to his High School (Laurinburg Institute) where he would later excel. He earned a scholarship to Providence where he would have a stellar career and become the #1 pick of the Detroit Pistons in the 67 NBA Draft.
>
> That kid's name was Jimmie Walker and he later had a son by the name of Jalen Rose who would change the face of college basketball as we know it

at The University of Michigan (along with the Fab 5).... Six degrees of separation is Real. The swag, outspokenness, style that we see today, can all be connected back to Mr. Sam Jones.... RIP LEGEND... Love you my man.[13]

John Wesley "Wes" Covington: World Series Champion

John Wesley "Wes" Covington was born in Laurinburg in 1932 and attended the Institute until 1950. At the Institute, Covington earned three letters in football, basketball and track. At first, he wanted to play professional football so he transferred to Hillside High in Durham, hoping the football scouts would notice his athletic talent. Fate intervened when Covington accepted an opportunity to play outfield in the 1951 North Carolina–South Carolina High School Baseball All-Star game.

The then Boston Braves scout Dewey Griggs spotted his talent and offered him a contract to play professional baseball. Still determined to play football with offers from North Carolina State and UCLA, Covington hesitated but changed his mind. He recalled: "You know how it is, I needed a few dollars, they had a few dollars. Good deal. Besides, my wife, then my sweetheart, asked me to play baseball instead."[14]

Like Sam Jones, he was one of the first athletes to integrate major league sports. After a two-year stint in the military, Covington joined the minor leagues with the Eau Clare Bears in 1952. He roomed with Hank Aaron, and they

John Wesley "Wes" Covington (1958), was one of the first blacks to integrate professional baseball, winning with the Milwaukee Braves the 1957 World Series (public domain).

remained friends over the years in the professional leagues. Covington, Aaron and Billy Brunton "became the field 'All-Black' outfield in the National League while with Milwaukee, continuing to fight baseball's color barrier that Jackie Robinson began to tear down just 10 years earlier."[15]

Covington joined the Milwaukee Braves in 1956 and was a major contributor to the Braves' 1957 World Series Championship over the New York Yankees, the first non–New York team to win a World Series since 1948. Covington had a life-time batting average of .279. His "pre-batting ritual described by *Baseball Digest* as a 'spike-knocking, cap-adjusting, hand-dusting, shoe-tying, uniform-tugging and bat-waggling production,' baffled opposing pitchers," and earned him five hits, a run batted in and a stolen base in the 1957 championship for his team.[16] As an outfielder in the 1957 World Series, Covington saved the home run hit by Yankee's Gil McDougald by a crashing-into-the-wall catch, which won them the fifth game of the championship.

Covington played with the Braves, Chicago White Sox, Kansas City Athletics, Philadelphia Phillies, Chicago Cubs, and the Los Angeles Dodgers. He played in three World Series, finally ending his career as a pinch hitter in the 1966 World Series game with the Los Angeles Dodgers. After that game, Covington retired due to knee injuries and he eventually moved to Edmonton, Alberta, Canada, where he owned a sporting goods store and was the advertising manager at the *Edmonton Sun* newspaper. Covington never forgot his roots in Laurinburg, where he visited each year until he died at age 79 in 2011.[17]

Sir John Swan: Premier of Bermuda

Besides outstanding musicians and athletes, the Institute under Emmanuel McDuffie prepared two other significant figures for a life in politics, Sir John Swan from Bermuda was one of them. Grachan Moncur and John Swan were classmates at the Institute in 1952. In a 2009 interview for Chris Everett's film *The Laurinburg Institute, Est. 1904*, Swan stated that the most significant aspect of his Institute experience was that he gained the confidence to go on to all-white schools and not be intimidated. The staff of the Institute not only taught academic subjects, but they also developed strength of character among their pupils who could stand up with pride and confidence in the wider world.

Swan was elected to the Bermuda Parliament in 1972, and served as Minister of Marine and Air Services (1975–1976) and Minister of Immigration and Labour (1976–1982). In 1982, Swan became the Premier of

Bermuda, a post which he held until he resigned in 1995. After leading the Tax Treaty with the United States in 1985, Swan enriched Bermuda by creating a leading offshore financial center and significant real estate developments, which stabilized the country and offered prosperity for many residents. Queen Elizabeth recognized Swan's contributions to his country and to the British Empire by knighting him in 1990.[18]

Sir John Swan (2007), was Premier of Bermuda (1982–1995). He was knighted by Queen Elizabeth in 1990 (courtesy of Sir John Swan).

North Carolina House of Representative Joy J. Johnson

Joy Johnson attended Laurinburg Institute for four years from 1933 to 1937. He gave an account of his life in his self-published book *From Poverty to Power* in 1976.[19] It gives us a good representation of the life and challenges for black citizens of North Carolina. Since the Institute was the only black high school in the county, located in Laurinburg, he was forced to travel 10 miles on foot or by hitching a ride to get to high school. Johnson was raised on a poor farm in Laurel Hill. So determined was he to get an education that he would rise in the dark to feed the animals and walk the distance to school. It was dark when he got home and still there were chores to do like chopping wood. Although the white kids had many school buses, not one mode of transportation was offered to the county black kids who needed them the most. This situation caused many black kids to stop school after the eighth grade. They also missed school because of the demands of harvesting crops. Tenant farmers needed their kids to work when the crops had to be harvested. Johnson recalled, "No Blacks attended any schools until the cotton was picked."[20] The last two years of his tenure at the Institute, a school bus was purchased through the efforts of parents and Mrs. W.F. Carlson, a faculty member. This change made his balancing act of chores and school more manageable.

Johnson was inspired by his teachers Frank and Mac McDuffie, Jr., Thelma Ervin Pugh, J.T. Speller and J.E. Melton. In spite of the challenges he faced, Johnson thrived at the Institute, graduating with honors, and determined to go to college. He and his family had no money so college seemed out of reach for him, but he had faith. Johnson said, "I heard a voice saying clearly, 'Have Faith, for All Things Are Possible, If You Only believe and Work Diligently.'"[21] Johnson began his ministry at age 16 at the Laurel Hill First Baptist Church. The members of the church raised money to send him to Shaw University, where he also received a scholarship.

The Laurinburg Institute graduate Joy Johnson was the second black man to be elected to the North Carolina House of Representatives since the Democratic white supremacist revolution in 1898. Johnson was a "firebrand Baptist minister," who served his community not only as a spiritual advisor, but also as an instrument of change. He served four terms from 1971 to 1979 and represented the 48th District which includes both Scotland and Robeson counties. The first black N.C. House Representative was Henry Frye, who was elected in 1969, and served Guilford County. They had little power, but together they pressured their white colleagues to make significant changes to Jim Crow laws such as banning the state's literacy tests which blocked black citizens from voting. Frye recalled, "Joy could preach to our colleagues and he would fire them up with his oratory, and then I would sit and negotiate with them."[22]

Joy J. Johnson (1973), was the second black man to be elected to the North Carolina House of Representatives. He led the fight to repeal Jim Crow laws. Portrait by Waller Studio.

Johnson's first effort in the assembly was to sponsor the 1971 Equal Opportunity Act, which required all state purchasing agencies to be open to bids from all people, particularly black people. The passing of that bill was encouraging but many other bills were an uphill battle. Johnson fought the sterilization program, which had passed in 1933 to force indigent citizens to bear no more children. By the 1970s, 7,686 women had been sterilized, 5,000 of them black. I personally knew a woman in Laurinburg who had been sterilized and crippled by the operation. Johnson fought against the Welfare Lien Act, which forced people on welfare to lose their homes. He also sponsored bills for prison reform, including restoration of citizen rights to felons who had served their time and minimum wages for prisoners who worked while in prison. He was also a strong advocate for the support of black state colleges, which never received funding equal to white schools.[23]

George W. Collins: Pioneering Newsman and Broadcaster

George Collins was born in Bennettsville, South Carolina, raised in Statesville, North Carolina, and attended the Laurinburg Institute as a boarding student. He graduated in 1944. After serving in the Air Force in communications and logistics from 1945 to 1947, Collins started his career in New York City as a reporter for *The People's Voice* founded by Adam Clayton Powell. He moved to Baltimore in 1950 and joined the *Afro-American Newspapers* staff as a reporter, working his way up to editor-in-chief over his 18 year tenure. As newspapers waned and television largely took over the reporting of news, Collins became the second black man hired by WMAR-TV, where he served as a news editor, political analyst, investigative reporter and editorial director. He also hosted two television programs that targeted the black community, called "Man-to-Man" and "Straight Talk." Dale Wright, manager of WMAR, said this about Collins: "He was one of the old-school news people who had the ability to write their own stories, get the facts, and make sure what they were saying was accurate. Collins' fellow broadcaster Andy Barth added "George had guts. He knew the power he had as a reporter, and he used it courageously to help right wrongs."[24]

Collins covered all the major civil rights stories and was instrumental in uncovering political corruption in Maryland. He achieved national prominence when he investigated the "Route 40 Caper." Several African diplomats, who were dressed normally, had been refused service at a restaurant along Route 40 from Washington to Baltimore.

The Kennedy Administration was embarrassed by the incident. Collins and two other reporters dressed up in elaborate African costumes and morning suits with top hats. They emerged out of a limousine and entered a number of restaurants along Route 40. None of the eating establishments refused service to those they thought were African diplomats, yet no ordinary black citizen could receive service. Collins exposed the class prejudices and racial inequities of the public establishments in Maryland. Two years later the State of Maryland passed laws banning discrimination against blacks in restaurants and hotels, the first state south of the Mason-Dixon Line to enact such laws.

During his long 65 year career as a newsman, Collins earned the respect of both his colleagues and his audiences. He made a difference for his race and for justice. In 2003, the Library of America, the National Committee for Excellence in Journalism and the Smithsonian Institution honored him jointly as "one of the best American journalists of the 20th century."[25]

The Laurinburg Institute influenced many young men and women, who went on to contribute richly to the raising of the black race in the eyes of the world. The alumni so far discussed were "shining lights in the darkness" of Jim Crow years, where "separate but equal" pretended to rule the day. They offered examples of the greatness that could be achieved when given the opportunity to engage and flourish in the wider white world. The next section, Part III, deals with the challenges of integrating into that world.

PART III

The Laurinburg Institute

Frank H. McDuffie, Sr.
(1954–1994)

14

The Cost and Legacy
of the Institute
to Public Education

The Civil Rights Movement put pressure on the Southern states to provide equal education opportunities for all. The Supreme Court 1954 Brown v. Board of Education decision dictated the complete integration of schools nationally. Schools often remained segregated merely by requiring students to attend schools where they lived, which for blacks was not in white neighborhoods. The Institute student Charlie Scott, who grew up in Harlem and became a member of the NBA Basketball Hall of Fame, remembered that in the North it was "segregation by diplomacy. You didn't know it but you were still segregated. Nothing had really changed; it's just that it wasn't talked about in the North. It was just a matter of where you lived."[1] By building schools in the black neighborhoods of Laurinburg, the school board managed to keep education segregated until 1966 when the fully integrated Scotland County High School was opened.

Four new Scotland County public black schools were built during 1952–53, including Lincoln Heights High School and Washington Park Elementary School in Laurinburg and Carver and Shaw in Scotland County. At long last, the Washington Park public school, which had been proposed by the developer in 1926 and had been supported by the Director of the North Carolina Division of Negro Education N.C. Newbold in countless pleas to the school board, was built in 1952–1953 to serve the black elementary and middle school children.

A former Institute student Mary Helen Speller recalled how badly the black children fared at the Laurinburg Institute which was "straining to meet the needs" of so many kids with so little support: "When I was going to school, we would get hand-me-down books. After the white children got tired of the books or they were torn or were outdated, the books were donated to the Laurinburg Institute. ... Desks we used, run down and in poor condition."[2]

The brand new schools were a great source of pride for the whole community. The students found a comforting continuity in their teachers who moved from the Institute to the public schools with ease.

The Institute Provides Teachers for the New Public Black Schools

The loss of students for the Laurinburg Institute was the gain of teachers for the four new Scotland County public black schools. In addition to the loss of the original campus, the Institute suffered the loss of its dean of 42 years, I. Ellis Johnson. Johnson became the principal of the new black public school Lincoln Heights. A number of former Institute teachers, including James Speller, Joy McDuffie, Ivory Smith and Isabelle Smith, followed Johnson into the public sector of education as well. The Institute phased out the lower grades over a period of time until only the ninth through the twelfth grades remained. A few out of the many Institute teachers who moved into the public sector are recognized below.

Dean and Principal I. Ellis Johnson and Amanda Johnson

Isaac Ellis Johnson was brought to the Laurinburg Institute in 1912 by Emmanuel McDuffie. They married sisters and were brothers-in-law. Like the McDuffies, the Johnsons had attended Snow Hill Institute. He served over forty years as dean and principal of the Institute. Johnson and four other faculty members were employed officially by the public school system and paid by State of North Carolina, long before he became the interim principal of the new Washington Park public school in 1952–1953, while still associated with the Institute.[3] He was in charge of all the public school students at the Institute. So, Johnson was the natural choice to take over the new black public schools. He already had a close relationship with the students and parents of Laurinburg.

When the new Lincoln Heights School was completed in the fall of 1953, Johnson was appointed principal of the school, which initially offered grades one through twelve and four trade courses. His wife

Amanda also taught there. His long time service to the Institute made him well prepared to take over the new public school. Johnson's granddaughter Thelma Dawson remembered him as "a great guy. Pretty calm and he cared a lot about his students.... He wanted to see everybody learn and get ahead.... A lot of people thought a lot of him. He helped a lot of people."[4]

At the time of his retirement in 1964, the school was renamed I. Ellis Johnson Elementary in his honor. By 1966, the school had integrated. The Laurinburg schools' Superintendent A.B. Gibson made this tribute to Johnson at his retirement celebration:

> The fact that Mr. Johnson has served here for 52 years is no little accomplishment in itself, but I must remind you that an understanding of this man lies far deeper in the complex issues of the heart. Mr. Johnson has erected his career of service to his fellowman without the slightest taint of selfishness. He has not permitted the harsh winds of controversy or the pressure of unkind circumstances to cause him to veer from the straight path. He has had many hard decisions to make and at times, no doubt, has had occasion to be troubled but nothing has affected the sweetness of his spirit. He has held his head high above the passions and prejudices of our age. As much as any man I have known, he has been and continues to be the captain of his own soul.[5]

I. Ellis and Amanda Johnson (center) between Superintendent A.B. Gibson (left) and Chair of Scotland County School Board Halbert Jones (right) at the Johnsons' retirement ceremony (1964), in Laurinburg, North Carolina. I. Ellis Johnson was principal of Laurinburg Institute (1912–1952), before directing the first public black high school Lincoln Heights (1953–1964) (courtesy of Beacham McDougald and *Laurinburg Exchange*).

Amanda Johnson was in charge of the public school lunch program at the Laurinburg Institute for many years. She cooked and supervised thousands of meals served to all the public school children who attended the Institute from 1912 to 1953. After her husband transferred to Lincoln Heights, she taught school there.

Sam Littlejohn, Sr.

Sam Littlejohn, Sr., first came to teach science and math at the Institute, but later he taught in the nearby public schools of Hamlet for 32 years. When he heard that a special federally funded class in astronomy was to be taught at St. Andrews Presbyterian College in Laurinburg, he tried to enroll in the class but was denied entry because of his race. Littlejohn confirmed the information he had concerning the federal funding and informed the college officials that they had no right to deny him entry because public funds were being used to fund the course. They apologized and enrolled him in the class, making Littlejohn the first black student to integrate St. Andrews Presbyterian College in 1960. Littlejohn recalled: "They were very nice to me. I worked hard in the course and made no mistakes. The other students didn't bother me."[6] He even brought his son to look through the class telescope and he helped set up a planetarium for the students. Littlejohn later was appointed to the Laurinburg City Council in 1971 and served as mayor pro temp in 1972.[7]

Anzell Harrell, Sr.

Anzell Harrell was the assistant principal of the Laurinburg Institute at the time of its transition. Harrell provided many of the photographs for this book. He continued his career as an educator in the Scotland County public schools, teaching at Shaw and I. Ellis Johnson before becoming an assistant principal at the integrated Scotland High School, where he taught driver's education to all students. At an event honoring Harrell in 2013, Terence Williams, president of the Scotland County NAACP chapter, summarized Harrell's contributions: "He was everybody's driver's ed teacher, and he was one that went above and beyond the call of duty in making sure that people locally began to start off with a good education, thus moving them forward. ... He did not mind sharing the knowledge so that everybody's family could be just as successful as he was."[8] Williams announced that the NAACP chapter

was establishing a scholarship honoring Harrell for
his life-long commitment to
educating the youth of Scotland County.

**Anzell Harrell (1952), was
assistant principal of Laurinburg Institute and later
became an assistant principal of the integrated Scotland
High School in 1966 (Anzell
Harrell Collection, courtesy
of Chris Everett).**

15

Reinventing the Institute as a Private Prep School

While many staff members migrated to the public school system, following their students, Frank and Sammie McDuffie remained committed to continuing the educational mission of the Institute, now as an entirely private preparatory school. Frank met his wife Sammie at North Carolina A&T State University. Frank was voted the "Most Versatile" in 1936 and Sammie, the "Most Pleasing Personality" three years in a row. She was also named the first "Miss A&T" for the 1934–35 school year. Sammie played basketball, sang in the choir and was a member of the student council.[1] Frank was captain of the tennis team. He went on to earn a master's degree from the University of Pittsburgh and was granted an honorary Ph.D. from North Carolina A&T State University. After finishing collage, they married and both taught at the Institute. Sammie taught home economics, math and science, and Frank taught history, choir and physical education. He also coached basketball. After leading the Laurinburg Institute for more than fifty years, Sammie Sellers McDuffie and Frank H. McDuffie, Sr., were awarded The Order of the Long Leaf Pine, the highest honor awarded by the Governor of North Carolina in 1996.

Frank and Sammie McDuffie had to reinvent the mission of the school. After the sudden loss of local students to the new public black schools in 1953, the Institute had only 87 boarding students and 14 teachers, half of whom were McDuffie family members. Originally the Institute served all the black students of Laurinburg and also boarding students from grades one through twelve, but when their numbers dwindled from 1100 to 87, the administration decided to gradually eliminate the lower grades, catering to their boarding students who usually came in at the high school level, offering only grades nine through twelve. Bishop McDuffie, who was a young child at the time, claims his parents closed each grade from one to eight as he finished each one so that he could be educated entirely at the Institute. Once the school was reduced to a high school only, they had to charge more substantial tuitions, which would support the school, and develop the patronage of the growing middle class of black patrons.

The McDuffies continued running the Institute as a private school. As their parents before them, they chose not to affiliate with a church denomination in order to gain financial support. Because they were no longer able to raise funds from Northern patrons based on the lack of a public school for black children, financial support dwindled, and the

Frank and Sammie McDuffie, Jr. (ca. 1960), began teaching and coaching at the Institute in the late 1930s. They later directed the Laurinburg Institute for forty years (1954–1994), (courtesy of Dr. Fran McDuffie Foster).

McDuffies could not keep up the maintenance of the Institute buildings. By 1958, the original buildings were in such bad repair that they were condemned.

With the help of generous donations from Dizzy Gillespie, the McDuffies, then, opted to tear down the old buildings and rebuild them across the creek from the old campus. The old buildings were torn down brick by brick and students moved the usable building materials to the new site. Those bricks had been handmade by students back when the industrial curriculum was emphasized in the early days of the Institute. The new buildings reflected the scaled down enrollment of the school, which had dropped from 1100 as a public school to 87 as a private boarding school.

The new building program began in 1958 with the cafeteria, where students were transported from their dorms on the old campus to have their meals. By 1960 they had reassembled the bricks into the buildings

E.M. McDuffie Administration and Classroom Building (1960), was built when the Institute dramatically lost the public enrollment of over 1000 students and transitioned to a 87–150 student private boarding high school (Anzell Harrell Collection, courtesy of Chris Everett).

on the new campus, which included boys' and girls' dormitories and an academic classroom building. Later on, a music building, a library, and a gymnasium with playing fields, a swimming pool and a tennis court were added to the new campus. These buildings were not as grand as the old ones, but they, along with the growing reputation of the Laurinburg Institute, provided enough to keep the school going.

Frank and Sammie McDuffie looked toward the future and realized that the way forward was to build a program that prepared their students to integrate into the wider world of opportunity in white institutions of higher education. Better academic training was one path forward and developing top athletic talent was another. Sammie led the academic program and Frank managed the athletic program. Both programs were designed to guarantee college acceptance not only to black colleges but also to predominantly white colleges.

Providing a Solid Foundation Academically: Faculty and Staff

Many fine Institute teachers migrated with their students into the new public schools, but others remained committed to the Institute. Certainly those who taught grades one through eight took public school jobs. However, those teachers, who taught at the high school level and chose to remain loyal to the Institute, had to make sacrifices for their loyalty. Andre Mack, a graduate of the Institute, put it this way:

Among us are people who declined better opportunities to instead work at Laurinburg Institute. They lived our motto: Deeds, Not Words.... Some worked at Laurinburg Institute for decades—Paul Baldwin, Peter Gomez, Vernon Johnson, Cynthia McDuffie, etc. Some were multi-subject teachers. They all gave multi-level instruction in terms of student comprehension. Our coaches, staff, and teachers quietly endured low pay without increases ... and no employment incentives....[2]

Frank McDuffie, Sr.

Beginning with the headmaster, Frank McDuffie, Sr., set the tone for rigorous student learning. His daughter Fran, who became a doctor, said her father repeated this mantra over and over: "Stay in college, graduate and become good tax paying citizens."[3] His leadership went beyond the classroom as one student, Dr. J. Gentile Everett, recalled:

Dr. McDuffie ... took me in like a son. He made me read the Harvard classics and I hated it, but every day for two hours he made me read this tremendous volume of books. Little did I know that he saw something in me that I never saw myself.... I am the person I am now because of The Laurinburg Institute. I'll tell anyone that.[4]

Everett went on to graduate in 1983 from St. Andrews Presbyterian College, and attended North Carolina A&T State University, Southeastern Baptist Theological Seminary and Duke Divinity School. He now is the head pastor at Mill Branch Baptist Church, an integrated congregation of a thousand or more people, in Fairmont, North Carolina. Everett has written four books including *The Making of a Life* (2011) and *The Eternal Divorce: Church History and Public Education* (2013), which has been adopted for classroom study at Wake Forest University, Duke University Divinity School and Shaw University.[5]

Another 1983 Institute graduate, Leon Rice, characterized his extracurricular learning experience with Frank McDuffie in this way:

At Laurinburg Institute every moment in the day was a teaching moment— way beyond the usual curriculum. I remember going to the store and a member of the faculty asked me, "Do you really need that?" He asked me to think about where I spent my money and what I spent it on. The question would become, "Is this a need or a want?" This lesson was taught to me by the Headmaster and President of the school, Dr. Frank McDuffie, Sr. He taught us that every dollar is power, capital power. He encouraged us to think about who we handed that power to, so we shouldn't blindly give it to those who didn't care about our community. That's a lesson every school should teach, that capital is the true power in the US.[6]

Sometimes Frank McDuffie had to play the role of protector as well as teacher for his students. Bishop McDuffie recalled one incident which illustrates this point. The young boy, aged 12, John Russell was walking through the colored section of Laurinburg in Washington Park. A white girl spat on him and he slapped her in response. He was arrested and brought up before a judge. Frank went to court with Russell and begged the judge to release him into his custody. Frank brought him back to the Institute and allowed him to live in the dormitory until he graduated. Russell went on to a career as a professional basketball referee in the CIAA. Through Frank's recommendation to UNC Coach Dean Smith, Russell became the first black referee in the NCAA. He is now in the North Carolina Basketball Hall of Fame.

Frank McDuffie became a passionate advocate for his basketball players, taking them to college campuses and pushing college coaches to offer them scholarships. Sam Jones was one such player, who won a scholarship to North Carolina College for Negroes under Coach John McLendon. McDuffie actively communicated with coaches at predominately white schools such as Providence, Davidson, UNC, N.C. State, and Wake Forest as well as the black college coaches. Always pushing his "great experiment," Frank McDuffie led the fight for equal opportunities for all races.

Besides his determination to promote and defend his students, McDuffie also encouraged them to find community and joy in musical associations. He conducted the Laurinburg Institute choir, which performed each Sunday morning for the local radio station WEWO. His sister Musa Butler provided the piano accompaniment.[7]

June Harrell

Mrs. June Harrell was given the first 2013 NAACP Legacy award in Laurinburg. She, along with her deceased husband Anzell Harrell, Sr., were honored at the event. Both taught at the Laurinburg Institute. June Harrell graduated from North Carolina A&T State University in 1956 and joined the teaching staff of the Institute in the same year. She taught business classes along with band and choir classes. Her college training included a business major as well as conducting classes, where she played the French horn.

Harrell recalled the seriousness of the academic atmosphere at the Institute and lamented the lack thereof in today's schools: "There's no comparison from when I started to what goes on today. ... I don't think kids value their education as they did then."[8] Harrell endeavored to be

Mrs. June Harrell's typing class (1960), with Bobbie Covington and William Holt (back row), George Whidbee and Renee McNeal (center row), Mattie Everett and Eugene Spencer (front row), (Anzell Harrell Collection, courtesy of Chris Everett).

fair with her students but also firm in her expectations of them: "I saw a change through the years as to the students.... But I never changed my tactics and the way that I dealt with my students, and it always worked." She eventually saw doctors and lawyers emerge from her classes. They often came to visit Harrell in her retirement, expressing their gratitude for her determined belief in their future accomplishments.

Frances McDuffie took students on trips to Europe, touring Germany, Italy, Switzerland and Austria. These trips widened the students' knowledge of the wider world and gave them a vision of boarder possibilities. Bishop McDuffie took students on tours of college campuses, such as Shaw, North Carolina A&T, Clark, Atlanta, and Spellman Universities. He wanted his students to believe that they could achieve a college degree if they worked hard in their classes and prepared for their SATs.

These invaluable teachers provided the foundation upon which students thrived. Expectations were high, with no excuses allowed. Each senior was handed a "Senior Syllabus," a packet of papers, which summarized the courses they had taken. Critical knowledge of the subject matter was required by all. The students were examined in an oral group exam, and they had to demonstrate their understanding of the material. The faculty would ask a question, and if the student answered the question incorrectly, the next student would attempt the answer until the correct response was elicited. The student could not graduate until he could demonstrate a complete understanding of the subjects. Student orations were also required of graduating students, demonstrating their ability to express their knowledge clearly.

Once graduation arrived, parents came from far and wide. The parents were put up in the dormitories since hotel space was still a problem for black travelers. The proud parents were treated to a Presidential luncheon in the yard, with white linen tablecloths, while the student awards, such as "Most Likely to Succeed," were announced.

16

Building Character
and Confidence

The one quality that almost all Laurinburg Institute graduates say they acquired was confidence or simply the belief in themselves to accomplish the things they desired. Character building was as much of the Laurinburg experience as academic or athletic training. The Reverend Dr. J. Gentile Everett, a 1979 graduate of Laurinburg Institute, explained: "They took me and said, just because you are born poor, doesn't mean you have a deficit. Just because you are born black, doesn't mean you have a handicap. I will never in my life forget that."[1] Leon Rice wrote in *Divergents Magazine* about his experience as a student at the Laurinburg Institute during 1979–1983.[2] His testimony also is worth repeating.

> ...very few [prep schools] prepare students the way Laurinburg Institute does. The institute teaches the whole person, explicitly teaching the skills you need to navigate the majority culture as well as academic skills and athletic skills, skills you find at most prep schools. They teach you how to carry yourself as an African American and be successful in life well after your high school days are gone.... [They] teach young black men how to handle adversity and setbacks as stepping stones to get to their goals.... Students learn to assess, adapt, and overcome the many challenges that young black men and women face.... The faculty would work with students one-on-one to get them up to speed.... Their model was to take each student where they were, and to work with her or him as a unique person.
>
> The Laurinburg Institute taught me how to live and thrive in America while being black.... So, students like me—struggling to find their confidence in a world of misunderstanding and institutional barriers—are transformed into confident, active members of society. We go out into the world armed with the tools of argument and research and evidence, as well as an understanding of the ways to fit into society ... to adapt and overcome, no matter what the obstacles we face. I learned that at Laurinburg, and it's a lesson that's lasted.[3]

Isaac Logan: A North Carolina Student's Life at a Private Boarding School (1959–1961)

Isaac Logan wanted to go to college. He grew up in Marion, North Carolina, and attended the public schools there. He realized that his education was "very limited in the sense that I was often helping other students there who were lagging behind in several subjects and there was very little incentive for me to try to learn more beyond what I was getting."[4] His father spoke to their minister, who suggested applying to Laurinburg Institute "for better opportunities for learning."

Coming to the Institute in 1959, he found the campus in a state of transition from the old, now condemned, campus to the new campus across the creek. Logan lived in the old boy's dorm and ate and attended classes on the new campus. He even helped to build the new boy's dorm on Saturdays by transporting bricks, which had been salvaged from the old buildings and cleaned by the students for one cent a piece, to the new campus in Dr. McDuffie's green Ford truck.

The school seemed to Logan like a "military school" because every minute of the day was scheduled with some class or activity. Isaac described his living conditions as "good, clean, and safe." After room inspections on week days, students went to the cafeteria for a breakfast of grits, fat back and powdered eggs. Then,

Roommates Issac Logan (left) from Marion, N.C., and Cornelius Starkley from New York, N.Y., 1960. Logan graduated valedictorian from the Institute and became an engineer managing the production of U.S. fighter jets for Northrop Grumman Aerospace in Los Angeles for 30+ years (Anzell Harrell Collection, courtesy of Chris Everett).

students went on to classes with a bag lunch with a sandwich and a piece of fruit. Sports, band and choir practice kept everyone busy until dinner time with a hot meal. Quiet time was observed for two hours of study time after supper. Saturdays were work days, when students could earn pin money for incidentals and snacks. Socializing occurred in the new student activity center, where they played board games and cards. On Sundays, breakfast was special, "grits with real eggs and bacon.... I love GRITS, even until today." Wednesday evenings and Sundays were filled with chapel, Sunday School, church and the student-run Christian Endeavors. Logan participated in band and choir, which Dr. McDuffie led and took around to both white and black neighborhoods during the Christmas season, singing carols.

Logan's favorite classes were math and science. He particularly liked trigonometry, which was taught by his favorite teacher Mr. Bryant. Logan strove to make all "A's" and eventually graduated first in his class. His grounding in math and the sciences prepared him well for a career in engineering, which eventually led to managing the production of U.S. fighter jets, such as the F-18, B-2, JSTARS, Global Hawk, and JSF-35, for Northrop Grumman Aerospace in Los Angeles for thirty-plus years. Logan said the most influential person in his life at the Institute was his teacher Bryant, who also lived in his dormitory as the Dean of Boys. Bryant advised him how to behave, "dating girls, getting your priorities straight and self control." He described the McDuffie family (Frank, his siblings Mac, Iva Melton and Musa Butler, and his wife Sammie) as "one excellent team and family with the same goals and purpose for building excellence in their students."

Confidence came with responsibilities well fulfilled. Logan said, "I think allowing me the opportunity to be trusted in a leadership position and given the responsibility that went along with that position" boosted my pride and self-confidence. The trust invested in Logan by giving him responsible jobs, such as driving the activity bus, the work truck and the brand new Buick owned by Mrs. Musa Butler, also demanded "accountability." Besides jobs, Logan was elected leader of the Sunday night Christian Endeavors program, which the whole faculty and student body attended. As president, Logan learned to prepare and present a lesson each week, which taught him the value of careful planning and good public speaking. The final honor awarded him was to memorize and deliver Booker T. Washington's 1895 Atlanta Compromise Speech at the graduation ceremonies in 1961.

Dr. Gerald Hassell: Clinical Psychologist and Laurinburg Institute Student (1971–1973)

Gerald Hassell remembers the date, September 8, 1971, when he left New York City for Laurinburg, because that was the day his son Nile was born.[5] He was only 17 years old at the time, and he recalled visiting the hospital to welcome his son just before boarding the bus for Laurinburg. That separation became the ground upon which he later built his career as a clinical psychologist.

Unlike Isaac Logan, Hassell came to Laurinburg Institute on a basketball scholarship. Frank McDuffie, who coached the basketball team up until 1970, had decided that the best way to get young black men into college, and particularly into white colleges, was through basketball. McDuffie set up a gap year for basketball players, who needed academic

Clinical psychologist Dr. Gerald Hassell (2023), a 1973 Institute graduate, specialized in supporting fatherless men through his clinical work and his book *The Impact of Father Absence on African American Boys*, 2023 (courtesy of Gerald Hassell).

as well as athletic coaching, in the early 1970s. Prior to that time, in the early 1960s, McDuffie formed relationships with Holcombe Rucker and other Harlem basketball stars, including Earl "The Goat" Manigault and Charlie Scott, who will offer their own Laurinburg stories in the following chapters. Hassell made the Institute connection through Howie Evans, a *New Amsterdam News* sports reporter, who encouraged him to apply.

A brand new boys' dormitory, Bidwell Hall, became his new home on the Laurinburg campus. Hassell described it as clean, carpeted and, most importantly, air conditioned. The South was like another country to a New Yorker. Besides the usual separate water fountains, bath rooms and seating in the movie theaters, Hassell experienced several memorable incidents which emphasized that fact. On an exploratory trip to see the campus at St. Andrews Presbyterian College, he and his buddies, who were on foot, were chased by a gang of white boys in a pick-up truck. He remembers hiding in the bushes as they passed, scared to death. On another occasion, Hassell was in a local department store as the radio announced that Governor George Wallace had been shot. Amongst the screaming and crying white customers, Hassell and his friend said, "Let's get out of here!" It didn't feel safe. Hassell also didn't feel safe among the local black men because they were jealous of his privileged education and his success with the local black girls.

The Laurinburg Institute campus was the only place that felt comfortable. There he dressed up New York style and was "clean to the bone." Most of the students were from up North, with a make-up of about 80 percent male and 20 percent female, which created a very competitive atmosphere for attention. The fact that the boys were not allowed on the girls' side of the campus didn't help either. Wednesday night was fried chicken night, when Hassell inevitably would beg in vain for an extra piece of chicken from Mrs. Lyle, the cafeteria cook. He remembers Frank McDuffie as a "no nonsense" kind of guy. When McDuffie entered the room, it got quiet. Everyone wanted his approval. And, Frank wanted his mother Tinny's approval, the true matriarch of the McDuffie family, a proud, stoic lady.

When it came to basketball, Hassell said: "It was the most competitive basketball in my life!" There was so much talent on the team that the practices were better than the games because there was so much rivalry between the boys from the NYC boroughs. Coach Ellis led the team locally, but when they went to play the freshmen teams from UNC–Chapel Hill, Duke, N.C. State, and Wake Forest, Frank McDuffie took over coaching.

In spite of the high level of play on the basketball team, by far the "biggest impact" on Hassell's life was the excellent academic program. It was the first time he had teachers who had graduate degrees, even Ph.D.s. It also was the first time he was expected to perform well academically as well as athletically. His New York school experience only emphasized athletic, not academic excellence. A high level of expectation coupled with rigorous practice and committed teachers gave him the tools to succeed in life. The courses required, particularly chemistry, physics and trigonometry, set him on a path bound for college. His New York education didn't offer him such opportunity. His favorite teachers were Mr. Gilchrist in chemistry and Mr. Melton in math, but his most feared and revered teacher was Mrs. Iva McDuffie Melton, his English teacher.

Hassell remembers that Mrs. Melton didn't smile a lot, but she was meticulous and demanding. She required excellence through persistent pressure to perform until you got it right. She would never let you give up. Her red pencil covered your paper, but, in the end you gained the knowledge and the confidence you needed to succeed. Hassell says, even to this day, he remembers "to dot my i's" because of her expectations. When he shares something he's written with a fellow Institute student today, and his friend finds an error, his friend always says, "You know Mrs. Melton ain't gonna like that!"

Mrs. Melton was in charge of the dreaded graduation orations. Hassell chose to memorize F.D. Roosevelt's presidential inauguration speech. Memorization was the easy part. Then, Mrs. Melton had you outline the speech, choosing key sentences, and write in your own words your interpretation of the speech. This exercise taught students how to organize and express their thoughts clearly and logically. Hassell says, when he defended his Ph.D. dissertation, the DNA that he had acquired from Laurinburg and Mrs. Melton kicked in, and he easily passed his examination.

After graduation, Hassell attended Virginia State University for a semester, but the love of his son drew him back to New York City, where "we grew up together." Eventually Hassell got a basketball scholarship to Talladega College in Alabama where he majored in psychology. After marrying a Talladega girl, he moved to Dayton, Ohio, where he graduated with a Ph.D. in clinical psychology from Wright State University. Hassell practiced clinical psychology for the states of New York and Georgia, as well as having his own private practice, until retirement. He specialized in treating fatherless black men, for whom he wrote the book *The Impact of Father Absence on African American Boys* (2023).[6]

Laurinburg Institute gave Gerald Hassell the strength of character and confidence he needed to succeed in life. It also built those qualities into many other students. The following discussion illustrates the many ways that the Laurinburg Institute constructed character and confidence in its students.

Good Appearance, Tidiness and Civility

Self-respect began at the Institute with appearance. The new prep school students wore school uniforms which distinguished them from

Confidence began at the Institute with creating a good appearance. Uniformed Senior Class (1979): (front row) Michael Colbert, Artie Gaines, Karry Causey, Garry Causey, Wayne Marshall, Eric Martin, Charles McKinney, (second row) Kevin Brinson, Peter McFarlane, Archie Steele, Shari Tobias, Benita Haynes, Denise Cooper, John Peterson, Maurice Lassen, Donchee Lockwood, Michael Francis, (third row) Kevin Duff, Myron Jones, Michael Stagger, Michael Armstrong, Reginald Reid, Albert Jefferson, Jeffrey Smith, Louis Levins, Anthony Thomas, Larry Howze, Keith Branch, Roy Jones, Jerry Clark, Pierre Tamba, John Woodbury, Abdoulie Jagne, Lloyd Javois (Anzell Harrell Collection, courtesy of Chris Everett).

others in town. Grooming and cleanliness were required at all times. The 1979 graduate Dr. J. Gentile Everett shared these memories concerning the importance of appearance in his book *The Making of a Life* (2011):

> Over and over again, in my mind I hear the voice of my mentor Dr. F.H. McDuffie constantly staying on me about achievement, and not just activity....
>
> Every Wednesday we were required to wear a school uniform, which consisted of gray slacks, a white shirt, and a dark blue blazer with the Laurinburg Institute seal, dark tie, dark socks, and black shoes. Similarly, the girls' outfit were along the same lines. Well, I thought that was nice, and I looked

forward to wearing it every Wednesday. We wore it all day for breakfast, lunch, dinner, and for the evening vesper services that were required for us to attend, without exception.[7]

Advice was given about how to carry yourself, posture and attitude. Shortie Hall told his students: "Never hold your head toward the ground. Keep your head up and hold your back straight. Men will respect you. You will appear tall even if you are short and you will appear beautiful even if you are homely."[8]

Everett also remembered that his teachers modeled distinguished appearances for the students. Anzell N. Harrell, Sr., the assistant principal of the school, taught "me much about how one should personally present oneself to the public as a professional.... He had a gift in color coordination, with just elegance and class.... I watched him every day, just to see what really nice outfit he would sport that day."[9] Everett could see how Mr. Harrell's "comportment coincided with his attire," and he wished to emulate not only Harrell's appearance but also his classy behavior.[10] He understood that appearance creates respect for oneself and gleans respect from others. Perhaps the most important advice Everett received from Mr. Harrell was "to tell me to be very careful, and don't put yourself in the position of being a father anytime soon" so that he could develop his full potential.[11]

Boarding students were also taught to keep their rooms tidy. Each morning before breakfast each student had to make their bed military style with crisp corners, sweep the floor, take out the garbage and generally clean up their room. The headmaster would inspect the results before they were allowed to go to breakfast. Should someone fail to pass review, they usually got a small fine or additional duty. Gentile Everett recalled: "When I was in school, you couldn't walk on the grass. ... You would be fined if you walked on the grass. (Frank McDuffie) kept that place like a hospital."[12]

Fines were doled out for using cuss words or speaking rudely to faculty as well. Everett remembered one incident he witnessed in Ms. Dorothy Stadler's grammar class:

> ... one day she was teaching about the subjunctive mood of the verb "be." One of our students was trying to sleep in class, and she asked him a question, and of course his answer was wrong. But his answer was not just wrong, he was very loud with it. Ms. Stadler said, "You see, you are loud and wrong." He replied, "Oh, woman, damn!" She said, "Damn? Well get your damn ass out of here!" She made sure the atmosphere was always conducive for those who had come to learn, and that was extremely important to her.[13]

Structure

When he first arrived at the Laurinburg Institute in 1959, Isaac Logan had the impression that it was like a military school:

> Well coming from a public school environment and then going to the Institute where you had to follow a fixed routine, such as getting up at a certain time, having your room ready for inspection on a daily basis, your clothes had to be in a certain order in your closet, a fixed time for every thing you did, and on many occasions having a specific uniform you were required to wear. This was my first impressions of it being like a military school compared to regular public school.[14]

Structure provided the ground rules upon which students could understand what was expected of them. Many complained at first, but quickly became accustomed to following the rules willingly. Even the hours after classes, evenings and weekends were structured. Sports, choir and band practice absorbed afternoon time after classes. After the evening meal, students were required to observe quiet time in order to do their homework and study from 7 to 9 at night. When all work was done, everyone would gather in the Campus Inn for a "Tute-a-fish sammich" (the nickname for the Institute was the "Tute"), Honey Buns or Moon Pie snacks and socializing before bedtime. Wednesday night was vespers led by the women faculty and Sunday night was the student-led program of "Christian Endeavors." Even Saturdays were often work days on the campus where maintenance and clean-up projects kept them busy.

Discipline

Discipline was often needed, especially for those unused to order at home. The mixture of cultural experiences among the students was quite varied: local versus boarding, country versus city, foreign versus American, North versus South, Muslim versus Christian, disciplined versus undisciplined children made for a wide variety of problems that required a great deal of management finesse. Classrooms, too, could be filled with a wide variety of ages and abilities. Teachers were sometimes younger than their students. Often each classroom was more like a one room school house, with many grades in one. So, consistent discipline was critical to maintaining order and creating a beneficiary learning environment.

Needless to say, bad behavior was not tolerated, yet getting control of bad behavior and turning it into respect was a tricky business for the faculty and the administration. Frances McDuffie, granddaughter of Frank and Sammie, shared that the lesson, which she quickly learned concerning discipline, was that she had to gain control of herself in reacting to her students' bad behavior. If she reacted in anger, calling out the student in front of his fellow students, "backing him into a corner," the ego of the student hardened and made him more resistant. Her fellow teachers advised her that "you don't have to hear everything they say." Sometimes you need to let it pass.

Gaining the trust of the student was paramount in creating respect and willingness to cooperate. A teacher could not embarrass a student in front of his peers. For instance, if you called on a student to read a passage in class and the student could not read, rather than admit his deficiency, he would refuse to read and disrupt the class. Rather than argue with the student, McDuffie learned to pass over the incidence and ask the student to come to her office after class or speak with him in the hall so that she could address the student's problem with reading. Bishop McDuffie's wife Cynthia McDuffie privately approached them with the question, "Why are you behaving like this?" Hoping to discover the underlying cause of the bad behavior, she then could offer solutions and join in solidarity with the student in managing his own behavior. If she could help the students understand that she actually cared about them, she could gain their trust and, then, their respect.

There were times, of course, when bad behavior persisted. When speaking privately to the student did not solve the problem, they would be sent to the principal's office for discipline. Most of the time the student would be given a task to perform such as washing floors or doing laundry or helping in the kitchen. Sometimes it was necessary to tell them to dig a ditch outside in front of the school. And they dug until they changed their attitude. Or, if they refused to dig at all, they would go without dinner, which usually changed their attitude for them.

Bishop McDuffie recalled two incidents when a student hit him with his fists. He stood and took the blows and, then, asked, "Are you through now? A few years ago I would whip you, but now I may have to have you arrested." One time he did call on the police to assist him. When riding home on a bus after an away basketball game, the "boys," who were sometimes older than he was at the time and usually much larger than himself, started throwing spitballs in the van and some hit the coach who was driving. They were generally misbehaving and Bishop could not settle them down. When they reached Wadesboro, Bishop drove to the police station and asked the boys "if they could behave or did they did they need to be taken into custody by the police for misbehaving?" After leaving the recalcitrant kids at the station, he took the team to get something to eat. When they returned to the station, Bishop asked the misbehaving kids if they could behave now: "Do you know what the words 'Stop' and 'No' mean now?" Teaching a person how to stop bad behavior was such a good lesson that many of the "bad" boys went on to impact the NCAA and the NBA.

Expelling a student was "never an option" according to Bishop. That would be abandoning them to society and to the outside world, which could be much crueler than the small, self-reliant school campus. Faculty and administration worked hard to earn the respect and trust of the students. Because they lived in a small, very controlled environment, students eventually were able to successfully conform to the community. Other students, who acted as examples for misbehaving newcomers, also put pressure on kids to behave properly and to make good decisions.

Bishop McDuffie wanted the experience of "going to the office" to mean more than just being punished. He was happy to "use the carrot instead of the stick" to encourage good behavior. He asked his teachers to "discover something each student did right each day and bring them to the office to be recognized for their good behavior." This reversal of "office-going" helped to build trust, self-confidence and self-respect.

Self-Discipline

Self-discipline produces self-respect as well. Sports demanded self-discipline above all. Of course, a player had to submit to his coaches' will if he wanted to play, but, above all, he wanted to play, so he quickly learned self-discipline. These guidelines were posted on the gymnasium bulletin board: "Drive, Determination, Desire, Discipline and Dedication." Players often had to show that they had finished their assigned homework in order to practice or play games.

Frances McDuffie said, "Self-discipline is the most important thing you can teach a student." She explained the harsh reality that in education, historically black culture depended more on following direct instruction rather than thinking for oneself. One was more likely to be asked to memorize numbers, words and facts than to be prompted to manipulate them critically. "You just had to follow instructions because there was no time to coddle. You were trained to do this now, without question. It was often a question of safety with no room for consideration of feelings."

Bishop remembered threats such as "I'm going to get hold to that boy and go up side somebody's head." By the time Frances taught at the

Building self-confidence and self-discipline included giving students leadership roles. Laurinburg Institute dormitory leaders (1979): (left to right) Keith Branch, Arnold Wilson, Denise Cooper, Darien Cipio, Roy Jones, Lloyd Javois (Anzell Harrell Collection, courtesy of Chris Everett).

Institute, physical punishment was not a disciplinary option so other motivating actions were needed. Perhaps the most motivating actions for the teacher were to learn self-control and patience, and, for the student, to learn that all was not hopeless and to believe that, with time, effort and help, they could fulfill their requirements and reach their goals. The small classes, racial consistency and structured environment worked together for the good of all. Eventually the student learned self-discipline, which produced confidence and self-respect, which earned the trust and respect of others.

Unmotivated students would complain that the class assignments were too hard and that they could not finish them. This attitude was always unacceptable. Many students had inferiority complexes, which they developed in their public school experiences, so they would not even try to do the work assigned. Frances McDuffie said they could not even "play the race card" at the Institute because it was an entirely black establishment. She explained that "you had to build them up to risk failure," that there was "no shame in failure." If you failed, you would not be ridiculed. The shame was in not trying. Shortie Hall told his whining students that he would work with them to accomplish what they viewed as impossible until they succeeded, but, if they didn't try, he had no patience for them. He illustrated his attitude with this homily:

> There are only two ways: the right way and the wrong way. "Almost" is always wrong. Don't tell me it's almost right. If you come to a river that's five feet wide and you jump four and one-half feet, you fall in and drown. You might just as well have jumped in from the bank of the river and saved your energy.[15]

One of the ways the faculty sought to instill self-discipline and self-respect in their students was to encourage them to see things from their perspective. Once a year the faculty exchanged places with the students. Frances McDuffie taught British literature at the Institute following her graduation from Duke University. She explained the theory behind the practice of exchanging places: "We do it for fun, but we also hold this exercise in order to give the students a feel for what it's like to be in our shoes for a day. Hopefully they will learn something from it as a result. ... We discuss the lesson plan with them the day before, and they will hopefully gain an appreciation for what it's like being a teacher."[16] Her students came from far and wide—Cameroon, Australia, Virgin Islands, Florida, and Washington, D.C. They had these comments to make: "Some of the kids were acting up, so I had to punish them. ... I have been doing all kinds of office work, which included making copies. It has been a blur." Booker T. Washington always taught that self-respect can be learned through the dignity of hard work. Understanding the demanding jobs of teaching and administration at the Institute gave the students both respect for their teachers but also a guide toward their own self-respect.

Cynthia McDuffie recalled that under her watch the Saturday morning dorm room inspections were conducted by herself and other faculty members, but also by representatives of the student body as well. By putting students in charge of critiquing other students' behavior in keeping their rooms tidy, they learned what was expected of their own behavior and taught them respect for those whose discipline guided them. Reversing role models was an effective way of teaching good behavior.

Standing Up and Speaking Out

Oration had always been required of Laurinburg Institute students from the earliest days. A newspaper reporter covered the 1914 graduation and was impressed especially with the student speeches, noting

Public speaking was a requirement for graduation from the Institute and a key component of building confidence for students. Christian Endeavors officers (1979): (left to right) Benita Haynes, Shari Tobias, John Peterson, Lloyd Javois, Denise Cooper (Anzell Harrell Collection, courtesy of Chris Everett).

that "These orations were far above the ordinary and the speakers in their selection of language, delivery and collection of subject matter reflected the great credit upon Prof. McDuffie and his teachers."[17] Public speaking was a method of teaching clear thinking, based upon solid research and sound argument. It was also a way to challenge students to stand up and speak out, which took courage.

Fran Foster recalled that one of the basketball players was so fearful of public speaking that he went to her father and begged him to "find something else he could do" so that he would not have to stand up in public and speak. Frank stood firm and said every student who graduated from the Institute since the beginning was required to memorize a speech by a significant black orator, and that this student would be no exception. It was a tried and true tradition, which changed the image of the speaker himself. Overcoming one's fears was an important part of his education. The student faced his fears and made the speech. Public oration, when successfully executed, gave students confidence. Another 1967 graduate Levester Flowers, nicknamed "Tulip," gave this testimony to a reporter about "a former teacher who required all students memorize a 10-page monologue before graduation": "When we were here we were inspired that there wasn't anything you couldn't do.... We saw people who we never thought would do it, succeed. Now they're talking about how kids can't achieve, kids can't do this—it's because no one is holding them accountable."[18] Flowers credits his five years at the Laurinburg Institute as the foundation that propelled him onto college and a career with Bank of America.

One of the venues that launched students into the spotlight were the Sunday evening services on campus called "Christian Endeavors." The students were entirely in charge of planning and executing the programs. It offered the opportunity for students to practice public speaking in front of their fellow students as well as the faculty. The weekly programs boosted the confidence of students as they assumed full responsibility and gave them the impetus to do research on the lives of inspiring black leaders.

Leon Rice remembered how Frank McDuffie saw him reading a book and asked him to prepare a book report. After he handed it in and went to assembly, McDuffie asked him to tell the whole student body about the book. He said, "What started as a book report turned out to be a lesson on being able to speak in public. By me being put on the spot, this experience taught me to rise to the occasion and get things done."[19]

Finding Strength Through Faith

Although the school never sought church affiliation, as so many private schools have done in order to survive financially, the McDuffie family found their own strength in their local church. The church and school always have been at the heart of the community. Emmanuel and Tinny McDuffie began their own journey in Laurinburg by joining a local Baptist church, Bright Hopewell, which allowed them to win the trust and support they needed in building a school. Their church offered more than just an entry into the local community, it also grounded them in faith that they could accomplish the seemingly impossible if it was God's will.

McDuffie hired the Rev. Larkin L. King, a fellow Snow Hill Institute graduate, as Chaplain of the Institute in 1912. Students were required to attend chapel every Wednesday night. The services taught more than Christian theology, offering a guide for a moral and a disciplined life. The vespers service was described in his book *The Making of a Life* (2011), by the Laurinburg Institute graduate Dr. J. Gentile Everett in the following way:

The Laurinburg Institute Mixed Chorus (1960), directed by Frank McDuffie, performed live Sundays on the local radio station WEWO and won many competitions (Anzell Harrell Collection, courtesy of Chris Everett).

The vespers services were where the school choir would sing, scriptures and prayers would be offered, and usually one of the local pastors would speak to the student body. This was every Wednesday at 7:00 p. m. And of course, who could forget Mrs. Butler, the sister to the school's President, Dr. McDuffie, who always played on the organ the closing song "Now the Day is Over." But for me the most impressive and moving part of the service was Mrs. S. [Sammie] E. McDuffie, the school's principal, when she would present her "By the Ways." The profundity and wisdom I saw in them shaped every facet of my life.

There I was every Wednesday going to a brief church service, and I wanted to do like the other student athletes and honor students as well as everybody else: just simply go to the brief service, and say and do nothing. But that never happened. At every Wednesday evening service, there I was in front of the student body, reading, praying, speaking, singing or playing the piano. Oh, how I wanted to be sitting with the other students, watching the clock, anticipating an earlier dismissal. But that was not to be. Dr. McDuffie never asked me to do anything. He simply told me what to do. And submitting to his instruction was not a problem, it was a pleasure. I was so in tune with having a meaningful life like his, I thought following his instructions was not only respectful, but essential to achieving the desired goals I had set for myself.

Dr. McDuffie, employing a type of falsetto to his voice, would look at my expression and interpret my perhaps discomfort at always standing in front of the student body, and he would say, "Jesse this is only a few minutes out of your life. Don't worry yourself. Just do what has to be done." Little did I know at the time that either through clairvoyance or a prophecy, he was laying the foundation of a principle that would serve me well in my future endeavors.[20]

17

Basketball Leads the Way

The NBA was founded in 1949. Professional athletics was available mostly to players who had trained previously in college athletic programs. Talented high school players had a better chance to play professional ball if they attended college. The Laurinburg Institute aimed to give academically underachieving black students, who showed athletic talent, the chance to attend college.

The history of basketball at the Laurinburg Institute really began just after World War II, when a black trucking company named the Red Ball Express was sent to dismantle the Laurinburg-Maxton Airbase, which had been commissioned as a training facility during the war. The Institute band leader, Shortie Hall, had worked there and entertained the officers with his musical performances. According to Bishop McDuffie, Vernon Echols, the guy in charge of the movers, discovered a cache of sports equipment at the base and donated it to the Institute.

Frank McDuffie believed in the power of sports to transform the rigid social rules of segregation. According to Bishop McDuffie, he pushed his own children into "the great experiment" of integration when they went to college in the 1950s and 1960s. But, in the 1940s things were different. Frank returned to the Institute to teach when he graduated from North Carolina A&T University in the late 1930s. The basketball equipment retrieved from the decommissioned airbase allowed him to form a team. The Tigers began competing among black high schools and even colleges.

Frank formed a friendship with Coach John McLendon at the North Carolina College for Negroes (now North Carolina Central University), in Durham, North Carolina, which expanded his coaching expertise considerably.[1] As a black student at the University of Kansas, McLendon had not been allowed to play but he managed the basketball team and learned much from the inventor of basketball, Coach James Naismith. Naismith wrote the original rule book for the game of basketball and founded the basketball program at the University of Kansas. After graduating, McLendon coached in North Carolina from 1941 to 1952. McLendon is credited by Bishop McDuffie and many others with revolutionizing the game of basketball with the invention of the fast break, the full-court press and the four corners offense. He was the first black coach to arrange a game with a white team. During the war, he matched his all black N.C. College for Negroes team with Duke's all white medical school team. This game has been described as "the secret game."[2] McLendon was the first black coach to lead a white team and the first black to coach in the NBA. He has been inducted three times into the Naismith Basketball Hall of Fame.

Frank McDuffie absorbed McLendon's vast knowledge of the game and applied it to his own Tiger team. He eventually led his team to the last national black high school playoffs in Nashville, Tennessee, in 1954. According to a 1960 Laurinburg Institute brochure, it was "the only team east of the Allegheny Mts. to ever win a National Basketball Championship." The Laurinburg Institute Golden Tigers defeated the

Homecoming Celebration (1952), with Jimmy Hardy, Homecoming Queen Margaret Gee and Betty Wilson. Laurinburg Institute won its first national basketball championship in 1954 (Anzell Harrell Collection, courtesy of Chris Everett).

Phyllis Wheatly High School team from Houston, Texas, winning the championship. The team travelled in the back of a pickup truck to get there.[3] Bishop McDuffie recalled that Emmanuel McDuffie was angry that his son Frank had taken the players out of school in order to play in the championship game.

The Celtic basketball star Sam Jones had put the Laurinburg Institute on the radar of black athletes as early as the 1950s. After graduating from the Institute in 1952, he attended North Carolina College for Negroes, no doubt because McLendon coached there. Unfortunately, Coach McLendon moved to Tennessee the year Jones arrived on campus. In spite of that drawback, Jones thrived at N.C. College for Negroes, which, upon graduation, propelled him into the NBA with the Boston Celtics and on to ten national championships. He also was inducted into the Naismith Basketball Hall of Fame in 1983.

Frank McDuffie had more than basketball championships in mind for his team. He often spoke of "the great experiment," which meant the integration of blacks into white institutions from which blacks had been excluded. In particular, he believed that university systems were the place to begin the "great experiment," and athletics offered the most reasonable opportunities for integration of the races. He contacted the University of North Carolina–Chapel Hill athletic department in 1962 and asked them to look at three Institute players, Skip Hayes, Jimmy Walker from Boston and Dexter Westbrook from upstate New York. The all-white

Jimmy Walker (1969) was the first Laurinburg Institute graduate, along with Dexter Westbrook, to integrate a white college basketball team at Providence College, Providence, Rhode Island, in 1964, and the first round draft pick of the Detroit Pistons in 1967 (courtesy of https://www.nytimes.com/2007/07/04/sports/basketball/04walker.html).

UNC program turned him down due to SAT test scores, but Frank managed to get Walker and Westbrook into an integrated basketball program at Providence College in Rhode Island in 1964. Both players went on to join the NBA. Westbrook was drafted by the Baltimore Bullets in 1967.

Walker was a first team All American and the leading scorer in the 1967 NCAA with 11,655 points. He still holds the highest scoring record with the Providence Friars in a single campaign and is "the lone New England college player to be selected No. 1 overall in the NBA Draft" in 1967.[4] He played for the Detroit Pistons, where he was a two-time All-Star, before moving to the Houston Rockets and the Kansas City Kings (1967–76). Walker was inducted into the National Collegiate Basketball Hall of Fame in 2022.

These athletes are among the 13 NBA basketball players who owe their successful start to the carefully crafted foundation laid by Frank and Sammie McDuffie of the Laurinburg Institute. After 1994, their son Frank "Bishop" McDuffie, Jr., continued their legacy with over fifty Division I players. Today the Laurinburg Institute ranks sixth in the nation among all high schools in producing the most NBA players.[5]

The following Laurinburg Institute graduates have gone on to play professional basketball:

Laurinburg Institute Golden Tiger Basketball Team (1979): (first row, left to right) F. Adams, R. Gumbs, (Tiny) Lassen, C. Myers, A. Shepperd, (second row) Coach Reynolds, A. Pickett, E. Vinson, J. Sprauve, S. Charles, L. Brown, D. Nichols. Frank McDuffie created an Institute gap year in the 1970s for basketball players to improve their academic training and prepare them for college (Anzell Harrell Collection, courtesy of Chris Everett).

Antonio Anderson: 2009 NBA Oklahoma City Thunder
Renaldo Balkman: 2006 NBA 1st round draft, New York Knicks
Spider Bennett: 1966 Hartford Capitals, 1968 ABA Dallas
    Chaparrals
Charlie Davis: 1971 NBA Cleveland Cavaliers
Joey Dorsey: 2008 NBA Houston Rockets
Robert Dozier 2009 NBA Miami Heat
Arvydas Eitutavicius: 2003 International Leagues
Mike Evans: 1978 NBA 1st round draft, Denver Nuggets
Chris Johnson: 2011 NBA Portland Trailblazers
Sam Jones: 1957 NBA 1st round draft, Boston Celtics, 10 times
    NBA champion, 5 times NBA All-Star, 1983 Naismith
    Basketball Hall of Fame
Quantez Robertson: 2009 German Basketball League
Magnum Rolle: 2010 NBA Oklahoma City Thunder
Robert Sallie: 2009 Israel Basketball League
Charlie Scott: 1972 NBA Phoenix Suns. NBA champion and 3
    times NBA All-Star, 2018 Naismith Basketball Hall of Fame
Jimmy Walker: 1967 NBA 1st round draft, Detroit Pistons
Chris Washburn: 1986 NBA 1st round draft, Golden State
    Warriors
Dexter Westbrook: 1967 NBA Baltimore Bullets
Shawne Williams: 2006 NBA 1st round draft, Indiana Pacers

Institute students Charlie Scott and the Jamaican track star Beverly McDonald represented the United States in the Olympics. Although many Institute graduates did not go on to careers in athletics, many did use their athletic abilities to gain entrance into college programs. Perhaps the greatest basketball player never to play in the NBA was the legendary Harlem street basketball player Earl "The Goat" Manigault, who did earn a scholarship to college after graduating from Laurinburg Institute.

Charlie Scott and Earl Manigault have recorded several accounts of their time at Laurinburg Institute and what it meant to them. Both life stories are representative of the fundamental goals of the Institute but in different ways. Frank McDuffie had his own reasons for supporting these two Harlem boys, who, because of their poverty and lack of family support, had no prospects for their amazing talents. He gave them a chance and provided them with the tools for success.

18

Holcombe Rucker and
Earl "The Goat" Manigault

Frank McDuffie was not the only man who encouraged black youth to succeed. In fact McDuffie's own success depended partially on a Harlem legend named Holcombe Rucker. Even today in Harlem, thousands gather each summer to honor Rucker's legacy at the Rucker Tournament. Professional basketball players, such as Wilt Chamberlain and Lew Alcindor (Kareem Abdul-Jabbar), match themselves against up-and-coming young basketball talents. Rucker Park is a prime scouting site for high school and college basketball coaches nationwide.

Many of the young players come from poor families with broken homes, ravished by drug and alcohol problems. Holcombe Rucker grew up among these difficulties and understood the enormous challenges that the Harlem kids faced. After serving in the armed forces during World War II, Rucker returned to Harlem determined to find a way to help youth climb out of the depths of addiction and poverty. He formed a youth basketball league with four teams in 1946.

Acquiring a job with the New York Department of Parks and Recreation, Rucker was assigned basketball courts to supervise and maintain. Although he appeared as a janitor, Rucker used this opportunity to mentor and encourage young boys to get an education and to learn discipline, responsibility and teamwork. Rucker maintained the courts while at the same time coaching and refereeing his team games. He required boys to show their passing report cards before they could play on his courts, and no boy escaped without a lecture concerning the importance of their getting an education. Countless young men owed their brighter futures to Holcombe Rucker. Some estimate that Rucker helped as many as seven hundred kids go on to college.[1]

Earl "The Goat" Manigault was one of those boys. Although he was already a basketball star at Benjamin Franklin High School, Manigault was expelled for smoking marijuana. Manigault himself claims that he had a falling out with the coach when he refused to compete in the long jump competition, and the coach had him expelled for arguing with him. Feeling down and out, Manigault went to shoot hoops at one of Rucker's courts. Rucker was sweeping the court and introduced himself. Manigault described his thoughts when he first met Rucker there in his autobiography *Double Dunk* (originally published in 1980), written with Barry Beckham:

> *This* is the dude everybody talks about? Scottie [Charlie Scott] used to talk about him all the time. Supposed to be a legend. Got all kinds of dudes in college. Supposed to be a father and friend to a lot of dudes

Holcombe Rucker (1960), founded the Harlem basketball youth leagues in 1946 and facilitated the enrollment of many players in the Laurinburg Institute (courtesy of www. HMdb.org).

> who were on their way or had been down the wrong path…. He is giving you pointers and talking as if he has all the patience in the world. You like this man, his voice, the way he looks you in the eye…. There is something very soothing and comforting about this moment and this man.[2]

Manigault never knew his father. He lived with his beloved mother who worked as a housekeeper in a hotel. He knew he had no way of affording or of getting into college with his bad academic record. He came to view Rucker as a father figure in his life and recalled that Rucker told him he could help him get into school at Laurinburg Institute, where he had sent over fifty boys including Dexter Westbrook and Charlie Scott, and, he was sure Manigault could get a scholarship. Rucker said:

Earl, I'll tell you a secret. Something I tell all the youngsters I work with. You determine yourself what kind of life you're going to live. Luck has its role of course, but if you decide you want to do something with your life and that nothing will stop you from doing it and that you *will* overcome every obstacle, you can't go wrong, son. I don't believe that hogwash about bad luck and can't get no breaks. Son, you got to *make* your breaks, do you understand me? We got no time to wait for luck.[3]

It is unknown how Rucker first became acquainted with the Laurinburg Institute. Perhaps Dizzy Gillespie spread the word in Harlem. Even during Gillespie's Institute time in the 1930s, boarding students came to the Institute from New York City. Perhaps Sam Jones, the Laurinburg Institute player who joined the Boston Celtics in 1957, had participated in the Rucker Tournaments. Rucker formed the Rucker Pro League in 1954, which invited professional players to compete against the winners of the local amateur competitions. In any case, Holcombe Rucker began sending boys to the Institute, particularly boys with basketball talent whom he mentored on his Harlem courts.

Many of these boys did not have the funds to attend a private school nor did they have enough public education to earn a scholarship to a college. Education was the key for access to NBA basketball careers. Rucker believed that education came first, though, even before talent; he always encouraged his boys to finish school. Rucker himself only managed to graduate from City College of NY in 1961. He taught English at a junior high school for four years before his death at aged 39 in 1965. By then, Rucker had sent many talented young men to the Laurinburg Institute including Charlie Scott and Earl "The Goat" Manigault. Their stories of the Institute will serve as examples for many other students over the next fifty years.

Earl "The Goat" Manigault (1944–1998)

At his NBA retirement celebration in 1989, Kareem Abdul-Jabbar was asked by a reporter, who was the greatest player he had ever played with or against in his career? Without hesitation Jabbar responded, Earl "The Goat" Manigault, the greatest basketball player never to play in the NBA. Abdul-Jabbar had played Manigault in the Rucker Tournament and in pickup games on the Rucker courts at 129th and 155th Streets. Jabbar remembered: "At the time there weren't a whole lot of people who could do the things with the basketball that Earl Manigault could do.... He was so agile, so quick. He used to make so many innovative moves to the hoop. Basketball was his total means of expression."[4]

Earl "The Goat" Manigualt at the Goat Park, New York City (1989), was the greatest basketball player never to play in the NBA. Photograph by Charlie Samuels.

Manigault was famous as an amazing talent at an early age. Manigault's nickname "The Goat" started as a pun on his name Manigault that sounded like "nanny goat," but quickly the nickname acquired "The Greatest of All Time" meaning it has among fans today. Even today he holds the New York City junior high scoring record of 57 points in a single game. Although he was short (6'1" for a basketball player, he could jump higher than anyone else. "With an astonishing 50-inch vertical leap, Manigault ... [boasted]: I was a little man, but I could fly with the big men.... There weren't too many guys soaring to the hoop and dunking on 6-9 and 6-10 guys."[5] People would put quarters or dollar bills on the top of the backboard and challenge him to grab them, which he could do.

During a Rucker Tournament, The Goat sealed his fame with a double dunk, which brought the game to a full stop. The crowd was stunned and broke out in pandemonium on the court. The Goat dunked the ball and caught it going down in time to redunk it before he hit the ground. Someone in the crowd shouted, "A motherfuckin' double dunk ... that shit's like walkin' on air."[6]

A film was made of Manigault's life in 1996 entitled *Rebound: The Legend of Earl "The Goat" Manigault.* The actor Eriq La Salle directed the film and HBO aired it. Today it is available on YouTube. The cast includes many of the leading black actors on stage and in film. Don Cheadle played Manigault. Forest Whitaker played Holcombe Rucker and James Earl Jones played Frank McDuffie, Sr. Some of the scenes take place in a much romanticized version of the Laurinburg Institute. The buildings resembled those on the first Institute campus more than those on the scaled-down campus Manigault attended. A pleasant lakefront was provided for the school, which never occurred in reality.

In 1963 Laurinburg looked to the New York City kid Manigault like one of those "Main Streets you see in the movies" with frame buildings, a post office, a catalog department store, a restaurant and a hardware store. On his arrival at the Institute, just three blocks from the bus stop, Manigault was underwhelmed by the brown grass and half dozen one-story buildings that "looks like a project development." However, he noticed that the students all wore school uniforms just as many prep school students did. The uniforms gave them an air of pride and seriousness. They also made them easily identifiable in town, giving them a modicum of respect. He cheered up when he suddenly was surrounded by seven of his old New York buddies. He said to himself, "Looks like half of New York goes to school here."[7] His friend Charlie Scott had also been sent down to Laurinburg Institute by Rucker earlier in the year.

While Manigault felt at home among his Harlem friends, he had some adjusting to do concerning the demands of the Institute. Discipline started early in the morning when the boys' dorm rooms were inspected by "Muffin," Manigault's nickname for Frank McDuffie. The morning routine included making your bed, sweeping the floor, emptying the trash and being ready for breakfast at seven a.m. Manigault remembered that McDuffie "comes in with his suit and tie. New suit every day almost. You got to line up against the wall. Everybody is half

Laurinburg Institute students (1960), taking a break between classes (Anzell Harrell Collection, courtesy of Chris Everett).

dead from fooling around the night before. You think you're in the army or something. Hands must be at your side when he comes into your room."[8] If something was amiss, the students were fined anywhere from twenty-five cents to twenty-five dollars, depending on the offense. Sneaking into the girls' dorm after hours usually carried the heaviest penalty.

McDuffie said, "we don't have any foolishness down here" and repeatedly asked his students "to behave like gentlemen," which included keeping their hair cut and attending Sunday services in the campus chapel. At the time Manigault griped, but later he came to see that "Muffin's outrageous shit, the rules, discipline that you complain about all the time…, [I] now see as necessary if you're ever to do anything sensible."[9]

Academics were not Manigault's strong point. In fact, when he was asked to read something out loud in English class, he tried to make a joke to cover his inability to read. After nine years in the New York City school system, Earl could not read. Manigault described his NYC school experience the following way:

> They didn't care about you when you was in school. They don't care about any of us. Shuffle through, that's all. You can't read or write or do nothing and you get promoted to the next grade where you still don't learn anything. Push them in, push them out. Next class, please. Ah, more dumb niggers here to play sports and smoke dope and talk shit to the white girls and raise hell with switchblades.[10]

His English teacher took him aside and privately told him she would teach him to read, that it was easier than he imagined. Manigault also had a girlfriend at the Institute named Yvette from New York who helped him with his studies. One of the remarkable things about the Laurinburg Institute was the fact that they met the students where they were and gave them the strength to believe in themselves. Then, they gave them the tools to overcome whatever obstacles stood in their way.

When Manigault arrived on campus his fellow basketball players told McDuffie, who was also the coach, that "He's the best player in New York."[11] Turned out he was also the best player in a good part of the South. The Laurinburg Institute Tigers not only played high school teams, but also college teams as well, and they won. Charlie Scott was three years younger than Manigault, but he held his own on the court alongside The Goat.

Manigault relished the attention the local newspaper the *Laurinburg Exchange* gave him. They did a feature article on him with his photograph and wrote coverage of his games with headlines like *Laurinburg*

Crushes Johnson, Manigault Stars and *Laurinburg Led by Manigault, Vanquishes Lions 80–65.*[12] Manigault averaged 30 points per game in his senior year.[13] Everyone on campus worshiped him. After his holiday visits home to Harlem, Manigault found himself "happy to get back to Laurinburg" even though the gym was like a barn and cockroaches roamed the dorms. He even looked forward to "the white lightning" that someone on the staff sold "to the students in mayonnaise jars."[14]

By the time Manigault graduated from the Institute two-and-a-half years later, he had offers for athletic scholarships from 73 colleges.[15] He decided to accept the scholarship offer from a coach he liked at Johnson C. Smith University in Charlotte, North Carolina, because he felt more comfortable going to an all-black college. Unfortunately for him, that coach had left before he got there and he never established a good relationship with the new coach. In fact, in spite of his high scoring, the new coach actually benched him for three games because he was so outstanding. He claimed Manigault needed to learn teamwork and called him a "troublemaker." At the same time, Holcombe Rucker died, and a dejected Manigault left school and returned to Harlem, never to play serious basketball again.[16]

The pressures of his life caused him to turn to drugs and, eventually, crime, which landed him in jail. At his lowest point, Manigault was reminded by a prison guard of how great his talent had been, asking him to sign a book with a chapter on his triumphs. He got off heroin in 1976 and took over Rucker's legacy of coaching boys basketball in the parks of Harlem.

Happy Warrior Playground in NYC's Upper West Side became known as Goat Park in his honor. He lived Rucker's motto "Each One, Teach One," repeating the mantras of Rucker and McDuffie which emphasized education above all. Manigault believed that "we teach each other.... I learn from them and they learn from me."[17]

Cal Griffin, who was one of the 13-year-olds Earl mentored, related that Earl would call his mother and grandmother and ask them to remind him to come prepared to play and to practice. Griffin recalled:

> I'm sure he regretted not playing pro ball but the impact that he had on the youth more than made up for that.... Earl Manigault was an advocate for me and all the youth he encountered.... It seemed like all Earl wanted to do was help kids avoid all the pitfalls that plagued our inner city. He created midnight basketball and drug awareness programs to help kids who have fallen victim to these issues. He did outreach at teen centers and fought vigorously to help steer kids away from the very thing that ultimately destroyed his life. He was the kind of guy that would give his last to a kid who needed it. He was a class act.... He's a once in a lifetime type of guy and they just

don't make people like him anymore.... It takes a very selfless person to do what he did for his community.[18]

Manigault started the "Walk Away from Drugs" tournament for boys before his death in 1998 at aged 53. The legend of The Goat grows with every passing year. His life was better because of Laurinburg Institute and the Institute's basketball fame grew because of him.

19

Charlie Scott, Charlie Davis, Chris Washburn and Beverly McDonald

Earl Manigault and Charlie Scott originally met on the basketball courts in Harlem when they were young boys. Earl was three years older than Charlie and already known as The Goat. Charlie was called Scotty by all who knew him. Both boys came from poor broken families, and both sought comfort and a sense of belonging on the basketball court. Scott claims that he was pretty much on his own by age 11. They spent all their spare time practicing and dreaming of success.

By the time Scott was 13, he was playing with Lew Alcindor (UCLA) and Norwood Todman (first black player at Wake Forest), among other college-bound athletes, and he played in the Rucker League in 1963. Rucker supported his dreams and, eventually, encouraged him to apply to Laurinburg Institute as he also had done for Manigault. Scott knew that Sam Jones, Jimmy Walker and Dexter Westbrook were Institute graduates who made it to the NBA, and he had watched them play in the Rucker games.

Unlike Manigault, Scott studied hard and made good enough grades to get in prestigious Peter Stuyvesant High School in downtown New York City. He traveled each day by subway from Harlem to City Hall because he was determined to find a way to go to college. He dreamed of becoming a doctor or lawyer, but soon realized that his basketball talent might be his ticket to a better life.[1]

When he heard about Laurinburg Institute, he asked his coaches to write letters of recommendation while he filled out an application and put it in the mail. His reputation as an up-and-coming young basketball player landed him a partial scholarship to the Institute. Scott said, "Mr. McDuffie made it possible for me to stay there, even though I had

UNC Coach Dean Smith with new recruit Charlie Scott (1966), who was the first black athlete to integrate UNC basketball (courtesy of Matt Bower, UNC–Chapel Hill).

no idea where it would lead. But, I knew I had a chance to go to college and get an education."[2]

Scott arrived at Laurinburg Institute in 1963 when he was only 14 years old. Besides what he wore, Scott owned only four pairs of pants, one jacket and one pair of black shoes. Having lived on his own in "survival mode" for some time, he was grateful for three meals a day and a roof over his head. Shortly after his arrival, Scott's father died of liver cancer. When he returned from the funeral, the McDuffies took him into their home and gave him the care and attention he craved. They became surrogate parents for him for the next three years. Frank McDuffie remembered:

> He was fresh from the streets of Harlem and he never had played real organized basketball. But all he wanted to do was play. He had no interest in his studies or his surroundings. He was a loner—a typical New York kid who didn't seem to like what he heard about the South. He hated white people, for instance, probably because he hadn't been around many for most of his life.... We learned that before arriving, he hadn't had a real meal in about two months.... About that time, my wife began to take a special interest. She could see promise in him that others couldn't.[3]

Sammie McDuffie was Scott's algebra teacher. She believed that he had as good a chance for an academic scholarship as for an athletic one so she put Scott on a rigorous study routine. He bloomed under her discipline. Sammie reported that Scott "...would head right to his dormitory when classes were over and worked until everything was done."[4] Frank, too, emphasized good study habits and good grades. Cynthia McDuffie reported that when a group of white coaches visited the campus to scout the basketball talent, Frank told the players not to be overly excited because they did not have good enough grades to get in those colleges. The players responded to the challenge and started taking their studies seriously. Scott's academic efforts paid off when he graduated valedictorian of his class in 1966.

Scott had good reason to dislike white people, as a traumatic experience he suffered in Laurinburg illustrates. Scott gave this account of his "culture shock":

> The first Saturday we were out of school, we were allowed to go downtown, and we went to the movies. We were told to sit upstairs, that we couldn't sit downstairs. Another Saturday, a couple of friends and I had walked off campus to go to the grocery store. We were picked up by the police because a White woman had been raped by three black men in the area. They took us straight to the house—not the police station—where this woman was raped and had her try to identify if we were the ones responsible. When we got there, her husband was standing outside with a shotgun. "Are these them?" That was the only thing they asked her. "No, they too tall." If that woman had said we were the guys, we would've been shot right then. That was an experience I had in the South; it made me understand the South.[5]

In spite of this traumatic experience, Scott learned that white Southerners were crazy about basketball, especially in North Carolina, and there Scott would rise to fame. During Scott's first year at Laurinburg Institute, he played second fiddle to Earl "The Goat" Manigault, who arrived shortly after he did. Earl was averaging 31 points per game and 13 rebounds. He got all the press reviews and praise, but coaches began to notice Charlie, especially Coach Charles "Lefty" Driesell at Davidson College.

Lefty Driesell had connected with Frank McDuffie early on. They both were on the lookout for great basketball talent. Frank saw that basketball was a potential gateway to integration in the South and he purposely recruited talented players whom he and his staff could develop academically well enough to gain entrance into the largely white university basketball programs. Starting with Jimmy Walker and Dexter Westbrook, Coach Frank McDuffie began his targeted integration strategy. They attended largely white Providence College in Rhode Island in 1963 and were drafted into the NBA in 1967. Scott knew these players from his Harlem days in the Rucker games.

Driesell invited McDuffie and Scott to the Davidson games at the Charlotte Coliseum. He courted Scott for two years knowing that Scott could be the player to put Davidson into the NCAA championships. Driesell gave Scott jobs at his summer basketball camps, took him out to eat, put him up at motels in Charlotte and even told him that he could pick his teammates.

Driesell asked Dr. Jim Richardson, the white Laurinburg surgeon and Davidson graduate, to lend his car to Scott so he could travel to the college games. Scott wrecked the car, but Richardson told him not to "worry about it." Scott loved Lefty and remembered that "it was the only time I felt wanted in my life."[6] Scott interviewed at UCLA, Villanova, Purdue, N.C. State, Duke and Wake Forest but he planned to sign with Lefty.

McDuffie had other ideas. Scott later realized that McDuffie had his sights on the basketball powerhouse at Chapel Hill. McDuffie knew it was asking a lot for a black boy to face the racism in these predominantly white schools, but he had faith in Charlie Scott, who put it this way:

> I was really the first Black scholarship athlete in the South…. I was really the only Black athlete below the Mason-Dixon Line then. That was a heavy burden, but it was something that my high school coach, Frank McDuffie, Jr., understood, and he pushed me in that direction. He was the one who thought I had the academic edge, the athletic ability and all the fortitude to be able to deal with it. I had offers to go to UCLA, but [UNC] wasn't my choice. I actually had committed to play for Lefty Driesell at Davidson, but Coach McDuffie saw the importance of, and understood the historical significance of, going to North Carolina.[7]

McDuffie understood that, if one of the top universities in the South accepted a black player who could succeed on the court and in the classroom, then, other schools would follow.

Coaches were aware of the talent that awaited them among the black community. The NBA showcased black talent like Sam Jones, who led the Boston Celtics to ten national championships. But, the difficulty for the coaches in the South was that most colleges were not yet integrated. Even if they were, most black athletes did not have the grades or SAT scores to get into those colleges. The UNC football Coach Jim Tatum was looking for talent for his team but knew he could not recruit black players. Instead, he "had an arrangement with a coach at Michigan State where if Tatum saw a good black football player in North Carolina he would refer him to Michigan State and the coach up there would refer down here the white football players who were not admissible at Michigan State that might be admissible here."[8] The UNC basketball Coach Frank McGuire asked the NAACP student group at UNC to help him recruit Lew Alcindor from New York. They wrote letters inviting Alcindor to visit the campus, but his father got a job in Los Angeles and he ended up at UCLA.

Daniel Pollitt, who was then faculty advisor to the NAACP student group at the University of North Carolina–Chapel Hill, recalled in an interview that the black students were searching for ways to get more blacks to apply to UNC. There were only about twenty black students at the time there, and most of them were in graduate programs such as law and medicine. They were housed in the same dorm, keeping them separate from the whites, and were segregated even at athletic games where they were forced to sit in obscure places like the end zone near the field house at football games. The UNC black students decided that their best shot at encouraging enrollment of other blacks was to focus on recruiting athletes, who could attract attention and act as role models for other black youth to follow. They met with Coach Tatum and Coach McQuire, who fully agreed with their strategy, but the coaches explained their untenable situation. Nonetheless, all agreed to work together to integrate the UNC athletic programs.

By the time the UNC basketball Coach Dean Smith took over in the 1960s, still no black athlete had joined a team. Frank McDuffie had heard Daniel Pollitt speak at the state convention of the NAACP where he spoke "on Brown against the School Board and what has happened since, or what has not happened since. So apparently he liked my speech."[9] McDuffie, whose mission was integrating college ball, called Dean Smith and invited him to bring Pollitt with him to meet their outstanding student and basketball player Charlie Scott. Although UNC's Coach Dean Smith got wind of Charlie Scott's abilities late in the game, Smith sent his assistant coach John Lotz to scout Scott's playing abilities, and Lotz reported that Scott was an amazing athlete, who was averaging 30 points a game and 12 rebounds in his senior year. Next, he sent another assistant coach Larry Brown to watch Scott play and heard about Scott's "bullet speed and slashing style" and that he was first in his class academically.

Smith had been trying for years to integrate his teams but was frustrated by the school requirements of minimal SAT scores, which Smith considered "culturally and economically biased," and by the lack of academic preparation black students suffered because of inadequate educational opportunities. When he heard that Scott had both qualifications, Smith told the *Daily Tar Heel:* "Scott's the first one to have both the academic and athletic qualifications. He will fit our system of run and pressure defense perfectly. He's quick as a cat. Great reaction time. And Charles is a fine boy, and first-line student ... not just a gladiator."[10]

McDuffie accompanied Scott to both Davidson and Carolina. Scott was leaning towards Davidson, but the McDuffies and Scott changed their minds when they had a bad experience at a Davidson restaurant called the Coffee Cup. They met Driesell there and, when the coach invited them to sit down and eat with him, the restaurant owner said, "We don't serve niggers." This insult made the McDuffies very angry.

Things were not that different in Chapel Hill. Water fountains and waiting rooms were racially separate. The university had begun admitting undergraduate black students under a court order in 1954. Blacks were allowed at football games, but they had to sit in a separate section. The Carolina Inn refused service to blacks. There were only about fifty black students at UNC when Scott was recruited. Coach Smith received threats from alumni if he integrated the UNC teams.[11]

When Dean Smith and Daniel Pollitt finally went to Laurinburg to meet Scott, they also brought along a black UNC medical student because they had heard Scott wanted to become a doctor.[12] They all sat at the McDuffie's kitchen table and openly discussed racial issues that might confront Scott at UNC and in Chapel Hill. Coach Smith orchestrated a nuanced recruitment of Scott, which included introducing him to black UNC students, sending him to a Smokey Robinson concert on campus, taking him to an integrated Baptist church and to the campus Rathskeller where black waiters served them. He also made sure he met the white guys who would be his teammates. Other prospective schools had avoided encounters with white fellow players. Scott also walked down Franklin Street on his own to test the racial waters in Chapel Hill and told Dean Smith he "didn't feel ostracized. I didn't feel strained.... The atmosphere was one where I wasn't intimidated if they didn't know I was a basketball player, so I felt comfortable."[13]

Much to the bitter disappointment of Lefty Driesell, and, with the strong encouragement of Frank McDuffie, Scott decided to sign with Carolina. And the rest is history. Scott was All-American in his junior and senior years. Carolina went on to win with him the ACC Championship in 1969 and made it to the NCAA's Final Four.

Daniel Pollitt tried to convince Scott to join the UNC Law School after graduation: "...you are bright and you'll probably be on the Law Review and you'll be one of the unique people and probably the Governor will want to hire you and you can really go a long way in law. ... [Scott responded] they just offered me four hundred thousand dollars to sign with them."[14] Scott played with the ABA Virginia Squires in

1970–1972 and with NBA Phoenix Suns in 1972–1975, when he was a three time NBA All-Star. He went on to win a NBA Championship with the Boston Celtics in 1976 and was inducted into the Naismith Basketball Hall of Fame in 2018. During and after college, Charlie Scott returned to Harlem to play in the Rucker Tournaments, becoming one of the 24 Rucker Park Elites. As promised by Dean Smith, two of Scott's children, Simone and Shawn, attended and graduated from UNC in later years.[15]

During negotiations for Scott's signing, two other requests by Frank McDuffie made a difference. McDuffie asked Smith to recommend John Russell, a lead official in the CIAA, to be the first black referee in the ACC. Russell served in that capacity for the next twenty years. He was inducted into the CIAA Officials Hall of Fame in 1992.[16] Smith also agreed to let the Laurinburg Institute Tigers play the UNC freshmen team each season. This agreement was honored until Frank McDuffie's death in 1994, and, even beyond.[17]

Future NBA Stars Charlie Davis, Mike Evans, Chris Washburn

McDuffie's dream of integrating white college athletics, particularly in North Carolina, was fulfilled also at Wake Forest University and North Carolina State University. The Laurinburg Institute graduate Charlie Davis was the second black athlete to play for Wake Forest University from 1969 to 1971. Davis paid this

Laurinburg Institute graduate Charlie Davis (1971), was the second black basketball player for Wake Forest University (courtesy of *The Howler*).

tribute to Laurinburg Institute in 2021: "I wouldn't have gotten into Wake Forest without going to Laurinburg Institute. People take that for granted now, but in 1967, there weren't places that African-Americans could go to do that. It just speaks volumes about Laurinburg Institute's place in history."[18]

Davis became the first black ACC Player of the Year. In 1984 Davis was inducted into the Wake Forest Sports Hall of Fame and his uniform (No. 12) was the third to be retired by the university. He still holds three Wake Forest records: career scoring average (24.94 points per game); career free-throw accuracy (87.3 percent); and single-game scoring, 51 against American University on February 15, 1969. After retiring from the NBA, Davis returned to Wake Forest to complete his college degree in 1990.[19]

The Institute graduates Mike Evans and Les Anderson were drafted into the basketball programs of Kansas State and George Washington Universities respectively in 1974. A later graduate Chris Washburn played for North Carolina State University in 1984. Both Mike Evans (1978) and Chris Washburn (1986) were drafted into the NBA as well.

Four Medal Olympic Track Star
Beverly McDonald

Among the many outstanding male athletic alumni, who attended the Institute under Frank McDuffie, Sr.'s, tenure, is the single female champion Beverly McDonald. McDonald was a member of the famed Jamaican Track Team before attending the Institute. She began competing when she was 15 years old and won first place in the 1985 CARIFTA games as a sprinter in the 100 m race and second place in the 200 m race. She competed and won in the CARIFTA games from 1985 to 1988. McDonald attended Laurinburg Institute for a gap year in 1988–1989. Her principal, Cynthia McDuffie, remembers McDonald as a shy and quiet young lady, who was also a good student, but she has no memory of her running at all.[20] Her goal at the Institute was acquiring enough education and SAT expertise to gain entry to a good university track program.

Upon graduation, McDonald won a scholarship to Texas Christian University, where she won gold in the 4 × 100 relay at the World Champion games in Tokyo. After graduating from TCU in 1993, McDonald continued to compete in the World Championships, winning two silver (1995, 1997) and two bronze (1999, 2001) medals in the 4 × 100 m relay games and one silver (1999) in the 200 m sprint. The crowning events for

McDonald's long track career were the 2000 Olympic games in Sydney, where she earned a silver medal in the 4 × 100 m and a bronze medal in the 200 m race, and the 2004 Olympics in Athens, where she won gold in the 4 × 100 m race. Texas Christian University honored McDonald with placement in their TCU Athletics Hall of Fame in 2008.[21]

PART IV

The Laurinburg Institute

Frank "Bishop" McDuffie, Jr.
(1994–Present)

20

The Responsibilities
of the McDuffie Legacy

The Laurinburg Institute owes its longevity to the McDuffie family. Four generations have kept it going, and not without cost. Bishop McDuffie, the third generation president of Laurinburg Institute, remembers that he wanted to attend Morehouse College when he graduated from Laurinburg Institute. His father came to him and said, "Your Mother and I have decided you are going to take part in the great experiment of integration."[1] When he heard "your Mother and I have decided," he knew he was in "high peril" if he did not follow their wishes. "The great experiment" meant attending a white school. At first, his father, "Mr. Frank," suggested attending Dartmouth, but Bishop said that was "too far away, too white, and too cold." Next his father told him he could attend any school, but, then, handed him "an admission ticket to the University of North Carolina–Chapel Hill, where my friend, Charlie Scott, was enrolled. The ticket represented a paid first year's tuition," which meant there was no more money for another school. Bishop's dream of being a big man in a black college vanished as he approached the challenges of integration at a big white university in 1969.

At the time of Bishop's arrival, there were only about 100 black students including graduate students. Although he felt confident in his ability to achieve academically, he knew he would have to face racial prejudices and social challenges. He got to his dorm room early and set up his side of the room. When his white roommate arrived, he said, "I'm not staying with a colored boy!" Bishop replied, "No problem, please remove your stuff while I go downtown to do some shopping." Reporting home that he felt unwelcome and begging his parents to let him go to Morehouse, still his father pressured him: "Do I need to come up there and help you unpack?" Again Bishop bowed to his father's wishes and remained alone in his room for the first semester.

The second semester another white boy was assigned to his dorm room. This time Bishop took no chances, as he drew a chalk line down the middle of the room instructing the white guy that this was his side and do not cross the line. Later, Bishop characterized this action as a little "racist" on his part. The white boy, Gerry Chapman, turned out to be the great-grandson of the famous author Joel Chandler Harris, who wrote *Uncle Remus: His Songs and Sayings* (1881). Before leaving to take a shower, Bishop told Gerry that he was expecting some friends and please ask them to have a seat. While Bishop was out of the room, Charlie Scott showed up knocking on the door looking for Bishop, followed shortly by Bill Chamberlain, both big basketball stars on campus. Chapman and other dorm mates were so impressed by Bishop's friends that social relations eased, and Bishop began to feel at home.

Bishop graduated in 1973 with a degree in history. His goal was to go to law school. He had taken his LSAT exam, doing well, in hopes of applying. Again, his family intervened, asking him to put off law school a year, and come home to help teach and administer the Institute and manage the "McDuffie Village Apartments, one of Laurinburg's first HUD sponsored units." Bishop recalled, "I was always the boy. Black parents always consider their children to be their 'boy' or 'girl,' even as grown individuals." It was not easy. Both his parents were "renowned coaches," who had no "hesitation in encouraging and criticizing him publicly," when he was coaching the winning basketball team. The promised chance to go to law school faded as his father's health diminished and more was

Frank "Bishop" McDuffie, Jr. (1979), taught history and economics and coached basketball. He became president of the Laurinburg Institute in 1994 and sent over 50 basketball players to Division I teams across the country, including 7 to the NBA (Anzell Harrell Collection, courtesy of Chris Everett).

demanded of him. Marriage and children added to his responsibilities. In the end he stayed at the Institute and assumed complete control as president in 1994, when his parents passed away.

Bishop continued to expand his knowledge as he sought to deal with problems the school faced. He took courses in substance abuse and crisis management at the University of Miami (1975), and in business management at UNC Management Institute (1977). He completed a masters' degree in education administration at University of North Carolina–Pembroke (1989). Bishop had to defer his dream of law school, which his daughter Frances eventually fulfilled.

The responsibilities of running the Institute also fell on the shoulders of the wives of the McDuffies as well. Bishop and Cynthia McDuffie were both students at UNC–Chapel Hill, where Cynthia earned a master's degree in psychology. After her marriage to Bishop, Cynthia taught psychology at St. Andrews Presbyterian College and Richmond Community College, but soon she, too, joined the faculty teaching English and psychology at Laurinburg Institute in 1985. She also took on the responsibilities of assisting Sammie McDuffie in the office. When Sammie passed away in 1994, Cynthia assumed the responsibilities of principal of the school. Since then, Cynthia claims she has not had a day off, except the one week when her mother died.

Bishop's daughter, Frances McDuffie, also felt the heavy burden of running the family school and keeping the family legacy alive. After graduating from the Institute, while taking extra courses at Scotland High School, Frances was accepted at Duke University in 1987. It must have been a great triumph for Frank McDuffie to see his granddaughter accepted at Duke University. He had dreamed of integrating all of the ACC teams

Cynthia McDuffie (2023), taught English and psychology and became principal of the Laurinburg Institute in 1994 (courtesy of Cynthia McDuffie).

Torie McDuffie (left) with her sister Frances McDuffie at her Laurinburg Institute graduation (1981). Frances taught English at the Institute for a decade. After subsequently receiving a law degree, she was appointed judge of the North Carolina Cumberland 12th District by Governor Roy Cooper in 2020 (courtesy of Frances McDuffie).

in North Carolina. Only one school stands out as a failure for him, Duke University. Frank McDuffie did live to see four grandchildren, including the two sons and a daughter of his daughter Dr. Fran Foster, graduate from Duke University. Frances graduated from Duke University in 1991 and returned home to teach British and American literature as well as ninth grade algebra at the Institute for a decade. She assumed the title of vice president. Both Cynthia and Frances McDuffie are discussed more thoroughly in the following text.

21

Keeping the Institute Alive as Other Black Schools Close

The third generation head of the Laurinburg Institute, Frank "Bishop" McDuffie, Jr., had his hands full when he assumed the lead after his father's passing in 1994. From approximately 100 black boarding schools open in the early 1900s to the 1960s, the Institute was one of the last six black boarding schools in the country still open. The other schools included Southern Normal in Brewton, Alabama; Pine Forge Academy in Pine Forge, Pennsylvania; Redemption Christian Academy in Troy, New York; Piney Woods Country Life School in Piney Woods, Mississippi; and Saints Academy and College in Lexington, Mississippi.[1]

One student illustrates the difficulties black students faced as black prep schools closed. After suffering a stray bullet wound on his way home in the Bedford-Stuyvesant section of Brooklyn in 1993, the pre-engineering Canarsie High student Jason Counts decided to seek a safer learning environment at Southern Normal School, where he became the student body president. By Christmas 1996, the school had closed and he enrolled in Ebon International Preparatory Academy in Forsyth, Georgia. Ten days later, that school closed and he enrolled in Laurinburg Institute, which had 45 students at the time. Counts said: "I kind of feel like a nomad, just roaming around trying to accomplish something. It's become real difficult. But what can I do? I'll just keep trying to get my diploma so I can get to college."[2] By 2004, only four black boarding schools survived.

The total integration of the United States public education system via the Supreme Court decision of Brown v Board of Education in 1954 presented both possibilities and problems for black education. Booker T. Washington's model of separate but equal schools served to quell the anxieties of the white population, especially in the South, but it did not

172

fulfill the promise of equal education for black students. Many schools in the South did not fully integrate until the mid–1960s, including those in Laurinburg. In the North, because of segregated housing, integration did not fully occur until the 1970s. Black public schools were established in Laurinburg only in 1952–1953, which caused the Institute the loss of almost a thousand students and many fine teachers who moved into the public education system. For black Laurinburg teachers this situation proved to be fortunate because they became integrated into the public system and were able to make the transition to fully integrated schools later in the 1960s.

Many black teachers lost their jobs or were demoted when integration occurred. As late as 1978 in North Carolina, "128 out of 131 white superintendents believed that it would be 'impracticable to use Negro teachers' in schools under their jurisdiction."[3] This prejudice remained in spite of the fact "that many southern Black teachers received advanced training in some of the best northern institutions, including Teachers College, University of Wisconsin–Madison, and University of Chicago making them better qualified than White southern teachers."[4] The Laurinburg Institute could boast that it had excellently trained teachers including Frances McDuffie, whose degree in English was from Duke University.

As black boarding schools closed all over the South, Bishop McDuffie fought to keep Laurinburg Institute open. Funding had never been great for the school, but it became critical by 1990 when the Institute's enrollment dropped to the low of 24 students. Believing that "black people should take responsibility for educating their own" and knowing that providing opportunities for young black students to study the proud history of the black struggle was important to enhance their self-esteem, McDuffie often had to make difficult choices.[5] Paul Baldwin, the Institute Dean of Students and chemistry-physics teacher, noted: "We sometimes get promises of payments that never materialize, but the parents beg us to keep (their children) here."[6] The school often ran on hope and a prayer.

All private schools struggle financially to keep their doors open unless they have a large endowment or they are located in a wealthy community where students can afford an expensive tuition. The Laurinburg Institute had neither option since the town of Laurinburg was small and the local black community was not wealthy. The school never had been funded by church support as so many private schools were. Although some boarding students could afford the relatively low tuition, most students depended upon scholarships. And scholarships depended upon relentless fund raising by the administration and generous alumni. By the time Bishop McDuffie took over, the school was in dire straits.

The U.S. Internal Revenue Service reviewed the Institute's accounts in 1994 and declared that the school owed $47,000 in back taxes. The "dire straits" of the school's finances became evident when the IRS delved into the records. McDuffie reported that the tax assessor looked at him and said, "You all are running a school with no money. You are losing money. How and why do you stay in business?" McDuffie's response was, "Because we have a mission. I could drop dead today, but the mission can't die."[7] Bishop McDuffie further explained, "We believe that everyone has the potential to succeed.... We have to prepare our children to cope and survive."[8] The Xerox Company donated $10,000 to keep the school open and legal arrangements were made to dip into the endowment fund.

With limited funds, do you fix a leaking roof or offer scholarships to students whose families cannot afford the school tuition? More often than not McDuffie chose to fix people rather than roofs. As a result, the physical plant of the Institute suffered. Beginning with the collapse of the gymnasium roof in 1997, gradually other buildings became condemned and closed. Hurricane Florence in 2018 finished off many of the buildings. Today the gym, dormitories, music building, and the library all are closed. Only the cafeteria and parts of the classroom building remain open for use.

Still, the McDuffies have persevered. And so did others, as Andre Mack discloses in his articles' admiration of the many Institute teachers, who continued to work for minimal wages and no benefits, and the students, who persevered in spite of the inconveniences of a deteriorating campus. There are stories after stories of students who came to the Laurinburg Institute as their last ditch effort to find a safe place to learn or to be seen at all. Nancy McLaughlin captured some of their stories in her 1994 article "Laurinburg Institute/Separate and Equal" for the *Greensboro News & Record.* She quotes them as follows.

Joseph Frazier of Chapel Hill sold drugs and got into fights before coming to the Institute. Frazier said, "I'm getting a fresh start.... I hadn't even thought about college before this." Adrian Black from Greensboro said, "It took a while for the teachers to get to me in Greensboro, and I gave up." Black's family sent him to the Institute because he could get the one-on-one teaching and learning experience he needed. Now he plans to be an engineer. Tisa James from Detroit said, "I see myself as having potential here. They brought out a better student in me. I got lost in the system at my old school." When 15-year-old Paul Baldwin from Philadelphia arrived at the Institute, his friends were starting to experiment with drugs. Baldwin said, "While that was happening, I was in a small town learning how to play the viola and trombone, marching in the band, singing in the choir and debating with the best of them. Instead of losing my youth, I was able to capture it." After earning a college degree in science, Baldwin returned to the Institute to teach and eventually became Dean of the school.

John Russell from High Point recalled, "Reading, writing and arithmetic isn't the only ingredient for a well-rounded person. We didn't finish the day at 3 or 4 in the afternoon. They kept us busy until it was time to go to bed. There was no crime on campus. There were no fistfights. We were too busy." Russell went on to become a high school principal in High Point, North Carolina.[9]

Ernest Holmes, director of the National Alliance of Black School Educators, made these insightful remarks in McLaughlin's article:

> The last vestige for many of our children is a residential setting somewhere like a Laurinburg Institute, where educators address such problems as low self-esteem. People ask why we need black boarding schools. That's what people say about historically black colleges and universities. They say, "Why do we need N.C. A&T when we have a Duke University?" Many of those students at N.C. A&T would not have been accepted at Duke for one reason or another ... maybe SAT scores. They say people who don't do well on those tests can't achieve, but they do at places like N.C. A&T.
>
> There is a gross misunderstanding and confusion about this whole quality issue. The difference is, you've got the advanced computers and we've got the old computers, but the brilliance of the faculty is the same. It's just a matter of resources.[10]

Four generations of McDuffies have invested in people more than things. They have invested their hard work and energy and their faith that everyone can succeed into thousands of young people. Since 1954, their proudest accomplishment has been the high rate of college acceptances earned by their graduates. Depending on the year, from 80 to 90 percent of their graduates went on to college or other professional training. No public school has such a remarkable record, white or black. The McDuffies can proudly say, "Mission accomplished!"

22

The Women of the Laurinburg Institute

The written records of the Laurinburg Institute largely preserve the voices and deeds of the men associated with the school. Yet, women were the backbone of the McDuffie family and the heart of the Institute. Bishop McDuffie's wife Cynthia McDuffie, who has been a teacher since 1985 and, later, principal of the Institute, and their daughter Judge Frances McDuffie, who attended the school (1986–1991), and taught there for a decade (2000–2010), have contributed to this account through lengthy interviews. The elder sister of Bishop McDuffie, Dr. Fran McDuffie Foster, and their first cousin Shirley McDuffie McCoy, the daughter of Reginald and Joy McDuffie, have also shared four generations of family memories and Institute recollections via oral accounts.[1]

The third generation of McDuffies, Bishop, Fran and Shirley, grew up on the Laurinburg Institute campus, where their parents taught school. Out of seven children, Emmanuel and Tinny McDuffie only had four grandchildren. Joel McDuffie passed away in 2000, but the other three are very much alive and engaged. Both Fran and Shirley recalled how their grandfather would allow the grandchildren to come to his office and get a nickel out of his desk drawer each day. The purpose of this temptation was so that Emmanuel would have the chance to visit with his grandchildren daily. Otherwise, they were scattered around the large campus, playing in the creek under the giant sycamore trees, rolling down the lawn, playing tennis or in school. There were many places to be on the 26 acre property.

In many ways, growing up in the Institute's self-contained village was ideal. Shirley recalled hearing her Aunt Dibba, otherwise known as Verdelle, playing the *Moonlight Sonata* in the dark at night. All the McDuffies have very happy memories of their childhood. Although, when they went to town, they were confronted with separate water fountains and bathrooms, and they had to sit in the balcony at the movie theater, the kids didn't think much about it. It was just the way things were. Shirley remembered their fun day trips to Atlantic Beach, the only beach open to blacks in North Carolina. She didn't feel she was denied anything and never really confronted the divide between the races until later.

It was only when Shirley came to know the local black kids that she realized things were different for them. She especially remembers getting to know James McCoy, whom she met in kindergarten and much later married, and discovering the difficult circumstances of his family. James lived in a house without plumbing and electricity. He had an absent father and a mother who worked as a housekeeper for the Catholic priest. He helped his mother raise his three sisters by shining shoes at the barber shop and cleaning Bob's Jewelry Store at night. Unlike Shirley, James also had a very different, not so good, experience with white people. He remained within the black community and became a Methodist minister in Brooklyn, New York and, later, Bishop of the A.M.E. Zion Church in charge of all churches in Florida and Alabama. After receiving a master's degree from Howard University, Shirley became a social worker for Veterans Administration hospitals in New York City and Alabama, where she worked with all races.

Co-Founder of the Laurinburg Institute Tinny McDuffie (ca. 1960), managed the care of boarding students and the physical plant. She was noted for her inspiring recitations at graduations (Anzell Harrell Collection, courtesy of Chris Everett).

Shirley recalled an incident when she went to Howard University that illustrates her early innocence. When she was hanging out with a bunch of girls from the North, Shirley heard them talking about Jews, Puerto Ricans, Italians, and Irish people, all of whom had their own discriminatory places in the girls' minds concerning prejudices. She asked, "What color are the Jews?" In her mind, all prejudices revolved around race, not ethnicity. In the South, there were simply white, black (usually called colored), and American Indian people. Ethnic distinctions did not exist.

Shirley explained how Bishop McDuffie came by his name. Bishop was born premature and had to be incubated in the hospital for a time. His mother Sammie said he made grunting noises that reminded her of an "old bishop." The name stuck, and to this day he is known as Bishop McDuffie. Shirley's mother Joy taught the cousins a song to sing to him when he came home from the hospital called "He's Such a Little Fellow." Shirley remembered that, as a child, Bishop used to run away from home to her house, riding in his fire engine truck.

Fran Foster had several memories of her grandfather Emmanuel from the perspective of a child. She said she believed he was some kind of prince because of the "stately" way he carried himself. She and her cousin Shirley would follow behind him and imitate his majestic walk. Her fondest memory was of her grandfather sitting outside the girl's dormitory in the late summer evenings cutting up a watermelon to share with anyone who happened to walk by.

As ideal as the lives of the McDuffie children seemed, Fran remembered that there were no privileges granted the McDuffie kids in class. In fact, she felt that her aunts and uncles, who were also her teachers, were much harder on her than on other students. When she got her papers returned from her English teacher Aunt Iva Melton, they looked as if "they were covered with blood" because they were so intensely corrected with red marks. Fran found it difficult to sit down to dinner with her aunt after being so viciously attacked. Of course, she later thanked her relatives' strict training when she arrived at college fully prepared and, later, when she got her medical degree, first as a family practitioner and, later, as a specialized ophthalmologist. Judge Frances McDuffie and Foster also recalled that when they weren't in class, they were often "slave labor" for their parents. This indentureship extended through the generations beginning with Tinny and Emmanuel.

Tinny Ethridge McDuffie was co-founder of Laurinburg Institute in 1904. As a graduate of Snow Hill Institute, Tinny never taught school but she provided the food and care needed for all the students beyond the classroom. Meanwhile, she raised seven children and originally hosted five other teachers in her home, providing food and shelter.

Bishop McDuffie pointed out that the two most important members of any school's staff are the cook and the janitor. Tinny's main job was "to care for humans," cooking, cleaning, doing laundry, and generally advising and consoling homesick students just as a mother would do. Cynthia McDuffie remembers that they called her "Great Mother," as Tinny lived to be over a hundred years old, passing away in 1983. "She gave everything she had to the school." Shirley recalled that her grandmother Tinny always smelled of lavender because she bathed with Yardley soap.

When the school raised enough funds to build the four story girl's dormitory Howland Hall by 1924, the McDuffie family lived on the first floor. Many teachers also lived in the dorm. Tinny fed and cared for the family members as well as the boarding school students. Because the school served both public and private students, all expenses were kept distinct by separating the tasks of feeding the public pupils, which were overseen by Tinny's sister Amanda Johnson, and providing for the boarding students, which Tinny controlled. The same division worked for the men as well. I. Ellis Johnson was in charge of the public school kids and Emmanuel McDuffie handled the boarding school students.

Tinny would work past daylight when the crops were harvested, putting up vegetables and preparing food for cold storage in the commercial local freezer in Evans' Quarters. As a young girl, Fran Foster remembers working with her grandmother all day and a good part of the night to make sure there would be food through the winter. She often complained she was too tired to continue working. Tinny would say, "That's what night is for. You can work past tired and you don't die." Foster said her grandmother never raised her voice or spoke much, but when she did, "wisdom flowed out of her mouth."

According to Frances McDuffie, the family was always "all hands on deck" at all times to keep the school running smoothly. She compared working at the Institute as to how a family runs a farm. Everyone had a role to play and everyone had multiple roles to play, especially when someone was ill or out of town. You could be a cook, a grocery shopper, a janitor, a chauffeur, a teacher, a guidance counselor, an administrator, a Sunday school teacher interchangeably and simultaneously. There was "no day off" except for Saturday evening when family and friends would gather in the McDuffie living room and play cards.

After the school moved to its new campus in the late 1950s, Frank McDuffie built a home adjacent to the campus for himself and his family and a home next door for Tinny, her first and only home to herself. Foster remembered that "Frank called her every day. He taught us how to love." When she became too old to live alone, Tinny moved in with

Frank and Sammie. Bishop remembers, although she was in a wheelchair by that time, she still would cook for the family.

At graduation, Tinny traditionally would recite a memorized poem. One of her favorites was by Douglas Malloch, "Be the Best of Whatever You Are." In her later years, Tinny would come to the graduation ceremonies in a wheelchair and give an encouraging speech, which mandated a college education for all graduates. This expectation included her children, grandchildren and great-grandchildren, all of whom went on to college and many of whom returned home to share their knowledge as teachers at the Institute. She was proud to see her grandchildren graduate from the University of North Carolina–Chapel Hill and Meharry Medical College, and her great-grandchildren, from Duke University, Duke Medical School and Harvard Law School. The ABC reporter Ted Kopple interviewed Tinny, along with Frank McDuffie and the Chairman of the Board Kermit Waddell, on his *Nightline* television program in the early 1980s. Tinny passed away in 1983, just before her 102nd birthday. She had witnessed great changes in her long time on earth, many of which she herself had brought about through her constant stewardship of the Laurinburg Institute.

Tinny passed on her position as Institute "mother" to her daughter-in-law Sammie Sellers McDuffie, who shared her home with Tinny in her failing years. She understood what it meant to build a life from scratch just as Tinny had done. Sammie was raised on a dirt poor farm in the South Carolina country. Her father was a carpenter and her mother Marie worked as a maid for white folks and took in laundry for college students. Sammie remembered watching her mother come home from work, walking across the fields side by side with a friend, both carrying laundry baskets balanced on their heads African style. Sammie picked cotton as a child, and said they were so poor, "I didn't know I had lived through the depression," Foster recalled. She never missed a day of school even though she had to walk several miles to get there. Her father moved the family to town and built a house for them so that Sammie could go to high school.

After graduating, Sammie went to New York City and found a job working for a Hollywood star. She earned enough money to pay her way to North Carolina A&T State College. Sammie was among the first women accepted into the college in 1934. She was a beautiful and popular young woman, who was elected the possibly first "Miss A&T." There she met Frank McDuffie, who was captain of the tennis team.

Sammie was hired by Emmanuel McDuffie as the teacher Miss Sellers. When Frank and Sammie secretly eloped, the students continued to call her "Miss Sellers." The name stuck long after their marriage became known. Frances McDuffie remembered that Frank and Sammie were so close that they shared a desk in the school office, Sammie on one side and Frank on the other. Sammie taught home economics at first but, when the school became exclusively private, she became a well-respected math teacher. The basketball player Charlie Scott benefited from her firm but encouraging support as his algebra teacher.[2] She acted as a counselor to the boarding students who "gravitated to her as a kind, loving and considerate" advisor, Foster recalled. Shirley described her as "like an angel walkin' on the earth." After attending summer school for four years, Sammie earned a principal's certificate and officially assumed the title, sharing the administrative responsibilities with Frank as president. Sammie also conducted the weekly vesper services every Wednesday evening.

Students, especially, were fond of Sammie's inspiring "By the Way" talks. These homilies often offered opportunities for sharing stories of black accomplishments. Frances remembered they began with a saying such as: "Shoot for the moon but, if you don't make it, you'll be among the stars," or "If you can't win the race, make the person ahead of you break the record," or "A good man dies when a boy goes wrong." Sammie would make the students write an essay on the topic of the day so that they could practice their writing skills and learn to apply the lessons, which she had presented, to their own lives. The combination of talk, writing, and application cemented those lessons in the minds and hearts of the students so much so that many can recall them today, still finding inspiration from those lessons long ago in their daily lives.

A local woman, Willa Robinson, told a story about Sammie McDuffie, who came to the rescue of Robinson's son, Fred. He had graduated from the all-black Robeson County Training School, and, having good grades, applied and was accepted into a college in Charlotte. He wanted to be a doctor. When Fred arrived on campus and the administration realized he was black, he was cut immediately because of his race. This event occurred two weeks before the college term began. Her son was devastated and begged his mother to help him get into another school. Fred told his mother, "If you just get me in there, I won't let you down. I won't let you down."[3]

Mrs. Robinson went to see Principal Sammie McDuffie, who made several calls to Howard University and asked them to accept Fred. Because Howard had a good relationship with Laurinburg Institute students and they trusted Sammie McDuffie's judgement, they granted her wish. This happened in spite of the fact that Fred was not an Institute graduate. Sammie's word was enough.

When Fred arrived at Howard University, he quickly discovered he was not prepared for his required courses, as he had been led to believe from his honor student status at his high school. He was "burning the midnight oil" just to keep up, much less excel. Through hard work, he made it, but no thanks to his "below par" public high school education. Laurinburg Institute students were better prepared for the Howard University experience. It was Sammie's belief in Fred's determination to succeed that paid off, not his training. The same belief propelled Charlie Scott and many other Institute students from low self-esteem and unpreparedness to confidence and success.

Cynthia McDuffie said Sammie was like a mother to her because she lost her own mother when she came to Laurinburg. It must have been a shock moving to the small provincial town of Laurinburg since Cynthia was raised in Durham, which had a thriving black middle class generated by big black businesses in insurance and banking. Cynthia's father was an attorney and her mother taught school.

Cynthia assisted Sammie in the office as well as teaching psychology and English. As a young student just out of the University of North Carolina–Chapel Hill with a master's in psychology, Cynthia was intimidated by the larger-than-life athletes whom she taught. She remembered asking the science teacher Mr. Gilchrist to walk her to class to give her confidence. Later, as Sammie aged out, Cynthia also attended four years of summer school to acquire her principal's certificate.

Her experience as a psychology major in college prepared her well for the emotional difficulties she encountered among the students. Once, Cynthia found a girl blocking her way to class and she touched her lightly to move her aside. The girl leapt backwards as if she were being attacked. Cynthia immediately recognized that the girl had serious emotional problems associated with touch. She learned to use humor, instead of anger, when students misbehaved in class. For instance, when Cynthia asked a student to quiet down, he talked back saying, "I'm not talkin'!" Her response was, "I'm not standin' here either."

Most of the students during Cynthia's term were boarding students living far away from home. She dealt with homesickness, grief from the death of parents, culture clashes between New Yorkers and Virgin Islanders and many other emotional difficulties. She opened her home to foreign students who had nowhere to go during the holidays. In addition to the problems of the students, she would have to broker reconciliations among battling faculty members as well.

Frances McDuffie, daughter of Bishop and Cynthia, was also a participant in the "great experiment" which Frank and Sammie envisioned. First, she attended the Institute, which largely consisted of boys. Once the school became entirely private, the majority of students were male.

Females were always less than 10 percent of the student body. In that situation, she learned to speak out in class and discovered that she could compete well in a male environment. Also, she would overhear the boys talking about girls, and she learned what it takes to be respected in the male world. Then, when Frances attended college at the prestigious Duke University, she had to learn how to feel "comfortable" in a white world. She explained: "There will come a time when you're going to be in the minority in a room. You have to learn how to get along with the majority." These lessons served her well in her future law profession.

Meanwhile, however, Frances McDuffie returned home after her college graduation, to continue the family legacy of teaching black youths. She taught English, American and British literature, and even ninth grade algebra for a decade. Frances explained, "so many people ... in my family were in education because that's a field where you can serve people." Saying she often learned more from her students than they did from her, McDuffie realized that "teaching just isn't about trying to present information to people.... It is also learning from the student about how best to present that information to them."[4] Frances realized that black boys are "an endangered species," who need protection in a controlled environment. Many of her students challenged her ideas and values, especially those who came from disadvantaged, inner city circumstances. She recognized that some students "came from unimaginable conditions," and she very much admired the "human resourcefulness it took to overcome those obstacles and achieve great things" through strength and determination. She was able to see that people can evolve and change for the better with care and attention to their natural gifts.

Although the Institute provided a carefully controlled and structured environment for the students, it also offered a lively mixture of cultures just like the real world. Frances illustrated this idea with two boys who roomed together. One was a fledging Southern pastor who often led the Christian Endeavor program. The other was a Northern Muslim. They would argue religious ideas endlessly. The Christian would say, "I can't believe you think women should be so controlled," and the Muslim would say, "I can't believe you think a virgin gave birth to Jesus!" These arguments spilled over into classrooms and snack time, but they were always respectful, offering excellent opportunities for nascent thinkers to strengthen their beliefs through questioning.

During Frances McDuffie's term at the Institute, the student body and faculty had evolved from a national representation of cultures to an international one. Both black and white students attended. Coach Chris Chaney was white. The math teacher, Peter Gomez, was from Gambia.

Coach Steve Levon was from Brazil and Coach Delaberra was from Senegal. Students came from the Virgin Isles, Yugoslavia, Australia, and Russia, among other countries. The Institute was indeed a truly small world.

In spite of its universal sophistication, the Institute was never a "posh" school, according to Frances McDuffie. It was never a status school. When parents made inquiries, the administration always tried to "manage expectations" prior to the student's enrollment. Frances told them that the school was about the individual and developing "character, leadership and integrity," not about material goods and making status connections. When a student bragged about his "Jorden shoes," a status symbol among black boys, or her Gucci handbag, a status symbol among all girls, Frances would query, "Why do you spend so much money for those things? Do you own stock in Adidas or Gucci?" She, herself, illustrated the qualities she admired. A Duke graduate, she could have had a high paying job, but she chose to serve her family legacy of educating black children. This meant living at home and driving a $700 car she purchased from a wealthier student.

When the school was reduced to a handful of students in 2006, Frances said she "did not want to be a burden to her family." She got a law degree, fulfilling the long deferred wishes of her father, Bishop, and took a job nearby in Fayetteville, North Carolina, as a public defender. Governor Roy Cooper appointed her as a judge in 2020 to the Cumberland District 12. Although she loves the law, Frances says she is often frustrated because she does "not have the time to solve problems" for the young people who come before her in juvenile court. She has seen what a long term commitment to a young person's education and developing character, in a controlled setting, can do.

23

Campaigning to Get the Word Out

Bishop, Cynthia and Frances McDuffie waged a vigorous campaign to increase the visibility of the Laurinburg Institute and, thereby, increase their flagging enrollment. They called on alumni to financially support their alma matter and to send their children to the Institute. The famed NBA player and Institute graduate Sam Jones led a group of alumni to meet with the McDuffies in April 1994. Their intention was to review the financial difficulties of the school and set up a plan to invigorate the school once more. Jones believed that the McDuffies "need some direction in how it should be run and what should be done to make it one of the top schools again."[1] Top among Jones' priorities for the school were paying off its debts, increasing enrollment and setting up a board of trustees to oversee the school's management. Bishop McDuffie negotiated with the IRS to pay off the school's delinquent taxes. In 2004, the Institute celebrated its 100 year anniversary with 135 enrolled students, each paying $14,000 per year for tuition.[2]

The Eriq La Salle film *Rebound* aired in 1996 on HBO, telling the story of Earl "The Goat" Manigault. It is still available on YouTube. The cast was a veritable who's who of well-known black actors including Don Cheadle, Forest Whitaker, and Clarence Williams, III. James Earl Jones played the part of Frank McDuffie, Sr. The Laurinburg Institute features prominently in the film, which no doubt helped to shine a light on its importance.

Frances McDuffie created a Facebook website for the National Alumni of Laurinburg Institute, which encourages graduates to keep in touch. Each year, the Institute recognizes accomplished black citizens, both graduates and non-graduates, and enters them into its Laurinburg Institute Hall of Fame. The stories of the Hall of Famers are available on the Laurinburg Institute website. The school sponsors a

Golf-A-Thon Day during the celebration weekend of the annual Institute Hall of Fame Ceremony. These events are major fund raisers to keep the school afloat.

The local *Laurinburg Exchange* newspaper reporter and Institute graduate Andre Mack wrote numerous articles about other graduates, such as Grachen Moncur, and Institute history in general. He believes the Institute deserves more recognition both locally and nationally, and calls for those who made that history to record it:

> Our school must also record its history. Centenary day, new campus construction in the 1950's, and the impact of social movements and world events on our school are all unrecorded.... The largest collection of Laurinburg Institute history, though, is archived in the memories of thousands of alumni throughout the Caribbean, Europe and the United States. We lived it! We are forever connected by the best of our Laurinburg Institute experiences.[3]

Danny Glover and Spike Lee

The McDuffies also sought the help of well-known Hollywood celebrities. The actor Danny Glover contributed to the support of the Institute and narrated a short film entitled *Laurinburg Institute (Edited)*, which is available on the school's website and on YouTube. He tells the story of the school's founding and 100 year history. Glover notes that a family member attended the Institute. The famed film director Spike Lee also has a

Actor Danny Glover (2020) narrated the video *Laurinburg Institute (Edited)* (photograph by John Mathew Smith).

connection with the McDuffies with whom he shares common ancestors, the slaves Mike and Phoebe.

The story of Mike and Phoebe has been passed down through their families for multiple generations. Mike and Phoebe originated in the Gambia/Senegal region of Africa. After their marriage, Mike and Phoebe were captured and sold into slavery in Charleston, South Carolina. Mike worked as an ironworker in Charleston while Phoebe was sold down river. As soon as Mike was able to buy his freedom, he searched until he found his wife Phoebe and purchased her freedom.[4] The book *Fallen Prince: William James Edwards and the Quest for Afro-American Nationality* (1989) by Donald Stone tells the remarkable story of Mike and Phoebe and traces the family tree down to the present day.

The descendants of Mike and Phoebe have met for regular reunions since 1980. In 2018, 74 descendants from all over the United States, including California, Texas, Utah, and New York, attended their family reunion at the Laurinburg Institute. Laurinburg Mayor Matthew Block spoke at the reunion. Mayor Block remarked:

> I know a lot of us in the city feel the importance of the Laurinburg Institute and of all the people that have been involved over the years to make it what it is. So to commemorate the extra special feelings we have for the

Film director Spike Lee (2007) considered making a film of the Institute story (photograph by Hans Reitzema).

Laurinburg Institute and the Descendants of Mike and Phoebe, on behalf of the city council, we wanted to bestow the key to the city.[5]

A spokesman for the group, Pamela Powell, said, "This is really huge for us—we've never had the mayor come and speak in such a respectful way. I think people had tears in their eyes. This has been one the best reunions we've ever had. Everyone has been so welcoming and receptive, we feel so appreciated."[6]

Spike Lee is a huge basketball enthusiast. According to Burnest Graham, a Laurinburg economic development official, Lee was impressed with the story of the Institute and considered creating a movie plan for that story. The agents of Danny Glover, Bill Cosby and Arsenio Hall also expressed interest in the project. Kukhautusha Croom, a former associate of Lee's production company, volunteered to write a script, at a greatly reduced price, for a movie about the Institute.[7] As yet, however, a Hollywood film has not been produced.

Chris Everett: Filmmaker

Meanwhile, a citizen of Laurinburg, Chris Everett began making a movie about the school called *The Laurinburg Institute, Est. 1904* (2009). Although Everett did not attend the Institute, graduating from Scotland High School in 2001 and studying at King's College in Charlotte, he was familiar with the Institute's contributions to the local community. He recalls that the Institute opened its recreation facilities to the local community during the summer.[8]

The Institute offered the local boys and girls their version of summer camp. For a dollar a day, kids could access a program of running, tennis, basketball, and swimming in the indoor pool. Snacks and soft drinks were sold to the kids in the gym, adding a little more income to the budget. Everett played basketball in the gymnasium and swam in the Institute swimming pool. During the painful period of integration, when black kids showed up to swim, the Laurinburg public pool had been closed and turned into a tennis court, so the Institute provided an important service to the parents and children of the local black community.

Everett grew up with Frances McDuffie and knew her family and many faculty members well. His grandfather attended the Institute and his godfather Anzell Harrell, a former principal of the Institute, gave him a stack of Institute photographs and mementos, which encouraged him to record the history of the Institute on film. While working in graphic design in Atlanta, he began work on the film.

The Laurinburg Institute, Est. 1904 trailer was posted on Facebook in November 2011, showing video clips and photographs. The film was to be made in the style of a Ken Burns film, with commentary over historic photographs interspersed with interviews with Institute students and staff. Everett documents the humble beginnings of the Institute, which began in a culture of repression where black children only had access to schools through the second grade, and ends with the triumphs of graduates such as Dizzy Gillespie and Sir John Swan, who credit the Institute with establishing the foundation they needed to succeed. Everett recognizes that the Laurinburg Institute "was the first place to give African-Americans in this area a chance at the American dream."[9]

Faced with a lack of records and photographs, Everett scoured the internet, eBay and Facebook for images, school annuals, newspaper clippings, yard sales, anything that documented the history of the Institute. Just before he passed away, Everett's godfather Anzell Harrell gave him many of the archival images that illustrate this book. Woody Shaw, grandson of an Institute graduate, praised Everett's efforts: "This film should raise a sense of responsibility and gratitude, and remind us of our debt to those who came before us and how much they sacrificed on our behalf."[10] Everett hopes one day to complete the film, confirming the legacy of the Laurinburg Institute.

Filmmaker Chris Everett (2020) made an unfinished film, *The Laurinburg Institute, Est. 1904*; clips available on Facebook (courtesy of Chris Everett and Southern Documentary Fund).

Everett established himself as a documentary filmmaker with his first feature-length film, the multiple award-winning *Wilmington on Fire* (2015). This film documents the 1898 Democrat white supremacist takeover of the Wilmington, North Carolina, city government and the massacre of many black elected citizens. Everett must have learned about Laurinburg's participation in that event while making his earlier film about Laurinburg Institute. The retired NBA basketball player David West proved to be Chris Everett's inspiration, just when he needed it the most.[11] When he heard about the *Wilmington on Fire* project, he contacted Everett and asked for a copy of the film. Everett said the film was stalled due to lack of funding. West provided the financial support so that Chris could finish the film.

The film won Best Documentary at the Culcalorus Film Festival (2015), Film SPARK, and North Carolina Black festivals (2016). Everett won Best Director First Feature Documentary at the 2017 Pan American Film Festival. He is now completing a second film that follows up on the reaction to his first film and shows how people can create change through honest discussion of traumatic historical events. Everett explained his reason for creating phase II of *Wilmington on Fire* as follows:

> We know the history, the past…. Now let's look at the present and see how people in Wilmington are trying to bring Wilmington back to that Fusion Period, to that period of 1897 [and] the work they're doing to do that. That's the story I want to tell, to give this story in history a complete circle. So people can see this happened in Wilmington, but look how not only the African-American community is rising up, the city of Wilmington as a whole is trying to rise up as well to become that city it was destined to be in 1897.[12]

Everett is now the program manager for the non-profit organization the Southern Documentary Fund in Durham, North Carolina. He has just completed a film documenting the life of a black judo expert, and is now preparing a film commissioned by Preservation North Carolina on black architects and builders.

24

Basketball, Basketball, Basketball

Frank McDuffie, Sr., created a systematic program to integrate college basketball, particularly in North Carolina. He knew that talent opened doors quicker than test scores at the largely non-integrated colleges in the South. Still, the test scores were a factor in getting players into those schools. Black players did not receive the academic encouragement and attention they needed in public school systems. Earl "The Goat" Manigault's story illustrates this failure in public education to address the academic gap for black athletes. Other challenges outside school, such as broken families, poverty, drugs and crime, added to the burdens of the black kids who wanted a college education. They often failed to achieve high enough scores on the required SATs for entrance into colleges.

The McDuffies, knowing that they could provide both the academic and the athletic support needed, targeted and recruited these talented, yet academically challenged players. They also raised funds to provide financial support for players to get a solid education. When funds were not available, the McDuffie family made personal sacrifices, such as forgoing a salary, so that they could serve the needs of others. Cynthia McDuffie said that the only vacation she has taken in the forty years that she has been associated with the Institute was a week off when her mother died. The relative isolation of the small town atmosphere of Laurinburg also helped to eliminate negative distractions and encourage concentration on studies.

Under Frank McDuffie, Sr.'s, leadership, at least nine Institute basketball players made it to college and eight players made it into the NBA. Frank added a gap year to the curriculum in the 1970s in order to help underachieving high school graduates meet college requirements. Three of four ACC college basketball programs in North Carolina accepted Laurinburg Institute graduates, including the University of North Carolina at Chapel Hill, Wake Forest University and the North Carolina

State University. Frank "Bishop" McDuffie, Jr., far exceeded his father's record with at least 53 Institute graduates who have been drafted into college basketball programs since 1994.

Jumping Through Academic Hoops

Professional sports have always depended on college programs to train their athletic candidates. College programs have also depended upon their athletic programs for financial support and visibility. Acceptances into college athletic programs have depended upon meeting academic requirements such as grades, curriculum and SAT scores. Yet, academic achievement has little or no relevance to athletic skill. The two systems exist in two different worlds. As the story of Earl Manigault illustrates, failing athletes can be the most outstanding players on a team.

Many athletic coaches have complained about the disastrous demands of academic requirements which barred many talented players from joining their teams. Imagine how many enterprising business and artistic careers would have been stymied by academic requirements! Not all talented, intelligent, creative people are right for an academic path. In fact, one might argue that academia often stifles talent, intelligence and creativity. The old saying, "Those that can, do, while those that can't, teach," sometimes rings true. School can dull the mind in the wrong hands. All of us have suffered boring classes that seem to have no relevance to us then or even later in life.

The focus required for greatness often demands eliminating all distractions, including irrelevant academic requirements. While many high achievers succeed without college degrees, in the case of athletics, many talented players have been blocked forever from a promising path. Maturity is also a factor. The NBA ruled in 2006 that players must be at least 19 years old and have one post–high school year before applying for the draft.

Early in the 1970s, Frank McDuffie added a gap year to the Laurinburg Institute curriculum in order to accommodate those players who wished to play professional ball without a college degree and to give those academically challenged players a chance to play college ball as well. The primary focus of this year was to teach players how to test well enough to make the grade. The SAT scores still remained a barrier. Nationwide the education system has become oriented toward teaching to the test, so focusing on successful test taking seemed the practical path forward for many players. The Institute faculty not only taught players how to jump academic hoops, but also raised them to excellence in basketball training and gave them the opportunity to mature and grow.

The story of Robert Dozier, a 2004–2005 student at the Laurinburg Institute, well illustrates the trials and tribulations he suffered to make good. This story has a happy ending because Dozier made the 2009 Miami Heat team, reaching the NBA at last, due to the support of the Institute, and, of course, dependent on his own talent and determination.

The University of Georgia recruited Georgia resident Dozier for their basketball team, but then, someone claiming to be on the faculty of Lithonia High School, from which Dozier graduated in 2004, reported that his SAT score was "fishy." The university asked Dozier to retake his SAT exam and found that the original score (1260) and the retested score (720) did not support the idea that the same person took both exams. A review by the SAT Educational Testing Services reported that the handwriting on the two tests did not match, indicating again that someone other than Dozier had taken the first test. Convinced by these facts, UGA withdrew their offer and Dozier was left suspended.[1]

Seeking a means to better his SAT scores, Dozier enrolled at the Laurinburg Institute in 2004. He was on the 2004–2005 Institute Tigers basketball team, winning a record 40–0 games and eventually the 2005 national prep school championship. Along with his fellow championship teammates Shawne Williams, Chance McGrady, Antonio Anderson, and Robert Sallie, Dozier signed with Coach John Calipari at University of Memphis. The dynamic combination of Dozier, McGrady and Anderson won 135 games from 2006 to 2009, the most of any NCAA Division-I players in a career, and, along with other Laurinburg Institute graduates Williams and Sallie, they took the Memphis Tigers to the 2006, 2007, 2008, and 2009 NCAA tournaments.[2] The jerseys of Dozier, McGrady and Anderson were retired in 2009 honoring their contributions to the most Division-I wins in four years by any team in the history of the NCAA.

Dozier graduated from the University of Memphis in 2009 with a degree in interdisciplinary studies and was drafted by the NBA Miami Heat. Since then, Dozier has played professional basketball all over the world (Greece, Spain, United Arab Emirates, Philippines, and Japan) and continues through the present. The Institute helped Dozier and many others overcome academic challenges while maintaining and encouraging their extraordinary athletic talents.

Bishop McDuffie shared the story of another Institute player, Renaldo Balkman, who had to confront racial prejudice concerning

University of Memphis 2009 Final Four with former Laurinburg Institute Golden Tigers Joey Dorsey (3), Antonio Anderson (5) and Robert Dozier (2), along with a referee and teammates (courtesy of author Beau B).

his academic qualifications. He was raised in Puerto Rico and came to the Institute, where he attracted the attention of university coaches as a member of the 2003 national prep school championship team. Balkman was recruited by the University of South Carolina Division I basketball team and gained acceptance to the school based on his academic record and his acceptable scores on the SAT. The athletic director refused to believe Balkman could have made such a good SAT score and insisted that he retake the exam. Balkman said, "I didn't cheat!" and testified that he had taken the exam with no outside help and, therefore, the grade was legitimate. Nonetheless, the director demanded that, if he wanted to play for the college team, Balkman would have to prove himself again under the USC's supervision. Downtrodden, Balkman returned to the Institute begging for a refresher course to prepare him to retake the exam. Bishop and his academic team worked with him for two weeks. Balkman, then, returned to USC and retook the test, making an even better score the second time around. Although he had to face the racial prejudices of a doubting coach, Balkman vindicated both himself and the Laurinburg Institute, which supported his victory.

Balkman was named the NIT Most Valuable Player of the Year in 2006. He was drafted in the NBA first round by the New York Knicks in the same year. Balkman has played ball continuously since then. The Institute prepared him well for his seventeen year career in professional basketball as it did for many other players. Recognizing the remarkable successes of the Laurinburg Institute, Richard Walker of the *Carolina Sports Hub* wrote:

> Since ... the inaugural 1946–47 NBA season, there have been 192 players [from North Carolina] to play in either the ABA or NBA.... Which school has produced the most players? Laurinburg Institute in Scotland County has that distinction—and it's not even close. The Tigers have produced 14 eventual NBA players, among them Hall of Famers Sam Jones and Charlie Scott and No. 1 overall pick Jimmy Walker. Jones is the first Basketball Hall of Fame inductee (1984) and the first African-American to be inducted into the N.C. Sports Hall of Fame (1969). Scott was inducted into the Basketball Hall of Fame in 2018.... Laurinburg Institute also produced hundreds of other eventual college standouts for schools all across the country.[3]

The list of colleges which have drafted Laurinburg Institute graduates include UNC, Wake Forest, NC State, Kansas State, LSU, Auburn, Cal State Bakersfield, Cal State Northridge, Nebraska, Wyoming, New Mexico State, UTEP, Texas A&M, Massachusetts, Rutgers, Indiana, South Carolina, New Orleans, Southern Mississippi, Arkansas Tech, Louisiana Tech, South Florida, Southern Utah, DePaul, Manhattan and many others.[4] The Institute certainly has established a national reputation for producing excellent basketball players with the skills and knowledge needed to compete at the national level.

Bishop McDuffie cultivated relationships with college coaches who spotted talent in the public schools, but who were also frustrated with their own schools' academic entry requirements, which prohibited underachieving draftees. The University of Memphis Coach John Calipari, who became an NBA head coach, was one of the coaches for whom McDuffie helped train potential college athletes for college acceptance. McDuffie also hired Coach Chris Chaney of basketball prep school fame. The combined efforts of Bishop McDuffie academically and Chris Chaney athletically made a dynamic duo.

Calipari found high school graduates who did not qualify for acceptance at his school, but who were outstanding athletes, and sent them to Laurinburg Institute for a year of post-graduate schooling. Chaney coached them in basketball and McDuffie's staff also coached them on how to take the SATs and make better grades. This system worked so well that the Laurinburg Institute Tigers won two national prep school championships in 2003 and 2005.

25

Coach Chris Chaney
and the Dream Team

Coach Chris Chaney, who is white, was the perfect fit for Laurinburg Institute's basketball program. Bishop McDuffie, a McDonald's All-American coach, recalled that he was set to hire a black coach to lead his Tiger team when the coach failed to show up for an interview. He noticed a white guy sitting in his car in front of the school. Asking if he could help him, McDuffie discovered that Chaney was waiting for the black coach to arrive and said he had been offered the opportunity to be his assistant. Discovering that the black coach hadn't shown up, Chaney asked McDuffie if he would give him a chance to coach the team. At first McDuffie hesitated because all basketball associates of the Institute had been family members or close friends who were black. The Institute took pride in being a completely black operation, one which was entirely self-reliant. However, Chaney's persistence, along with the support of Cynthia and Frances McDuffie, convinced McDuffie to give Chaney a try.

Chaney not only led the Tigers to two national championships in 2003 and 2005, but, because he was white, other coaches agreed to play the Institute team, opening up venues which, until that time, had been closed to them. Chaney also provided opportunities for white players to join the team, particularly players from other countries such as Russia, Czechoslovakia, Yugoslavia, Australia and Spain. Today Chaney's record is most impressive: winning 850+ games, more than any coach his age in history; winning several national championships with teams ranked number one in the country seven times; coaching 140 Division I players, 70-plus players who have played pro ball internationally, and 19 NBA players. According to the Scotland Campus Sports page:

> He also coached what many experts call the best pre-college team of all time (was in *Sports Illustrated*), the 40–0 Laurinburg Institute team in

ESPN Seth Greenberg (left) with Coach Chris Chaney (2012), who led the Laurinburg Institute Golden Tigers to two national championships in 2003 and 2005 (courtesy of Chris Chaney).

2005. That team had 15 Division I players and 5 players that either played or got drafted in the NBA and they won by an average of 40 ppg, including the National Championship game vs. Hargrave Military.[1]

Antonio Anderson was among the 2005 players who won the Institute championship game. He later went on to play for Coach Calipari at Memphis and is now a head high school coach in Massachusetts. Anderson says about Chaney: "He's the basketball doctor, man. A kid needs help academically, needs help developing? He's the No. 1 option. It's a no-brainer."[2] Chaney's reputation as a top notch coach for aspiring young players spread beyond our national borders to Europe, Russia, the

Caribbean and Africa. Under his watch, the Laurinburg Institute successfully integrated and gained international prominence.

Coach Chaney spent four years at Laurinburg Institute from 2001
to 2005. Unlike most basketball prep schools, the Institute did not have
an impressive campus filled with large buildings and fine equipment. In
fact, the Institute campus was fairly rundown, particularly the gymnasium, which was closed due to a partially collapsed roof over the indoor
pool. Chaney said the campus was not the thing that attracted him, it
was the people. He has very fond memories of both the staff and the
players he coached. Chaney described Cynthia McDuffie as "the sweet-
est lady" performing an "unreal job" preparing her students for SATs
and college acceptance. "Caring for the kids has got to be number one,"
Cynthia told him.[3] Chaney saw the academic roles played by the McDuffie family, including Bishop and Fran McDuffie, as key to the successful
lives of his players beyond the basketball court. He said, "One day, my
players' careers as athletes will end. They will need good habits to succeed off court, starting with being on time and earning good grades.
We encouraged them to be the best version of themselves they can
be." Chaney was grateful to Bishop McDuffie, who has a "big heart, he
gave us all opportunities to succeed." Twenty years later, Chaney still
receives a phone call from Bishop on his birthday.

Because most of Chaney's players were only at the Institute for one
year between high school and college, both the staff and the coaches had
to give 100 percent of their concentrated attention to the development
of their students, whether on the court or in the classroom. A constant
repetition of mantras, such as be on time, pick up the trash, respect others, be a responsible worker, earn good grades, be a good leader, was
drilled into the students. Good habits produced good results. Many students later did well in college.

As far as basketball was concerned, Coach Chaney recognized the
challenges facing his students, many living far from home for the first
time, with a new coach and new fellow players. He reminded them that
time went by quickly and that this was only the beginning of a series of
changes that they would have to face in the future. They would need to
learn the lesson of making adjustments as they faced new situations.

The adjustments Laurinburg Institute students made in order to
succeed were many. For the basketball players, the most difficult obstacle to overcome was the loss of the gymnasium in 1997 when the roof
caved in over the attached swimming pool. Coach Chaney found other
courts to utilize, some as far away as 30 miles. The team ran five miles
to their borrowed ball court on the campus at St. Andrews Presbyterian College for team practices. When St. Andrews got new weight

equipment, they donated their old equipment to Laurinburg Institute for their use during offseason. Coach Chaney particularly worked with his players during offseason when he had more time to devote to them individually. Chaney said, "I think we work harder than anyone in the country. I'm not saying that other teams don't work hard because I know they do, but I think we outwork them."[4]

Players complained about the living conditions of roach-infested, condemned dorms and the "meager food." Gone were the days when the school was self-sufficient, raising its own crops and building its own housing. Yet, under Coach Chaney, the players persevered and won college attention by winning game after game. Chaney never lost a single player in spite of the challenges they faced. Adversity seemed to make them stronger. Chaney described his challenge to his players in this way:

> Is the campus brand new? No. Is it all that? No. But it's kind of like who we are, blue collar. You're living away from home, new coach, new system. At the end of the day, we don't want anything easy. We get kids to buy into a culture.... That's why we make them tough. After a couple of months, I hate to say it, it's like brainwashing. But it's brainwashing for good. Like, "I have to outwork everybody, I have to be different." ... We've proved we can win on a very high level with under-the-radar guys (who work harder than others). We joke about it. We want you to have two hearts, we don't want just one.[5]

One big adjustment the players had to make was setting aside their egos and learning what real teamwork meant. The sports writer Jeff Goodman pointed out that going undefeated, winning 40–0 in a season, is as much about coaching as it is about talent: "People would assume it's easy to run the table when you've got as much talent as Chris Chaney had at Laurinburg. But trying to manage all the personalities and get that many talented players on the same page is no easy task."[6]

Chaney said, "all the players were stars in their high schools." They were used to being "the guy" who led the team. Now they were all "the guy" who had to make sacrifices for the sake of the team. He told them they would probably play more in college as freshmen than they would for his team, which was so extraordinarily talented. The player Antonio Anderson recalled: "I thought everyone was going to be out for themselves. ... And at first it was definitely like that. But after the third game, Coach Chaney sat us down and told us we weren't going to win the championship. That's when we started to come together."[7]

Chaney "treated practices like games" because he had the depth on his team to create opposing teams with equal talent. Chaney taught his team to trust each other and respect his leadership. Another player

Robert Sallie made this comment: "I'm a big believer in going unde-feated, but I've watched plenty of great teams slip up. ... The thing about our team is that if our starters didn't show up, our second unit was ready to play. ... We never had a drop-off at any position and that's what made our team spectacular."[8]

The players learned to sacrifice their own egos for the good of the team. They were "unselfish" and "didn't care who scored as long as the team scored." Chaney told them, "Our goal is not to win the national championship, but to be undefeated." Of course, being undefeated would mean winning the national championship, which the 2002–2003 team did accomplish by being ranked No. 1 nationally.

All their games were played off campus, which involved many hard miles of traveling. The sports reporter Michael Gilliland described the incredible "masterpiece season" with a 40–2 record as follows:

> This season the prep squad logged over 16,000 miles and over 225 hours on the road. The Tigers traveled to destinations such as Canada, Buffalo, Rhode Island, Maryland, Virginia, Washington, D. C., Florida and Min-nesota to play their games, with Minnesota being the only trip taken by aircraft.
>
> The Tigers played at the Target Center in Minnesota—otherwise known as the home of the National Basketball Association's Minnesota Timber-wolves, and the Dean Smith Center in Chapel Hill, where they defeated the Tarheels junior-varsity squad on Jan. 22.[9]

The 2003 outstanding players included Koundjia from the Cen-tral Africa Republic, Keith Banks, Boubacar Coly and Renaldo Balk-man from Puerto Rica. They would matchup against such players as the now famous LeBron James of St. Vincent–St. Marys. The NBA scouts attended 20 of their games. After the season, the players signed with LSU, Texas A&M, Xavier and USC respectively. Jim Quinn in *Slam Magazine* wrote that "Laurinburg is one of the biggest, deepest, and most talented teams in the country. Chaney has players on his 2003–2004 team who have already committed to powers such as Oklahoma, Memphis, the University of Southern California, and Miami."[10] *Slam's* attention garnered them such notoriety that high school players were clambering to join the next Institute squad.

Over the following two years Chaney built his veritable dream team. He also got to know the famous Boston Celtic Sam Jones, who always came to the Institute graduation ceremonies. Jones had attended Chaney's games when he was a coach at Newport Prep in Maryland before his arrival in Laurinburg. Chaney and Jones got to be friends and talked on the phone often, exchanging ideas on draft picks, games and potential players. Chaney understood that relationships, more than winning, mattered. He described his personal evolution in the following manner:

> That's the best thing I have, in my opinion, is the relationships with my kids. My players are like my family. They're part of my life for the rest of my life. The reason I love coaching is just to change peoples' lives. It's really grown for me the last 10 years. Early in my career it was more winning, winning, winning. As I mature I see the ultimate goal is to make these guys into the best version of themselves. That gives me more of a peace of mind....[11]

In talking about his relationships, Coach Chaney used as an example the Laurinburg Institute student Quantez Robertson, whom he coached in the 2005 championship team. Chaney had coached him before coming to the Institute and knew he was a high level player. In spite of Chaney's support, Robertson could not get even a Division II school interested in him.

Chaney encouraged Robertson to go to Laurinburg Institute for a prep year. There, Robertson went on to win the 2005 championship under Coach Chaney and gain enough academic support under Bishop McDuffie and his staff to gain entrance to Auburn University.[12] Chaney described Robertson as a real leader, who encouraged his fellow players to "come on time, pick up the trash, and generally develop good habits." Robertson, under Coach Jeff Lebo at Aubrun, was named three times Outstanding Defensive Player between 2005 and 2009, when he signed with the German BBL Fraport Skyliners in Frankfurt. According to Chaney, every time Coach Lebo, now assistant coach at UNC, sees him, he says, "Send me another one like Robertson!"

Robertson played for

Quantez Robertson, playing for the BBL Fraport Skyliners (2023), also played on the Laurinburg Institute 2005 championship team and was a star player for Auburn University (courtesy of Sandro Halank).

the Skyliners for a decade, leading them to win the 2016 FIBA Europe Cup title. A reporter for Euro Cup Basketball declared, "Quantez Robertson is a ball magnet! All [his moves] were the kind of plays that make a difference because they show desire and leadership, just like Robertson has been doing for a decade in a city far from home."[13] As of 2024 Robertson was still playing professional ball in Europe.

Robertson played on the 2005 national championship team. Chaney's relationships solidified "what some experts consider the best precollege team in history," according to Kelli Anderson writing in *Sports Illustrated*.[14] Zach Smart wrote in his sports blog that Coach Chaney created "a veritable prep 'Dream Team' … [which] reached unprecedented success and simultaneously re-wrote the pages of high school sports history. The team posted a 40–0 overall record en route to the 2005 national prep championship [and had] a record 15 Division-I signees."[15]

Four of the Institute 2005 championship winners—Antonio Anderson, Kareem Cooper, Robert Dozier, and Shawne Williams—went on to play for Coach Calipari at the University of Memphis. Calipari

LAURINBURG INSTITUTE'S SEASON OF DOMINATION

Date	Opponent	Score
Oct. 5	Brunswick CC	93-51
Oct. 16	Spark Academy	108-64
Oct. 22	Cape Fear	85-48
Nov. 2	Virginia Tech JV	99-59
Nov. 5	Virginia Tech JV	108-58
Nov. 6	Genesis Christian	92-51
Nov. 6	Genesis Christian	85-59
Nov. 10	Bonner Academy	100-57
Nov. 12	Bonner Academy	111-58
Nov. 17	Italian Jr. National	86-47
Nov. 19	Notre Dame Prep	101-69
Nov. 20	Bridgeton	99-77
Nov. 21	Brewster	96-92
Dec. 1	Eldon Academy	113-66
Dec. 4	Mt. Zion	101-64
Dec. 9	London All-Stars	146-46
Dec. 10	TAPS	85-70
Dec. 11	Beal	107-50
Dec. 11	St. Clair	87-45
Dec. 12	West Hill College	132-64
Dec. 12	Philly Lutheran	102-74
Dec. 14	Prince Ave. Prep	89-59
Dec. 16	Coastal Christian	93-68
Dec. 17	Charis Prep	95-54
Jan. 11	Louisburg	102-70
Jan. 16	Lutheran	84-81
Jan. 18	Austrailian All-Stars	101-51
Jan. 26	Denmark Tech CC	101-46
Feb. 1	Charis Prep	87-70
Feb. 4	St. Andrews	116-58
Feb. 8	VMI	132-50
Feb. 8	Virginia Tech JV	129-64
Feb. 11	Redemption Christian	95-69
Feb. 12	St. Thomas More	70-59
Feb. 13	Winchenden	102-79
Feb. 17	Philadelphia Christian	Forfeit
Feb. 18	Pfeiffer JV	101-61
Feb. 19	UNC JV	101-54
Feb. 22	Prince Ave. Prep	123-60
Feb. 25	Hargrave Military	95-83

Final record: 40-0
Points scored: 3,952
Avg. points: 101.3
Points allowed: 2,405
Avg. allowed: 61.6

The Dream Team record of the 2005 Championship season (40–0), for the Laurinburg Institute Golden Tigers (courtesy of Chris Everett and *Laurinburg Exchange*).

had drafted Joey Dorsey from the Laurinburg Institute team the previous year and was impressed with the training they had received. Bishop McDuffie reported that he had asked Coach Calipari to take five players, but Calipari said: "You're crazy, no Division I college has ever taken seven student athletes from the same school. I just want Joey Dorsey!" He ended up taking five players that year, who joined two previously recruited players, many of whom, in their freshman year, played for the varsity team that reached second place in the 2006 NCAA Final Four Championship. McDuffie boasted, "Those young men represented the winningest Division I team in the history of the NCAA."

When asked how such a young team managed to play so well together, Shawne Williams said that being at the Institute "helped us at lot. It was good that we could all go to the same school so that we could become acquainted with each other. It seemed like everybody on that team was at Laurinburg to be together. We learned what to say to each other and how to act around each other."[16] Williams told *Sports Illustrated*: "That's how we have fun—we look for each other."[17]

second national championship in three years

MICHAEL GILLILAND/SPORTS EDITOR

The Laurinburg Institute claimed its second national championship in three years with a 95-83 win over Hargrave Military Academy on Friday in Boone. Friday marked the first ever prep national championship game. Laurinburg finished ranked first in the prep polls in 2002-03.

The 2005 National Championship Laurinburg Institute Golden Tiger Team, photograph by Michael Gilliland (courtesy of Chris Everett and *Laurinburg Exchange*).

After a year with Memphis and taking his team to the NCAA Final Four, Williams opted to place his name in the ring for the NBA draft. He took advantage of a rule that players who were unrepresented by agents could return to school if they were not selected. The Indiana Pacers drafted him. Larry Bird, the president of the Pacers basketball operations, explained: "We were just hoping our guy would get to us, and we got very fortunate tonight.... (Williams) has a lot of talent. We feel he'll be able to play the 4 (power forward position) in time."[18]

Calipari characterized his championship freshmen team with this praise: "They think they're supposed to win.... But the things that make them so good are that every one of them are so unselfish and they're all so competitive. When you're insecure about yourself, other people's success can affect you. But these guys are all secure in themselves and they'll sacrifice whatever it takes to win."[19]

After winning two national championships with Laurinburg Institute, Chris Chaney won National Coach of the Year awards for 2003, 2005 and 2006. He took a job at the Patterson School in Lenoir, North Carolina, and later, he coached for six years at Scotland Campus Sports in Scotland, Pennsylvania, from 2015 to 2021. As of 2024 Chaney is now coaching at The Academy of Central Florida in Orlando, Florida. He continues to coach winning USA Select teams in international tournaments. There is no doubt that his championship years at the Laurinburg Institute spotlighted both his career as a coach and the school as well. Forty of the 60 Laurinburg Institute basketball players to be drafted by Division I teams were coached by Chris Chaney.

26

Charter School
and NCAA Woes

North Carolina began its charter school experiment in 1997. The schools were limited to 100 statewide. Hoping to right the Laurinburg Institute ship, Bishop McDuffie applied for charter status, which was granted in 1998. The Institute was one of four black charter schools in the state. With that status, the Institute received funding from the state and federal governments for North Carolina students. Expectations included financial accountability, gradual enrollment growth, adequate testing results and good graduation rates. The Institute made progress from a 1997 enrollment of 100 to 152 students in 2002. Eight teachers were employed from 2000 to 2006.[1] Unfortunately, in 2006, Laurinburg Institute fell to the lowest performance rate of 15.3 on end-of-grade test scores among all charter schools in the state. It ranked fifth lowest in graduation rates among charter four-year cohort high schools.

Frances McDuffie explained that the local charter students, some of whom had been expelled from the public school, were more difficult to control because they went home at night and did not follow the strict study habits required of the boarding students. Parents, who sent their children to the Institute as boarding students, had more desire to encourage good behavior and good study habits than did the parents of local day students. The state insisted that the students' age be matched to their grade even though they did not have the academic ability to function at that grade level. As a result, many kids graduated from the public high school with a certificate of completion rather than with an academic diploma. Bishop was concerned with this situation, but confirmed that behavior issues among the charter students posed a problem for the school as they had done also for the public schools. Some students "couldn't stop bad behavior, didn't even know they had it." One kid "wanted to take his clothes off if he got excited."[2] As a result of these problems, the school's charter was not renewed June 2006.[3] After which, school enrollment dropped precipitously from 152 to 50 students.

Reasons given for non-renewal were governance, finance and enrollment. However, as early as September 2004 the Office of Charter Schools Director Jack Moyer recommended the revocation of the Institute charter, due to:

> ... a broad range of findings, including an audit exception for the school's drawing state funding of $102,539.76 for 24 out-of-state students in fiscal year 2002–03. In addition, the Charter School Advisory Committee found irregularities in the school's administration of state accountability testing. "The Committee was not satisfied that, in light of the years of inadequate, if not evasive procedures, the School has the ability or the desire to rectify the situation."[4]

Bishop McDuffie refused to accept the Charter School Advisory Committee's charges. He hired attorney Ted Edwards to represent the Laurinburg Institute and took the case to court. The accountant Les Merritt had kept strict records which separated the financial accounts of the North Carolina students from those of out-of-state boarding students. Finding no wrongdoing, the judge ruled in favor of the Laurinburg Charter School and the charter was restored. However, trust in the North Carolina Office of Charter Schools had been broken, and the Laurinburg Charter School Board opted to submit its charter back to the NC State Board of Education.

Bishop McDuffie's troubles were not over yet. In addition, the NCAA reviewed the academics and curriculum of the Laurinburg Institute in 2006–2007 and 2007–2008. The NBA instituted new draft regulations in 2006, which allowed players at least 19 years old and one year removed from high school graduation to be drafted without college experience. So-called "basketball academies" in particular were reviewed for irregularities as well as the transcripts of potential players from those schools. Dramatic improvement in grades and taking sequential courses at the same time were considered red flags. After their review, the NCAA declared Laurinburg Institute, along with 60 other schools, "not cleared" in 2009. McDuffie has been unsuccessful in finding out from the NCAA why they terminated their relationship with his school or what he could do to reinstate it. Bishop McDuffie defended his school in the following statement:

> We here at Laurinburg have always said the proof is in the pudding. Concern started here over whether we were teaching school or not. I don't know of any kid who's left here who has flunked out of college. Almost all of our kids have stayed eligible, and the ones who were eligible to graduate have either graduated or left because of reasons that kids leave school

for anyway. They've either got a job like you or I, or have gone on to become multimillionaires. If we are going to take credit for failure, we also get to take credit for our success. They call us a "diploma mill," but how do the two go hand in hand? If we're a diploma mill, then how could our kids be finishing college?[5]

The implication of this statement is that the Institute prepared his players to succeed in college or, if not, then colleges themselves are complicit in bending academic rules in order to benefit from winning teams. Nonetheless, there can be no doubt that the Laurinburg Institute opened doors for many talented students who otherwise would have been left out in the cold. Not only did they gain entry into the closed system of academia and Division-I basketball, but many were drafted by professional teams both in the United States and around the world. For those who did not achieve careers as professional players, college offered them the opportunity to succeed in life off the court as well.

McDuffie recognized that the NCAA's "not cleared" decision "has cost us many things." Enrollment dropped from 104 in 2004 to 35 in 2009, including 7 due to graduate in 2010. According to tax revenue reports, income dropped from $146,734 in 2006 to $63,162 in 2008.[6] Chris Chaney resigned in order to join the coaching staff at Patterson School in Lenoir, North Carolina. After a decade of teaching at the Institute, Frances McDuffie decided to go to law school because she believed a law degree would help her administer the school once she became the fourth generation to run the Institute.

Frances graduated from the only black law school in the state, North Carolina Central University, in 2013. Instead of returning to administer the Institute, however, McDuffie accepted an assistant public defender position with Cumberland County in Fayetteville, North Carolina. Again she encountered disadvantaged people within the criminal justice system and, thanks to her experience as a teacher at the Institute, she was able to serve them well. In 2020 Governor Roy Cooper appointed her as a district court judge for Judicial District 12, which serves Cumberland County. Frances McDuffie continues the family tradition of service to others in her capacity as judge, where she brings a wider perspective to justice in our country through her dedication to lift others through education and compassionate understanding.

27

Struggling to
Keep the Ship Afloat

The effects of losing charter status, the "not cleared" decision of the NCAA, the loss of students and teachers and, the final blow, the destruction of the campus by Hurricane Florence in 2018 have virtually closed the school. The last boarding students graduated in 2014. The decision not to enroll boarding students for the 2014–2015 school year was a difficult one for Bishop McDuffie. He said, "I had every board member mad at me, parents mad at me, they said I was destroying the school. ... But it's kind of like when we said Christopher Columbus was going to fall off the end of the world. Change is hard. Change is not easy. It's cumbersome and it's hard. But you have to have it."[1] In spite of all these challenges, Bishop McDuffie poured all his energy into raising funds to keep the school afloat so that it could continue the McDuffie legacy of educating black students. He instigated a series of learning opportunities, beyond the usual curriculum, reviewed below.

As early as 2007, a local service group called MELO, Men Enhancing the Lives of Others, offered a semester-long course in brick masonry on the Laurinburg Institute campus. Echoing the original intentions of Booker T. Washington, the course was "designed to teach students marketable job skills while also modeling values such as accountability, discipline, professionalism and responsibility." The class instructor Lawrence Rush, a professional brick layer, expressed his pleasure at seeing how successful the class had been: "(I'm) trying to make these young men productive in society.... Rather than sitting in a classroom, I think we get more progress out of the students by being hands on with the material.... They've already learned a lot.... I'm totally impressed."[2]

In 2011 the Institute partnered with One on One Academic Services of Miami, Florida, in order to offer a summer outreach program for elementary children. Campbell's Soup, a local production company, sponsored the program hoping to encourage successful learning for potential employees. The program emphasized the need to prepare students for standardized testing by offering them a support network which included counseling, academic tutoring and family support. The objective was to create an atmosphere conducive to learning which reached beyond mere academic instruction to the creation of an environment inspiring confidence in one's ability to learn and succeed in test taking.[3]

The next project that McDuffie tackled was an attempt at forming a post–high school prep football team in 2012. Just as his father and grandfather before him, Bishop McDuffie recognized that sports offered opportunities for young black men to attend college and, eventually, to create a career for themselves. "Once the ink dries on their high school or GED diploma," often these men had "seen their time run out on them," according to McDuffie.[4] College was unattainable because of "grades, income or an unstable family." The Institute would offer college courses and SAT coaching while further developing football skills. Prospective students were invited to a combine on the Institute campus where they would try out under the watchful eye of Jim Webster, a former University of North Carolina assistant football coach.

By 2016, McDuffie was trying another tactic to keep the Institute afloat. This time he announced a 10 week program at the LNII Center for Technological Training and Certification Programs on the Institute campus. Recognizing the need for a new kind of economic development in Scotland County, "where traditional industry has been replaced by advanced manufacturing," McDuffie raised funds for computer equipment that would support this training. A cultural training course would be added to this program which would teach prospective job seekers how "to act and interact with one another" said McDuffie.[5]

In the fall of 2018, McDuffie started a STEM—science, technology, engineering, and mathematics—program at the Institute with Saturday classes, which he hoped to turn into an after school program and summer workshop program. A program director Denise Cozart said that the classes will teach knowledge that will be applicable to the public school's common core curriculum and, yet, "be a fun learning experience." Marcus X, an instructor with the HVAC program at Richmond Community College, helped to fund the STEM program and is partnering with the Institute to offer drone courses with FOCUS Unmanned Aerial System based in New Jersey.[6] Unfortunately the equipment that supported this training program and others was destroyed in the fall of 2018 when Hurricane Florence damaged the roof of the academic building. McDuffie immediately set up a GoFundMe website in order to repair the damages and get the school running again by the second semester. He explained, "Everyone has been put on hold. We have had a loss of some students because they had to enroll in other schools.... It has been a tough loss on us all.... Even though we had this tragedy, we are still excited to serve people."[7] Taking a new tack, McDuffie announced plans to start a new program focused on choir classes for local pupils.

Always looking for ways to educate and stimulate learning, the McDuffie family continues its mission to lift a race through encouragement and education. Cynthia McDuffie still teaches online a few students. Recently, with the Covid shutdown, Bishop McDuffie has searched for ways to educate kids virtually:

> We already know the devastating impact the [Covid-19] pandemic has had on all high school students, most particularly African-Americans. Excellent teaching in tough times is what we've always done very well at Laurinburg. We have master teachers who are tremendous at taking students from wherever they are and elevating them to where they need to be.... My appeal is to parents who know their children better than anyone else and know their students are struggling.... Parents, you also know that finding better academic options and opportunities for a better life for your children is not the child's responsibility or the school's responsibility ... it's yours. I hope you will allow the Laurinburg Institute to help. It's private school at a public school cost.[8]

Recognition and Gratitude

Frank H. McDuffie, Sr., and Sammie Sellers McDuffie received the highest honor bestowed by the governor of North Carolina in 1996, The Order of the Long Leaf Pine.[9] The North Carolina General Assembly passed a resolution honoring the contributions of Frank and Sammie McDuffie in 2005, and the Congress of the United States officially recognized the Laurinburg Institute in 2009, the resolutions of which are reproduced in the following appendix.

The State of North Carolina, represented by the state Office of Archives and History, installed a permanent historic marker close to the Laurinburg Institute grounds on North Main Street in Laurinburg, North Carolina, on August 25, 2014.

In 2020, Laurinburg Mayor Jim Willis proposed naming the area once owned by the McDuffie family between Railroad, Gill, Main and Roper streets, where the courthouse sits, McDuffie Square. The Laurinburg City Council unanimously concurred.[10] Over a hundred years have passed since Laurinburg honored the first white educator, W.G.

Historic Marker (2014), recognizing the Laurinburg Institute was installed by the North Carolina Office of Archives and History, close to the school on North Main Street (courtesy of Chris Everett and *Laurinburg Exchange*).

Quakenbush, with a granite memorial on courthouse grounds. Willis stated that the square will be an appropriate place to memorialize the Laurinburg Institute and the four generations of McDuffies who have dedicated their lives to the education of black youths locally, nationally and internationally. It has been a privilege to preserve the memories of that institution, its teachers and students, and, especially, the McDuffie family.

Appendix

The North Carolina General Assembly recognized the outstanding contributions of Frank and Sammie McDuffie in a 2005 resolution.[1] The Congress of the United States also expressed their gratitude to the Laurinburg Normal and Industrial Institute in the Congressional Record of 2009.[2] The texts of these well-deserved honors, from the highest branches of our government, will illustrate what has been discussed at length in this book.

GENERAL ASSEMBLY OF NORTH CAROLINA
SESSION 2005
RATIFIED BILL

RESOLUTION 2005–43
SENATE JOINT RESOLUTION 1178

A JOINT RESOLUTION HONORING THE LIFE AND MEMORY OF FRANK HOWE MCDUFFIE, SR., AND SAMMIE SELLERS MCDUFFIE, NORTH CAROLINA EDUCATORS, HUMANITARIANS, COACHES, CIVIL RIGHTS LEADERS, AND RECOGNIZING THE ESTABLISHMENT AND WORK OF THE LAURINBURG NORMAL AND INDUSTRIAL INSTITUTE, INC.

Whereas, on September 15, 1904, Emmanuel M. McDuffie and his wife, Tinny Etheridge McDuffie, came from Alabama to Laurinburg, North Carolina, responding to the call of Dr. Booker T. Washington of the Tuskegee Institute and William Edwards of the Snow Hill Institute to help to provide "suitable education and training in the common pursuits of life for the black people of the area"; and

Whereas, on September 15, 1906, Emmanuel M. McDuffie, J.H. Davis, and Robert Leach incorporated the Laurinburg Normal and

213

Industrial Institute at Laurinburg, North Carolina, for "the instruction of colored teachers and youth in the various common, academic, and collegiate branches, the best methods of teaching the same, and the best methods of theoretical and practical industry in their application to agriculture and the mechanics arts"; and

Whereas, upon the death of the Emmanuel M. McDuffie, Sr., his son Dr. Frank H. McDuffie, Sr., became the President of the Laurinburg Institute and his wife, Sammie Sellers McDuffie, its Principal, and together they built a new campus, integrated the faculty and student body, developed its foreign student program, and built and coached a worldwide recognized athletic and music program; and

Whereas, Frank and Sammie McDuffie were the recipients of the Order of the Long Leaf Pine and various other awards and accolades; and

Whereas, some of the alumni of the Laurinburg Institute alumni played pivotal roles in integrating athletic teams and the university systems of the South, including Charlie Scott who played basketball at the University of North Carolina at Chapel Hill and John Russell who served as a referee; and

Whereas, the Laurinburg Institute provided total secondary educational facilities to black boys and girls in Scotland County for more than 50 years; and

Whereas, the Laurinburg Institute provides its students with special training in numerous technical fields as well as providing and nurturing thousands to "Work hard, stand up, be somebody, be the best"; and

Whereas, Frank and Sammie McDuffie and the Laurinburg Institute have provided invaluable services to the people of the area, as well as educational services to black people from the State, the region, and foreign countries; and

Whereas, the Laurinburg Institute could not have survived and developed without the vision, dedication, and devotion of Frank and Sammie McDuffie; Now, therefore,

Be it resolved by the Senate, the House of Representatives concurring:

> SECTION 1. The General Assembly honors the memory of Dr. Frank H. McDuffie, Sr., and Sammie Sellers McDuffie for the service they rendered and recognizes and expresses its profound appreciation for their contributions to Eastern North Carolina and the State of North Carolina.

> SECTION 2. The Secretary of State shall transmit a certified copy of this resolution to the family of Dr. Frank H. McDuffie and Sammie Sellers McDuffie.

SECTION 3. This resolution is effective upon ratification.
In the General Assembly read three times and ratified this the 28 day of July, 2005.

Marc Basnight
President Pro Tempore of the Senate

Richard T. Morgan
Speaker Pro Tempore of the House of Representatives

October 21, 2009 CONGRESSIONAL RECORD—
HOUSE H11536-H11538

RECOGNIZING LAURINBURG NORMAL INDUSTRIAL INSTITUTE

Mrs. DAVIS of California. Mr. Speaker, I move to suspend the rules and agree to the resolution (H. Res. 660) recognizing the distinguished history of the Laurinburg Normal Industrial Institute, as amended.

The Clerk read the title of the resolution.

The text of the resolution is as follows:

H. RES. 660

Whereas the Laurinburg Normal Industrial Institute (referred to as the "Laurinburg Institute") was founded on September 15, 1904, in Laurinburg, North Carolina, by Emmanuel McDuffie and his wife Tinny Etheridge McDuffie at the request of Booker T. Washington of the Tuskegee Institute and William Edwards of the Snow Hill Institute;

Whereas the Laurinburg Institute is the oldest of only four historically African-American boarding schools still remaining in the United States;

Whereas the Laurinburg Institute was founded to help provide suitable education and training in the common pursuits of life for African-Americans in the area of Laurinburg, North Carolina;

Whereas, on September 15, 1906, Emmanuel McDuffie, J.H. Davis, and Robert Leach incorporated the Laurinburg Institute at Laurinburg, North Carolina, for the instruction of African-American teachers and youth in various academic branches of study and in the best methods of theoretical and practical industry applicable to agriculture and the mechanical arts;

Whereas in 1956, the Laurinburg Institute began to build a new campus, integrated its faculty and student body, expanded its foreign student program, which consisted of students from Russia, Africa,

South America, Brazil, Portugal, the Caribbean, and other countries, and further solidified its nationally and internationally recognized athletic and music programs;

Whereas since 1904, the Laurinburg Institute has graduated students of color, and since 1954 many graduates have finished college or other post-secondary training;

Whereas the Laurinburg Institute's distinguished alumni include Sir John Swann, the former Premiere of Bermuda and one of the first blacks to be a head of state in the Western Hemisphere, Joy Johnson, one of the first African-Americans elected to the North Carolina General Assembly after the Reconstruction era, John Birks "Dizzy" Gillespie, an internationally renowned jazz trumpeter, and Charles "Charlie" Scott, the first African-American scholarship athlete at the University of North Carolina at Chapel Hill, who later became a National Basketball Association (NBA) All-Star where he played for such teams as the Boston Celtics, Denver Nuggets, Los Angeles Lakers, and Phoenix Suns, winning an NBA championship with the Boston Celtics and a gold medal in the 1968 Summer Olympics;

Whereas in 2005, the North Carolina General Assembly passed Senate Joint Resolution 1178 which honored the lives of Frank and Sammie McDuffie, who were the second generation of McDuffie's to serve as administrators of the Institute, and the work of the Laurinburg Institute in producing educators, humanitarians, athletes, and civil rights and leaders;

Whereas in 2009, the Laurinburg Institute's President and Chief Executive Officer is Frank "Bishop" McDuffie, Jr., and his daughter, Frances McDuffie, serves as the Institute's Vice President and President; and

Whereas Frank "Bishop" McDuffie and Frances McDuffie are the third generation of McDuffie administrators of the Laurinburg Institute: Now, therefore, be it

Resolved, That the House of Representatives—

1. recognizes the distinguished history of the Laurinburg Normal Industrial Institute;
2. acknowledges the Laurinburg Institute's remarkable contribution to the education of African-Americans and other people in the State of North Carolina and the Nation; and
3. commends the enterprise and dedication of the McDuffie family in creating and sustaining the Laurinburg Institute.

The Speaker pro tempore. Pursuant to the rule, the gentlewoman from California (Mrs. DAVIS) and the gentleman from Tennessee (Mr. ROE) each will control 20 minutes.

The Chair recognizes the gentlewoman from California.

GENERAL LEAVE

Mrs. DAVIS of California. Mr. Speaker, I request 5 legislative days during which Members may revise and extend and insert extraneous material on House Resolution 660 into the record.

The SPEAKER pro tempore. Is there objection to the request of the gentle-woman from California?

There was no objection.

Mrs. DAVIS of California. Mr. Speaker, I yield myself such time as I may consume.

Mr. Speaker, I rise in support of House Resolution 660, which recognizes the historical significance of the Laurinburg Institute, one of the Nation's oldest African American boarding high schools in the United States.

In the early 1900s, there were few educational opportunities for black students. The Laurinburg Institute, along with other African American boarding schools, answered the needs of many African Americans desiring an education.

The Laurinburg Institute was founded on September 15, 1904, in Laurinburg, North Carolina, by Emmanuel McDuffie and his wife, Tinny Etheridge McDuffie, at the urging of Booker T. Washington and William Edwards. Since then, the McDuffie family has remained committed to the school's mission, devoting their lives to its service for more than three generations.

The school has developed and created exceptional music and athletic programs. Over the years, Laurinburg Institute has graduated renowned musicians and professional athletes, most notably NBA All-Star Charles Scott. Other prominent alumni include musician Dizzy Gillespie and professional basketball player Sam Jones.

Today, this school offers a unique atmosphere for all students to succeed. The McDuffie family, through generations of hard work and dedication, has implemented a curriculum for their students to succeed. The institute has an enrollment capacity of 135 students and has a student body comprised of young men and women from across the country and the globe.

Once again, I support this resolution and thank Congressman KISSELL for bringing this bill forward. I urge my colleagues to support this bill.

Mr. Speaker, I reserve the balance of my time.

Mr. ROE of Tennessee. Mr. Speaker, I yield myself as much time as I may consume.

Mr. Speaker, I rise today in support of House Resolution 660, recognizing the distinguished history of the Laurinburg Normal Industrial Institute founded in 1904 by Emmanuel McDuffie and his wife, Tinny. Laurinburg Institute is the oldest of only four historically African American boarding schools still in existence in the United States. It was founded to help provide suitable education and training in the common pursuits of life for African Americans in the Laurinburg, North Carolina, area.

At the turn of the century, Laurinburg Institute instructed African American teachers and youth in various academic branches of study and in the best methods of theoretical and practical industrial applications for agriculture and the mechanical arts. In 1956, the Laurinburg Institute built a new campus, integrated its faculty and student body, and expanded its foreign student program, which consisted of students from Russia, Africa, South America, and the Caribbean. It also further solidified its nationally and internationally recognized athletic and music programs. The Laurinburg Institute has graduated over 50,000 students.

Today, we recognize the distinguished history of the Laurinburg Institute and acknowledge its remarkable contribution to the education of African Americans. I commend the dedication of the McDuffie family in creating and sustaining the legacy of Emmanuel and Tinny McDuffie. Congratulations to its third-generation administrators, president and CEO, Frank McDuffie, and his daughter, Frances McDuffie, who serves as vice president and chief operating officer, as well as the faculty, staffs and students of Laurinburg Institute.

Mr. Speaker, I reserve the balance of my time.

Mrs. DAVIS of California. Mr. Speaker, I am pleased to recognize for 10 minutes the gentleman from North Carolina, the sponsor of this legislation, Mr. KISSELL.

Mr. KISSELL. I would like to thank my colleague from California for yielding time to me.

Mr. Speaker, as we look at the Laurinburg Institute, or its official name, Laurinburg Normal Industrial Institute, there is a story to be told here that goes beyond some of the information that we have already received.

If you can imagine back prior to September 15, 1904, when the Laurinburg Institute was officially founded, if you could imagine the conversations that took place when Booker T. Washington at Tuskegee Institute came to the McDuffies, Emmanuel and Tinny Etheridge, and said, I have got an opportunity for you. They weren't talking about how they could become millionaires or how they could invest moneys.

No, it was something much more important than that. They were talking about education. They were talking about educating African American youth at a time before Brown v. Board of Education, a time when we did not talk about equality of education. In some cases we didn't talk about education of African American youth at all.

This was a time in the early 1900s only 40 years after the Civil War. We know our Nation was going through some tough times, and these people were talking about education.

There must be something that runs strong in the McDuffie family in terms of their genetics, because not only is this one of only four such schools that have survived till today; it is still run by the same family that started it. Four generations later of McDuffies, they are still running the same school. They are still concerned about education.

We know that the opportunity of education is to influence young people for generation upon generation because that influence never stops. Teachers know, and one of the great rewards of teaching is that they know that who they affect may not be the person who is in their classroom; it may be someone two or three generations down that is affected directly by someone that they had taught and inspired.

This is what the McDuffie family has offered to us, Mr. Speaker: 50,000 graduates. Think of all of the families and all of the people that were affected by these 50,000 that would not have been if Booker T. Washington had not convinced the McDuffies that the best investment they could make is in education.

Now, we have heard a couple of the graduates mentioned. I would like to add a couple more names to that list. Sir John Swan was a premier of Bermuda, one of the first people of color that was a head of state in the Western Hemisphere. We mentioned Charlie Scott, who was the first African American ever to be awarded an athletic scholarship to the University of North Carolina. Now, as a Wake Forest graduate, I also have to mention another basketball player, Charlie Davis, who was the first African American Player of the Year in ACC history in basketball in 1971.

Once again, we are talking about thousands of people that came through this institute, thousands of people that were affected. Once again, the great joy of education is that its influence never ends.

I congratulate the McDuffie family. I congratulate the faculty and alumni and students of this great institution because they have survived, and they have made a difference in the lives of not only the people of Scotland County, which I am fortunate enough to represent as part of North Carolina's Eighth District, but they have also influenced the State of North Carolina and this great Nation of ours.

Mr. ROE of Tennessee. Mr. Speaker, just to dovetail, I do remember, I believe Charlie Scott played in the old ABA for the Virginia Squires. I have seen him play many times, a great athlete and a great human being.

As my colleague Mr. KISSELL from North Carolina clearly stated, an education doesn't just affect one person. It affects a family, it affects a community, it affects a nation. So this family that has had this commitment to education for over a century is to be commended.

I urge my colleagues to support this resolution.

Mr. Speaker, I yield back the balance of my time.

Mrs. DAVIS of California. Mr. Speaker, I am honored. I certainly want to thank Mr. KISSELL for really giving us a more expanded view of the Laurinburg Institute. I appreciate his passion and interest in it.

I want to encourage my colleagues to support this resolution, House Resolution 660, recognizing the historical importance of the Laurinburg Institute.

Mr. Speaker, I yield back the balance of my time.

The SPEAKER pro tempore. The question is on the motion offered by the gentlewoman from California (Mrs. DAVIS) that the House suspend the rules and agree to the resolution, H. Res. 660, as amended.

The question was taken.

The SPEAKER pro tempore. In the opinion of the Chair, two-thirds being in the affirmative, the ayes have it.

Mrs. DAVIS of California. Mr. Speaker, on that I demand the yeas and nays.

The yeas and nays were ordered.

The SPEAKER pro tempore. Pursuant to clause 8 of rule XX and the Chair's prior announcement, further proceedings on this motion will be postponed.

Chapter Notes

Chapter 1

1. Margaret Calhoun and John Hudson, eds., *Heritage of Scotland County North Carolina—2003* (Laurinburg, N.C.: Scotland County Heritage Book Committee and Scotland County Historical Association, Inc., 2004), 58.

2. "Whipping Record 1823–1844," Special Collections, Laurinburg, N.C.: Scotland County Memorial Library.

3. John McCormick, "Impressions and Recollections of Laurinburg in Earlier Days," *Laurinburg Exchange*, 15 December 1932, 1.

4. Maxcy L. John, "Historical Sketch of Laurinburg," *Laurinburg Exchange*, 15 December 1932, 5.

5. McCormick, 1.

6. McCormick, 3.

7. Nettie McCormick Henley, *The Home Place* (New York: Vantage, 1955), 7.

8. John, 5 and 8.

9. Henley, 5.

10. Walter Hurley, "The Hanging of Willis Lytch, a Negro Slave, During the Civil War, in Laurinburg (Scotland County), North Carolina," unpublished paper in the collection of records for Marilyn Wright's *Sketch Book of Scotland County*, Laurinburg, N.C.: Scotland County Memorial Library, Special Collections, 1964, 2.

11. Hurley, 2.

12. John G. Barrett, *Sherman's March Through the Carolinas* (Chapel Hill: University of North Carolina Press, 1956), 137.

Chapter 2

1. Henley, 8.

2. Gael Graham, "'The Lexington of White Supremacy': School and Local Politics in Late- Nineteenth-Century Laurinburg, North Carolina," *The North Carolina Historical Review* 89, no. 1 (January 2012): 27–31; Maxcy L. John, "Know Your History: Answers," *Laurinburg Exchange*, 8 March 1934, 6.

3. Roger Martin McGirt, "The Development of Public Education in Scotland County" (master's thesis, University of North Carolina at Chapel Hill, 1931), 46.

4. McGirt, 48–49.

5. Joyce M. Gibson, *Scotland County Emerging 1750–1900* (Laurel Hill, N.C.: J.M. Gibson, 1995), 166–171.

6. Graham, 27–58.

Chapter 3

1. Graham, 40; Gibson, 205.

2. John, 5.

3. Maxcy L. John, "Know Your History: More about the Red Shirts," *Laurinburg Exchange*, 15 March 1934, 6.

4. Graham, 43; Gibson, 215; John, "Historical Sketch of Laurinburg," 8.

5. Gibson, 206 and 191–192.

6. Adrienne LaFrance and Vann Newkirk, "The Lost History of an American Coup D'État," *The Atlantic*, 12 April 2017.

7. John, 15 March 1934, 6.

8. Graham, 44.

9. Henley, 16–17.

10. Graham, 44; Gibson, 213; John,

"Know Your History: More about the Red Shirts," 6.

11. Dockery v Bellamy contested election record, Gibson, 214–215.

12. Gibson, 215.

13. Graham, 49.

14. Graham, 48.

15. LaFrance and Newkirk; Chris Everett, dir., *Wilmington on Fire* (Speller Street Films, Double7 Images, and Blackhouse Publishing, 2015): DVD.

16. Gibson, 207; Graham, 52.

17. Walter P. Evans, "What the Best Negroes Will Do," *News and Observer*, 26 July 1899, 4.

18. Graham, 55.

Chapter 4

1. A.B. Caldwell, ed., *History of the American Negro: North Carolina Edition IV* (Atlanta: A.B. Caldwell Publishing Company, 1921), 803.

2. Calhoun, 243; Mary Modlin, "Walter Parsley Evans, 1863–1937," https://www.usgaarchives.net, retrieved 15 July 2021.

3. Gibson, 189; Calhoun, 243.

4. "Evan's White Front Department Store," *Laurinburg Exchange*, 15 May 1924.

5. Walter P. Evans, "Colored People of Laurinburg Make Progress," *Laurinburg Exchange*, 15 December 1932, 6.

6. Walter P. Evans, "What the Best Negroes Will Do," *News and Observer*, 26 July 1899, 4.

7. Calhoun, 243.

8. Marylin Wright, ed., *A Sense of Place, Part II* (Laurinburg N.C.: Walsworth Publishing Company, 1996), 188.

9. Caldwell, 805.

10. J.J. Melton, "A Story of Success: W.P. Evans Built a Business in the Downtown Area Starting in 1884," *Laurinburg Exchange*, 19 February 2021, 1; Modlin.

11. Rena McNeil and Scotland County NAACP Youth Council, *A Diamond Eventually Shines: Scotland County's African-American Pioneers* (Kearney, N.C.: Morris Publishing, 1999), 37.

12. Graham, 53–55.

13. McGirt, 61.

14. Maxcy L. John, correspondence to Nathan C. Newbold, 19 August 1927, Raleigh: North Carolina Archives, Department of Public Instruction, Division of Negro Education, Box 4.

15. All accounts consulted list Walter Evans as the one who wrote Booker T. Washington, with one exception. William Maize reported that Milton McKennon wrote the letter in his master's thesis "An Interpretative History of Laurinburg Normal and Industrial Institute, Laurinburg, North Carolina" (Rutgers University, June 1948), 21.

Chapter 5

1. Booker T. Washington, *Up from Slavery: An Autobiography* (Reprint: Digireads.com Publishing, 2016), originally published 1900.

2. Helen W. Ludlow, *Armstong's Ideas on Education for Life* (Hampton, VA: Hampton Institute Press, Reprint, 1945), 12–13.

3. Francis Greenwood Peabody, *Education for Life: The Story of Hampton Institute* (Garden City, N.Y.: Doubleday, Page, 1926), 99–100.

4. Washington, 63.

5. Washington, 69.

6. Washington, 98.

7. Washington, 104–105.

8. Washington, 110.

9. Washington, 87–88.

10. Thomas W. Hanchett, "The Rosenwald Schools and Black Education in North Carolina," *The North Carolina Historical Review* 65, no. 4 (October 1988): 387–444.

11. Bishop McDuffie, interview with Elizabeth Jones, Laurinburg, N.C., 20 May 2021.

Chapter 6

1. William Edwards, *Twenty-Five Years in the Black Belt* (Columbia, S.C.: Reprint, 2021), 39–41.

2. Edwards, 39.

3. Edwards, 68–70.

4. Donald P. Stone, *Fallen Prince: William James Edwards, Black Education and the Quest for Afro-American Nationality* (Snow Hill, AL: Snow Hill Press, 1989), 157.

5. "The Laurinburg Normal and Industrial Institute," *Laurinburg Exchange*, 15 December 1932, 6.

6. Wright, 119.

Chapter 7

1. Edwards, 40.
2. Bishop McDuffie, interview, 20 May 2021.
3. Bishop McDuffie, interview, 20 May 2021.
4. Frank McDuffie in Wright, 119–120.
5. Frances McDuffie, interview with Elizabeth Jones, Laurinburg, N.C., 26 February 2023.
6. Johnny Baxter Hodge, Jr., "A Biography of Phillmore Mallard Hall with Particular Emphasis on His Contribution to the Development of Black School Bands in North Carolina" (PhD diss., The American University, 1977), 74–76.
7. Marylin Wright, ed., *A Sense of Place* (Laurinburg, N.C.: St. Andrews Press, 1991), 198.
8. Hodge, 77.
9. Hodge, 78.
10. Hodge, 78.
11. Monroe N. Work, *Industrial Work of Tuskegee Graduates and Former Students During the Year 1910* (Tuskegee: Tuskegee Institute Press, 1911), 55.
12. Maize, 38.
13. Maize, 65.
14. Maize, 65.
15. Washington, 28–29.
16. Maize, 57.
17. Maize, 56.
18. Work, 55.
19. Maize, 61.
20. Ullin W. Leavell, *Philanthropy in Negro Education* (Nashville: George Peabody College for Teachers, 1930), 73.
21. Maize, 38.
22. "Many Negroes Hear Their Famous Leader," *Laurinburg Exchange*, 19 November 1910, 1.
23. "Negros Pay Respect," *Laurinburg Exchange*, 18 November 1915.
24. Maize, 59.
25. Maize, 38–39.
26. Hodge, 85.
27. Maize, 31.
28. Calhoun, 68–72.

29. Emmanuel McDuffie, *The Ninth Annual Report of the Principal and Treasurer of the Laurinburg Normal and Industrial Institute* (Laurinburg, N.C.: Laurinburg Institute Print, 7 May 1914), 8. Laurinburg Normal and Industrial Institute (Laurinburg, N.C.), n.d. [Announcements, bulletins, programs, etc.]. Chapel Hill: University of North Carolina, Wilson Library, North Carolina Special Collections.
30. Emmanuel McDuffie, 5.
31. Emmanuel McDuffie, 5.
32. Maize, 69.
33. Emmanuel McDuffie, 7.
34. Maize, 108.
35. "Successful Institutions of the Colored People," *Laurinburg Exchange*, 15 May 1924, 3.
36. "Evan's White Front Department Store," *Laurinburg Exchange*, 15 May 1924, 3.
37. Dot Coble, "County's first African-American physician, a legend in his own right," *Laurinburg Exchange*, 23 February 2007, B1.
38. Calhoun, 290.
39. Wright, *A Sense of Place, Part II*, 201.
40. Coble, B1.
41. "Doing a Great Work," *Laurinburg Exchange*, 14 May 1914, 2.
42. Caldwell, 182.
43. "Doing a Great Work," 2.
44. "Doing a Great Work," 2.
45. Edwards, 41.
46. Hodge, 127.
47. Edwards, 41.
48. Edwards, 40.
49. Stone, 242.
50. Stone, 239–242.
51. Wright, *A Sense of Place, Part II*, 123–124.
52. "The Colored Civic League, Incorporated," *Laurinburg Exchange*, 15 December 1932, 6.
53. Wright, *A Sense of Place*, 165–166.
54. Wright, *A Sense of Place*, 166.
55. "Teachers' Institute," *Laurinburg Exchange*, 12 August 1915, 1.
56. Emmanuel McDuffie to Nathan C. Newbold, 15 October 1915, Raleigh: North Carolina Archives, Department of Public Instruction, Division of Negro Education, Box 4.

57. Nathan C. Newbold to Emmanuel McDuffie, 23 October 1915, Raleigh: North Carolina Archives, Department of Public Instruction Records, Division of Negro Education, Box 4.

58. Nathan C. Newbold, "Report of N.C. Newbold, State Agent Negro Rural Schools for North Carolina, For the Month of December, 1915," Raleigh: North Carolina Archives, Department of Public Instruction, Division of Negro Education.

Chapter 8

1. Nancy Green, "Among Our Graduates," *The Eastern Searchlight* 29, no. 10 (Laurinburg, N.C.: Laurinburg Institute, 1949), 2, Laurinburg, N.C.: Scotland County Memorial Library, Special Collections.

2. M.H. Harding to Nathan C. Newbold, Director of the State Division of Black Education, 23 January 1931, Raleigh: North Carolina Archives, Department of Public Education, Division of Negro Education, Box 4.

3. Harding, Box 4.

4. "Hard Hit," *Seward Daily Gateway*, 13 February 1931, 2.

5. I. Ellis Johnson to Partinari, 13 January 1945, https://www.artsandculture.google.com.

6. Edwards, 40.

7. Caldwell, 182.

8. "Emily Howland," https://www.wikipedia.com, retrieved 16 March 2023.

9. "Antique Real Photo Postcard—Emily Howland Girls Institute Laurinburg NC—RPPC," 5 November 1912, https://worthpoint.com, retrieved 6 March 2023.

10. "B.N. Duke has authorized a gift," *Robesonian*, 4 September 1925, 2.

11. Jessie Benson, "Outstanding Negro Achievements Guided by Laurinburg Institute," *Wellesley College News*, 27 September 1943, 3.

12. "Drive Aids New Item: After Year's Wait Negro School Gets Place on Drive List," *Vassar Miscellany News* XXV, no. 7, 16 October 1940, 1 and 3.

13. Hodge, 84.

14. *Application for Admission to the Laurinburg Normal & Industrial Institute*, 191–192, Laurinburg Normal and Industrial Institute (Laurinburg, N.C.), n.d. [Announcements, bulletins, programs, etc.]. Chapel Hill: University of North Carolina, Wilson Library, North Carolina Special Collections.

15. Maize, 77.

16. Maize, 76.

17. Hodge, 116.

Chapter 9

1. Louis Harlan, *Separate and Unequal: Public School Campaigns and Racism in the Southern Seaboard States, 1901–1915* (Chapel Hill: University of North Carolina Press, 1958), 186.

2. Diane Ravitch, "A Different Kind of Education for Black Children," *The Journal of Blacks in Higher Education* no. 30 (Winter 2000–2001): 99–100.

3. Hanchett, 392.

4. W.A. Robinson, "Report of School Situation for Negroes in Laurinburg," 8 July 1926, Raleigh: North Carolina State Archives, Department of Public Instruction Records, Division of Negro Education, Box 4.

5. Hanchett, 394.

6. Hanchett, 407.

7. G.E. Davis to Nathan C. Newbold, 16 February 1924, Raleigh: North Carolina Archives, Department of Public Instruction, Division of Negro Education, Box 4.

8. G.E. Davis to Nathan C. Newbold, 14 May 1924, Raleigh: North Carolina Archives, Department of Public Instruction, Division of Negro Education, Box 4.

9. McGirt, 66; Calhoun, 58–59.

10. "Successful...," 3.

11. John, correspondence to Nathan C. Newbold, 19 August 1927.

12. Nathan C. Newbold to Maxcy John, 24 August 1927, Raleigh: North Carolina Archives, Department of Public Instruction Records, Division of Negro Education), Box 4.

13. Nathan C. Newbold to Jackson Davis, 18 July 1927, Raleigh: North Carolina Archives, Department of Public Instruction Records, Division of Negro Education, Box 4.

14. Newbold to Jackson Davis, 18 July 1927.

15. Newbold to Jackson Davis, 18 July

1927; W.A. Robinson to Walter White, 26 August 1927, Raleigh: North Carolina Archives, Department of Public Instruction Records, Division of Negro Education, Box 4.

16. McGirt, 66.
17. McGirt, 67.
18. McGirt, 70.
19. McGirt, 84–85.
20. Walter P. Evans to Nathan C. Newbold, including copy of letter to Dr. Shaw, 12 August 1927, Raleigh: North Carolina Archives, Department of Public Instruction, Division of Negro Education, Box 4.
21. Maxcy L. John to Nathan C. Newbold, 19 August 1927, Raleigh: North Carolina Archives, Department of Public Instruction, Division of Negro Education, Box 4.
22. John, "Historical Sketch of Laurinburg," 8.
23. Rev. Larkin King to Newbold, 1 September 1927, Raleigh: North Carolina Archives, Department of Public Education, Division of Negro Education, Box 4.
24. Maxcy L. John to Nathan C. Newbold, 26 September 1927, Raleigh: North Carolina Archives, Department of Public Instruction, Division of Negro Education, Box 4.
25. Newbold to John, 24 August 1927.
26. W.A. Robinson, "Report of School Situation for Negroes in Laurinburg," 8 July 1926, Raleigh: North Carolina State Archives, Department of Public Instruction Records, Division of Negro Education, Box 4.
27. Calhoun, 72.
28. Newbold to John, 24 August 1927, Box 4.
29. Nathan C. Newbold, Correspondence to G.E. Davis, Supervisor of Rosenwald Buildings, 14 September 1927, Raleigh: North Carolina Archives, Department of Public Instruction Records, Division of Negro Education, Box 4.
30. Robinson, "Report...."
31. Maize, 154.
32. McNeil, 5.

Chapter 10

1. William S. Maize, "An Interpretative History of Laurinburg Normal and Industrial Institute, Laurinburg, North Carolina," master's thesis, Rutgers University, June 1948.
2. Maize, 71.
3. Maize, 22.
4. Calhoun, 328.
5. Dizzy Gillespie with Al Fraser, *To Be, or Not ... to Bop* (Minneapolis: University of Minnesota Press, 1979), 39.
6. McNeil, 16–20. Laurinburg NAACP youth interviewed significant members of the Black community, including Speller, for the information presented here and elsewhere.
7. Hodge, 118.
8. McNeil, 19.
9. Hodge, 115.
10. McNeil, 20.
11. Gillespie, 36.
12. Wright, *A Sense of Place*, 167.
13. Gillespie, 36–37.
14. Maize, 43–55.
15. Maize, 89.
16. Isabelle Smith and Ivory Smith, *Life Lines: A Collection of Inspiring Poetry and Prose* (Laurinburg, N.C.: I. and I. Smith, 1952), v.
17. Smith and Smith, vi.
18. Frances McDuffie Foster, interview with Elizabeth Jones, Durham, N.C., 26 March 2023.
19. Foster interview, 26 March 2023.
20. "Scotland Has No Farm or Home Agent But I. H. Smith Adequately Fills In," *The Carolinian*, 1 August 1959, 16.
21. Maize, 25.
22. Maize, 80.
23. Maize, 72.
24. Maize, 93.
25. Maize, 94.
26. Maize, 82.
27. Maize, 92.
28. Maize, 79.
29. Leroy McLeod, interview with Elizabeth Jones, Laurinburg, N.C., 1 March 2023.
30. Daniel H. Pollitt, "Interview with Daniel H. Pollitt," L-0064-4 *Southern Oral History Program Collection* (#4007), *Documenting the American South* (Chapel Hill: University of North Carolina, 15 February 1991), 4.
31. Maize, 22.
32. Isaac Logan, interview with Elizabeth Jones, Black Mountain, N.C., 16 March 2023.

33. Andre Mack, "Life and times of Henrietta Davis," *Laurinburg Exchange*, 17 May 2019.

34. Beth Lawrence, "Inspirational Scotland County educator dies at 101—Family reflects on a life well lived," *Laurinburg Exchange*, 2 January 2018.

35. Lawrence.

36. Lawrence.

37. Maize, 122–125.

Chapter 11

1. Johnny Baxter Hodge, Jr., "A Biography of Phillmore Mallard Hall with Particular Emphasis on His Contribution to the Development of Black School Bands in North Carolina" (Ph.D. diss., The American University, 1977), 70–160.

2. Hollie I. West, "Dizzy And the Dean," *Washington Post*, 5 February 1981.

3. West.

4. Hodge, 96.

5. Hodge, 81–82.

6. Hodge, 84.

7. Hodge, 86.

8. Hodge, 86.

9. Hodge, 88.

10. Hodge, 90.

11. Hodge, 93.

12. Hodge, 94.

13. Hodge, 89.

14. Hodge, 89.

15. Hodge, 90–91.

16. Maize, 111.

17. Hodge, 91.

18. Hodge, 91.

19. Hodge, 95.

20. Hodge, 127.

21. Hodge, 129.

22. Hodge, 95.

23. Hodge, 107.

24. Hodge, 95.

25. Hodge, 96–97.

26. Hodge, 97.

27. Hodge, 97.

28. West.

29. Hodge, 98.

30. Hodge, 115.

31. Hodge, 133.

32. Hodge, 125.

33. Hodge, 132.

34. Hodge, 145.

35. Hodge, 133–134.

36. Hodge, 149–150.

37. Hodge, 154.

38. Hodge, 151–154.

39. Hodge, 157.

40. Hodge, 142.

41. Richard Harrington, "A Day for Dizzy," *Washington Post*, 17 November 1983.

42. Everett Goldston, "A Giant Passed Our Way: Phillmore Millard Hall, 1905–1984," *The Carolina Times*, 26 January 1985, 10–11.

Chapter 12

1. Dizzy Gillespie with Al Fraser, *To Be, or Not … to Bop* (Minneapolis: University of Minnesota Press, 1979).

2. West.

3. R.B. Wright, "Conversations with John Birks 'Dizzy' Gillespie, Pioneer of Jazz," *The Black Perspective in Music* 4, no. 1 (Spring 1976): 85.

4. Gillespie, 34.

5. Gillespie, 35.

6. Gillespie, 35.

7. Gillespie, 38.

8. Gillespie, 38.

9. Gillespie, 38–39.

10. Hodge, 100.

11. West.

12. Gillespie, 36.

13. West.

14. Gillespie, 40.

15. West.

16. Gillespie, 39–41.

17. West.

18. Gillespie, 43–44.

19. Hodge, 123.

20. Gillespie, 347.

21. Gillespie, 304.

22. "'The Clown Prince' Dizzy Gillespie: Music starts in the rear," *Winston-Salem Chronicle*, 4 October 1984, 19.

23. Adam Fairclough, *A Class of Their Own: Black Teachers in the Segregated South* (Cambridge: The Belknap Press of Harvard University Press, 2007), 212.

Chapter 13

1. Sandra Davidson and Wayne Martin, "50 For 50: Eddie Ray," *Come Hear*

North Carolina (North Carolina Arts Council, 23 July 2019), http://www.ncarts.org.

2. Davidson and Martin.

3. Andre Mack, "Artist Captures Jazz Legend Grachan Moncur III," *Anson Record*, 7 September 2021.

4. "Moncur, Grachen III," *Wikipedia,* retrieved 11 October 2021, http://www.wikipedia.com.

5. Calhoun, 328.

6. Foster interview, 26 March 2023.

7. Bishop McDuffie, interview with Elizabeth Jones, Laurinburg, N.C., 1 March 2023.

8. "Hall of Famer Sam Jones, winner of 10 NBA titles, dies at 88—Attended high school at Laurinburg Institute," *Laurinburg Exchange*, 31 December 2021.

9. "Hall of Famer Sam Jones."

10. "Hall of Famer Sam Jones."

11. Calhoun, 300–301.

12. Drew Lindsay, "From Out of a Swamp: A School's Tale of Faith," *Education Week* 13, no. 35 (25 May 1994), http://www.edweek.org.

13. Levelle Moton, "Tribute to Sam Jones," post on Laurinburg Institute Facebook page, 31 December 2021.

14. Andy Sturgill, "Wes Covington," *Biographies*, Society for American Baseball Research, http://www.sabr.org, retrieved 2 February 2023.

15. Matt Smith, "From the Cheap Seats," *Laurinburg Exchange*, 27 July 2011.

16. Smith.

17. J.J. Melton, "Our Major Leaguer Wes Covington went from football to baseball career," *Laurinburg Exchange*, 16 April 2021.

18. "Sir John Swan," Wikipedia, http://www.wikipedia.com, retrieved 20 October 2021.

19. Joy Johnson, *From Poverty to Power: An Autobiography of Dr. Joy Joseph Johnson, The Practical Preacher Politician* (Fairmont, N.C.: J.J. Johnson, 1976).

20. Johnson, 5.

21. Johnson, 7.

22. Milton C. Jordan, "Black Legislators: From Political Novelty to Political Force," *North Carolina Insight* (December 1989), 41.

23. Johnson, 21–25.

24. Frederick N. Rasmussen, "George W. Collins, pioneering broadcaster," *Baltimore Sun*, 4 August 2014.

25. Rasmussen.

Chapter 14

1. Barry Jacobs, *Across the Line: Profiles in Basketball Courage; Tales of the First Black Players in the ACC and SEC* (Guilford, CT: Lyons Press, 2007), 105.

2. Wright, *A Sense of Place*, 219.

3. McNeil, 55.

4. Cheris Hodges, "A Strong Legacy: I. Ellis Johnson left a positive mark on Scotland County's educational system," *Laurinburg Exchange*, 17 December 2021.

5. Calhoun, 295.

6. Wright, *A Sense of Place*, 212.

7. Wright, *A Sense of Place, Part II*, 131.

8. Mary Katherine Murphy, "Educators' legacy honored," *Laurinburg Exchange*, 28 February 2013.

Chapter 15

1. "Bluford Library Archives: Rediscovering a Lost Queen of N.C. A&T," *A & T Alumni Times*, 22 November 2017, www.relations.ncat.org.

2. Andre Mack, "The Reunion of Laurinburg Institute," *Laurinburg Exchange*, 12 March 2019.

3. Foster interview, 26 March 2023.

4. Abbi Overfelt, "Alumni celebrate installation of Institute's historical marker—Headmaster looks to the future," *Laurinburg Exchange*, 16 May 2014.

5. Mary Katherine Murphy, "Pastor adds voice to church-state debate," *Laurinburg Exchange*, 8 February 2013.

6. Leon Rice, "The Laurinburg Institute," *Divergents Magazine*, https://www.divergents_magazine.org, retrieved 10 September 2021.

7. Foster interview, 26 March 2023.

8. Mary Katherine Murphy, "Educators' legacy honored," *Laurinburg Exchange*, 28 February 2013.

Chapter 16

1. Overfelt, "Alumni."
2. Rice.
3. Rice.
4. Isaac Logan, interview with Elizabeth Jones, Black Mountain, N.C., 16 March 2023.
5. Gerald Hassell, telephone interview with Elizabeth Jones, 30 April 2023.
6. Gerald Hassell, *The Impact of Father Absence on African American Boys* (Orlando: Gerald Hassell, 2023).
7. J. Gentile Everett, *The Making of a Life* (Fairmont, N.C.: Xlibris Corporation, 2011), 19.
8. Hodges, 92–93.
9. Everett, 29.
10. Everett, 31.
11. Everett, 29.
12. Overfelt, "Alumni."
13. Everett, 31.
14. Logan interview, 16 March 2023.
15. Hodge, 92.
16. John Lentz, "Students learn as teachers," *Laurinburg Exchange*, 14 May 2009.
17. "Doing a Great Work," 2.
18. Overfelt, "Alumni."
19. Rice.
20. Everett, 19–20.

Chapter 17

1. Bishop McDuffie interview, 1 March 2023.
2. Scott Ellsworth, *The Secret Game* (New York: Back Bay Books, 2016).
3. Lindsay.
4. Bill Koch, "Friars legend Jimmy Walker to be inducted into college basketball Hall of Fame," *The Providence Journal*, 30 June 2022.
5. Ross Kelly, "Top 40 High Schools that Have Produced the Most NBA Players," 20 August 2021, https://www.stadiumtalk.com, 70–71.

Chapter 18

1. Jarrod Jonsrud, "Harlem's Unsung Hero: The Life and Legacy of Holcombe Rucker," *Journal of Sport History* 38, no. 1 (Spring 2011): 26–27.
2. Barry Beckham, *Double Dunk: The Story of Earl "The Goat" Manigault* (Silver Spring: Beckham Publications Group, 1993), 55.
3. Beckham, 56.
4. Vincent Mallozzi, "King of Kings," *SLAM Magazine*, 12 June 2010, https://www.slamonline.com.
5. Mallozzi.
6. Beckham, 102.
7. Beckham, 65–67.
8. Beckham, 71.
9. Beckham, 82–83.
10. Beckham, 137.
11. Beckham, 67.
12. Beckham, 83 and 77.
13. Art Chansky, *Game Changers: Dean Smith, Charlie Scott, and the Era that Transformed a Southern College Town* (Chapel Hill: University of North Carolina Press, 2016), 44.
14. Beckham, 82 and 105.
15. Beckham, 83.
16. Beckham, 105–108.
17. "Earl 'The Goat' Manigault on CNN," *The Sporting Life*, 8 October 2012, available on YouTube.
18. Cal Griffin, "Earl Manigault: The Greatest of All Time," https://www.allthingshoops.com, retrieved 10 October 2021.

Chapter 19

1. Chansky, 9–11.
2. Chansky, 41–42.
3. Larry Keech, "Laurinburg's McDuffie Put Scott on Road to Success," *Greensboro Daily News*, 11 March 1969, B3.
4. Chansky, 43.
5. Charlie Scott with Mark Wright, "Going Through Hell to Get into the Hall of Fame," 21 October 2019, https://www.ozy.com.
6. Chansky, 44 and 71.
7. Scott.
8. Pollitt.
9. Pollitt.
10. Jacobs, 5.
11. Chansky, 69–72 and 25–27.
12. Pollitt.
13. Chansky, 75–76.
14. Pollitt.
15. Chansky, 10 and 78.

16. "MEAC Official Makes Bid For NC House Seat," *The Carolinian*, 21 April 1992, 10.

17. Chansky, 78.

18. Charlie Davis, comment on Laurinburg Institute Facebook page, retrieved 11 October 2021.

19. "Wake Forest Hall of Fame: Charlie Davis," https://www.godeacs.com, retrieved 28 November 2021.

20. Cynthia McDuffie, interview with Elizabeth Jones, Laurinburg, N.C., 3 March 2023.

21. "Beverly McDonald," *TCU Athletics Hall of Fame*, 2008, https://www.tcufrogclub.com; "Beverly McDonald," Wikipedia, https://www.wikipedia.com, retrieved 15 March 2023.

Chapter 20

1. Bishop McDuffie, interview with Elizabeth Jones, Laurinburg, N.C., 1 March 2023.

Chapter 21

1. Nancy McLaughlin, "Laurinburg Institute/Separate and Equal," *Greensboro News and Record*, 10 December 1994.

2. David J. Dent, "Black Boarding Schools Suffer Unexpected Closings," *New York Times*, 5 March 1997.

3. J. Haney, "The Effects of the *Brown* Decision on Black Educators," *The Journal of Negro Education* 47 (1978): 88–95.

4. Gloria Ladson-Billings, "Landing on the Wrong Note: The Price We Paid for Brown," *Educational Researcher* 33, no. 7 (October 2004): 3–13.

5. McLaughlin.

6. McLaughlin.

7. Lindsay.

8. McLaughlin.

9. McLaughlin.

10. McLaughlin.

Chapter 22

1. Cynthia McDuffie, interview with Elizabeth Jones, Laurinburg, N.C., 3 March 2023; Frances McDuffie, interview with Elizabeth Jones, Laurinburg, N.C., 26 February 2023; Frances McDuffie Foster, interview with Elizabeth Jones, Durham, N.C., 26 March 2023; Shirley McDuffie McCoy, telephone interview with Elizabeth Jones, 1 May 2023. Quotes from these interviews are identified within the text.

2. Chansky, 43.

3. Malinda Maynor, "Poor high school resources leave black students unprepared for college," interview U-0014 with Willa V. Robinson, *Southern Oral History Program Collection* (#4007), 14 January 2004, https://docsouth.unc.edu/sohp/U-0014/excerpts/excerpt_655.html.

4. John Henderson, "Former Teacher, Public Defender Appointed to Fill Cumberland Judgeship," *Fayetteville Observer*, 6 May 2020.

Chapter 23

1. Lindsay.

2. Fairclough, 212.

3. Andre Mack, "115 Years of Black History," *Laurinburg Exchange*, 14 February 2019.

4. Katelin Gandee, "Descendants of Mike and Phoebe Given Key to the City," *Laurinburg Exchange*, 16 July 2018.

5. Gandee.

6. Gandee.

7. Lindsay.

8. Chris Everett, interview with Elizabeth Jones, Wilmington, N.C., 2 March 2023.

9. Mary Katherine Murphy, "Film sheds light on Institute," *Laurinburg Exchange*, 21 October 2011.

10. Murphy, "Film."

11. Jon Evans, "Chris Everett: Filmmaker Working on the Follow-Up to His Award-Winning 'Wilmington on Fire' Documentary," podcast *1 on 1 with Jon Evans*, 11 December 2020.

12. Jon Evans.

Chapter 24

1. Michael Gilliland, "Source said former Institute player Dozier had 'fishy' SAT scores," *Laurinburg Exchange*, 5

June 2009; Michael Gilliland, "Dozier's SAT score fell dramatically on retake." *Laurinburg Exchange,* 9 June 2009.

2. Michael Gilliland, "Dangerous Memphis team still led by Laurinburg Institute talent," *Laurinburg Exchange,* 17 March 2009.

3. Richard Walker, "From N.C. High School Basketball to the NBA: It's a Well-Worn Path that Continues Today," *Carolinas Sports Hubs,* 5 March 2021, www.carolinashportshub.com.

4. "Laurinburg Institute, Laurinburg (NC) Players," https://www.basketball.realgm.com, retrieved 21 October 2021.

Chapter 25

1. "Basketball Coaches: Chris Chaney," https://scotlandcampus.org, retrieved 10 November 2021.

2. Frank Bodani, "Why Is This Great Coach at a Tiny Pa. Prep School?" *York Daily Record,* 7 April 2021, https://www.heraldmailmedia.com.

3. Chris Chaney, interview with Elizabeth Jones, High Point, N.C., 27 March 2023. All further quotes from this interview are identified within the text.

4. Michael Gilliland, "Tigers prep team finishes year ranked No. 1 nationally," *Laurinburg Exchange,* 10 March 2003.

5. Bodani.

6. Jeff Goodman, "Laurinburg Is Numero Uno," *National Recruiting Analyst,* 8 May 2005.

7. Goodman.

8. Goodman.

9. Gilliland, "Tigers prep team."

10. Jim Quinn, "In the Gym with Jim—Checking in with Marriott," *Slam Magazine,* 19 December 2003.

11. Bodani.

12. Bodani.

13. "Robertson at Heart of Skyliners Win," 4 October 2018, https:www.eurocupbasketball.com.

14. Kelli Anderson, "Whiz Kids: Skilled beyond their years, fearless freshmen are boosting many top teams—none more than Memphis," *Sports Illustrated,* 9 January 2006, 72.

15. Zach Smart, "For Chaney, Illustrious Prep Career Continues at Scotland Campus Sports," 21 July 2017, https://www.zachmart.com.

16. Mark Schlabach, "Memphis Fab Freshmen Run Well Together: Top-Seeded Tigers Are Sparked by Our Players from Same High School," *Washington Post,* 22 March 2006.

17. Anderson.

18. Michael Gilliland, "Former Institute ballers drafted in NBA's first round," *Laurinburg Exchange,* 29 June 2006.

19. Schlabach.

Chapter 26

1. "Laurinburg Charter (Closed 2007)," https://www.publicschoolreview.com, retrieved 5 December 2021.

2. Bishop McDuffie interview, 1 March 2023.

3. John Manuel, "Charter Schools Revisited: A Decade after Authorization, How Goes the North Carolina Experience?" *North Carolina Insight* (May 2007): 52, 27 and 59.

4. Manuel, 54.

5. Michael Gilliland, "NCAA finds Laurinburg Institute unfit as academic establishment. School has appealed, but if decision stands, Laurinburg courses would no longer count toward college eligibility," *Laurinburg Exchange,* 3 April 2009.

6. Peter Galiczka, "NCAA Scrutiny Helps Hasten Decline of Tradition-Rich Black Prep School," *Diverse: Issues in Higher Education,* 10 May 2010, www.diverseeduction.com.

Chapter 27

1. Overfelt.

2. Erin McDermott, "MELO's brick masonry class provides life skills for students," *Laurinburg Exchange,* 23 February 2007.

3. Mary Katherine Murphy, "Outreach program targets elementary school students," *Laurinburg Exchange,* 12 August 2011.

4. Jason Chisari, "The Laurinburg Institute to unveil new prep football team," *Laurinburg Exchange,* 17 May 2012.

5. Mary Katherine Murphy, "Laurinburg Institute to honor alumni," *Laurinburg Exchange*, 18 May 2016.

6. Katelin Gandee, "Laurinburg Institute to serve as site for tech." *Laurinburg Exchange,* 10 May 2018.

7. Jael Pembrick, "Book gives glimpse into local black history," *Laurinburg Exchange*, 22 February 2019.

8. "Laurinburg Institute extends a legacy of learning to students," *Laurinburg Exchange*, 12 January 2021.

9. The Order of the Long Leaf Pine Society, https://www.longleafpine society.org, retrieved 6 May 2023.

10. Katelin Gandee, "Project—Parking area named McDuffie Square," *Laurinburg Exchange*, 16 December 2020.

Appendix

1. "A Joint Resolution Honoring the Life and Memory of Frank Howe McDuffie, Sr., and Sammie Sellers McDuffie," General Assembly of North Carolina, Resolution 2005–43, Senate Joint Resolution 1178, 2005, www.ncleg.gov.

2. "Recognizing Laurinburg Normal Industrial Institute," House Resolution 660, *Congressional Record* 155, no. 153 (October 21, 2009): H11536–11538, www.govinfo.gov.

Bibliography

Anderson, Kelli. "Whiz Kids: Skilled beyond their years, fearless freshmen are boosting many top teams—none more than Memphis." Sports Illustrated, 9 January 2006.

"Antique Real Photo Postcard—Emily Howland Girls Institute Laurinburg NC—RPPC." 5 November 1912. https://worthpoint.com. Retrieved 6 March 2023.

Application for Admission to The Laurinburg Normal & Industrial Institute, 191–192. Laurinburg Normal and Industrial Institute (Laurinburg, N.C.), n.d. [Announcements, bulletins, programs, etc.]. Chapel Hill: University of North Carolina, Wilson Library, North Carolina Collections.

"B.N. Duke has authorized a gift." *Robesonian*, 4 September 1925.

Barrett, John G. *Sherman's March Through the Carolinas.* Chapel Hill: University of North Carolina Press, 1956.

"Basketball Coaches: Chris Chaney." https://scotlandcampus.org. Retrieved 10 November 2021.

Beckham, Barry. *Double Dunk: The Story of Earl "The Goat" Manigault.* Silver Spring: Beckham Publications Group, 1993. Originally published 1980.

Benson, Jessie. "Outstanding Negro Achievements Guided by Laurinburg Institute." *Wellesley College News*, 27 September 1943.

"Beverly McDonald." *TCU Athletics Hall of Fame*, 2008. https://www.tcufrogclub.com. Retrieved 15 March 2023.

———. Wikipedia. https://www.wikipedia.com. Retrieved 15 March 2023.

"Black Boarding Schools: A Vanishing Breed." *The Journal of Blacks in Higher Education* 14 (Winter 1996–1997): 27–29.

"Bluford Library Archives: Rediscovering a Lost Queen of N.C. A & T." *A & T Alumni Times*, 22 November 2017. www.relations.ncat.org.

Bodani, Frank. "Why Is This Great Coach at a Tiny Pa. Prep School?" *York Daily Record*, 7 April 2021. https://www.heraldmailmedia.com.

Caldwell, A.B., ed. *History of the American Negro: North Carolina Edition, IV.* Atlanta: A.B. Caldwell Publishing Company, 1921.

Calhoun, Margaret, and John Hudson, eds. *Heritage of Scotland County North Carolina—2003.* Laurinburg, N.C.: Scotland County Heritage Book Committee and Scotland County Historical Association, Inc., 2004.

Chaney, Chris. Interview with Elizabeth Jones. High Point, N.C., 27 March 2023.

Chansky, Art. *Game Changers: Dean Smith, Charlie Scott, and the Era That Transformed a Southern College Town.* Chapel Hill: University of North Carolina Press, 2016.

Chisari, Jason. "The Laurinburg Institute to unveil new prep football team." *Laurinburg Exchange*, 17 May 2012.

"'The Clown Prince' Dizzy Gillespie: Music starts in the rear." *Winston-Salem Chronicle*, 4 October 1984.

Coble, Dot. "County's first African-American physician, a legend in his own right." *Laurinburg Exchange*, 23 February 2007.

"The Colored Civic League, Incorporated." *Laurinburg Exchange*, 15 December 1932.

Davidson, Sandra, and Wayne Martin. "50 For 50: Eddie Ray." Come Hear North Carolina, 23 July 2019. North Carolina Arts Council. http://www.ncarts.org.

Davis, Charlie. Comment on Laurinburg Institute Facebook page. Retrieved 11 October 2021.

Davis, G.E. Correspondence to Nathan C. Newbold, 16 February 1924. Raleigh: North Carolina Archives, Department of Public Instruction, Division of Negro Education, Box 4.

_____. Correspondence to Nathan C. Newbold, 14 May 1924. Raleigh: North Carolina Archives, Department of Public Instruction, Division of Negro Education, Box 4.

Dent, David J. "Black Boarding Schools Suffer Unexpected Closings." *New York Times*, 5 March 1997.

"Doing a Great Work." *Laurinburg Exchange*, 14 May 1914.

"Drive Aids New Item: After Year's Wait Negro School Gets Place on Drive List." *Vassar Miscellany News* XXV, no. 7, 16 October 1940.

"Earl 'The Goat' Manigault on CNN." *The Sporting Life*, 8 October 2012. Viewable on YouTube.

Edwards, William. *Twenty-Five Years in the Black Belt*. Columbia, S.C.: Reprint, 2021. Originally published 1918.

Efkarpides, George. "Fraport Skyliners Keep Quartez Robertson." 24 July 2018. https://www.eurohoops.net.

Ellsworth, Scott. *The Secret Game*. New York: Back Bay Books, 2016.

"Emily Howland." Wikipedia. https://www.wikipedia.com. Retrieved 16 March 2023.

Evans, Jon. "Chris Everett: Filmmaker Working on the Follow-Up to His Award- Winning 'Wilmington on Fire' Documentary." Podcast *1 on 1 with Jon Evans* 11 December 2020.

Evans, Walter P. "Colored People of Laurinburg Make Progress." *Laurinburg Exchange*, 15 December 1932.

_____. Correspondence to Nathan C. Newbold including copy of letter to Dr. Shaw, 12 August 1927. Raleigh: North Carolina Archives, Department of Public Instruction, Division of Negro Education, Box 4.

_____. "What the Best Negroes Will Do." *Raleigh News and Observer*, 26 July 1899.

"Evan's White Front Department Store." *Laurinburg Exchange*, 15 May 1924.

Everett, Chris. Interview with Elizabeth Jones. Wilmington, N.C., 2 March 2023.

_____, dir. *The Laurinburg Institute, Est. 1904*. Speller Street Films, 2009. Clips from film available on https://www.facebook.com.

_____, dir. *Wilmington on Fire*. DVD. Speller Street Films, Double7 Images, and Blackhouse Publishing, 2015.

Everett, J. Gentile. *The Making of a Life*. Fairmont, N.C.: Xlibris Corporation, 2011.

Fairclough, Adam. *A Class of Their Own: Black Teachers in the Segregated South*. Cambridge: The Belknap Press of Harvard University Press, 2007.

Foster, Frances McDuffie. Interview with Elizabeth Jones. Durham, N.C., 26 March 2023.

Galiczska, Peter. "NCAA Scrutiny Helps Hasten Decline of Tradition-Rich Black Prep School." *Diverse: Issues in Higher Education*, 10 May 2010. https://www.diverseduction.com.

Gandee, Katelin. "Descendants of Mike and Phoebe Given Key to the City." *Laurinburg Exchange*, 16 July 2018.

_____. "Laurinburg Institute to serve as site for tech." *Laurinburg Exchange*, 10 May 2018.

_____. "Project—Parking area named McDuffie Square." *Laurinburg Exchange*, 16 December 2020.

Gibbons, Bob. "Laurinburg Wins U. S. Prep National Championship." https://basketballrecruiting.rivals.com, 26 February 2005.

Gibson, Joyce M. *Scotland County Emerging 1750–1900*. Laurel Hill, N.C.: J.M. Gibson, 1995.

Gillespie, Dizzy, with Al Fraser. *To Be, or Not ... To Bop*. Minneapolis: University of Minnesota Press, 1979.

Gilliland, Michael. "Dangerous Memphis team still led by Laurinburg Institute talent." *Laurinburg Exchange*, 17 March 2009.

———. "Dozier's SAT score fell dramatically on retake." *Laurinburg Exchange*, 9 June 2009.

———. "Former Institute ballers drafted in NBA's first round." *Laurinburg Exchange*, 29 June 2006.

———. "Former Institute standout, now at Memphis, suspended after drug charges." *Laurinburg Exchange*, 25 January 2006.

———. "Former Laurinburg Institute players from Memphis, USC declare for NBA Draft." *Laurinburg Exchange*, 1 May 2006.

———. "NCAA finds Laurinburg Institute unfit as academic establishment. School has appealed, but if decision stands, Laurinburg courses would no longer count toward college eligibility." *Laurinburg Exchange*, 3 April 2009.

———. "Source said former Institute player Dozier had 'fishy' SAT scores." *Laurinburg Exchange*, 5 June 2009.

———. "Tigers prep team finishes year ranked No. 1 nationally." *Laurinburg Exchange*, 10 March 2003.

Goldston, Everett L. "A Giant Passed Our Way: Phillmore Millard Hall, 1905–1984." *The Carolina Times*, 26 January 1985.

Golen, Jimmy. "Hall of Famer Sam Jones, winner of 10 NBA titles, dies at 88." 31 December 2021. https://www.cbc.ca>sports>basketball>nba>nba-hall-of-famer-sam-jones-dies-at-88-1.6301552.

"A Good Investment." *Laurinburg Exchange*, 10 November 1910.

Goodman, Jeff. "Laurinburg Is Numero Uno." *National Recruiting Analyst*, 8 May 2005.

Graham, Gael. "'The Lexington of White Supremacy': School and Local Politics in Late-Nineteenth-Century Laurinburg, North Carolina." *The North Carolina Historical Review* 89, no. 1 (January 2012): 27–58.

Green, Nancy. "Among Our Graduates." *The Eastern Searchlight* 29, no. 10. Laurinburg Institute, 1949. Laurinburg, N.C.: Scotland County Memorial Library Special Collections.

Griffin, Cal. "Earl Manigault: The Greatest of All Time." https://www.allthingshoops.com. Retrieved 10 October 2021.

"Hall of Famer Sam Jones, winner of 10 NBA titles, dies at 88- Attended high school at Laurinburg Institute." *Laurinburg Exchange*, 31 December 2021.

Hanchett, Thomas W. "The Rosenwald Schools and Black Education in North Carolina." *The North Carolina Historical Review* 65, no. 4 (October 1988): 387–444.

Haney, J. "The Effects of the *Brown* Decision on Black Educators." *The Journal of Negro Education* 47 (1978): 88–95.

"Hard Hit." *Seward Daily Gateway*, 13 February 1931.

Harding, M.H. Correspondence to Nathan C. Newbold, Director of the State Division of Black Education, 23 January 1931. Raleigh: North Carolina Archives, Department of Public Education, Division of Negro Education, Box 4.

Harlan, Louis. *Separate and Unequal: Public School Campaigns and Racism in the Southern Seaboard States, 1901–1915*. Chapel Hill: University of North Carolina Press, 1958.

Harrington, Richard. "A Day for Dizzy." *Washington Post*, 17 November 1983.

Hassell, Gerald. *The Impact of Father Absence on African American Boys*. Orlando: Gerald Hassell, 2023.

———. Telephone interview with Elizabeth Jones. 30 April 2023.

Henderson, John. "Former Teacher, Public Defender Appointed to Fill Cumberland Judgeship." *Fayetteville Observer*, 6 May 2020.

Henley, Nettie McCormick. *The Home Place*. New York: Vantage, 1955.

Hodge, Johnny Baxter, Jr. "A Biography of Phillmore Mallard Hall with Particular

Emphasis on His Contribution to the Development of Black School Bands in North Carolina." Ph.D. diss., The American University, 1977.

Hodges, Cheris. "A Strong Legacy: I. Ellis Johnson left a positive mark on Scotland County's educational system." *Laurinburg Exchange*, 17 December 2021.

Hurley, Walter. "The Hanging of Willis Lytch, a Negro Slave, During the Civil War, In Laurinburg (Scotland County), North Carolina." Unpublished paper in Collection of Records for Marilyn Wright's *Sketch Book of Scotland County*. Laurinburg, N.C.: The Scotland County Memorial Library Special Collections, 1964.

Jacobs, Barry. *Across the Line: Profiles in Basketball Courage; Tales of the First Black Players in the ACC and SEC*. Guilford, CT: Lyons Press, 2007.

John, Maxcy L. Correspondence to Nathan C. Newbold, 19 August 1927. Raleigh: North Carolina Archives, Department of Public Instruction, Division of Negro Education, Box 4.

_____. Correspondence to Nathan C. Newbold, 26 September 1927. Raleigh: North Carolina Archives, Department of Public Instruction, Division of Negro Education, Box 4.

_____ "Historical Sketch of Laurinburg." *Laurinburg Exchange*, 15 December 1932.

_____. "Know Your History: Answers." *Laurinburg Exchange*, 8 March 1934.

_____. "Know Your History: More about the Red Shirts." *Laurinburg Exchange*, 15 March 1934.

"John Wesley Covington." Wikipedia. https://www.wikipedia.com. Retrieved 10 October 2022.

Johnson, I. Ellis. Correspondence to Partinari, 13 January 1945. https://www.artsandculture.google.com.

Johnson, Joy. *From Poverty to Power: An Autobiography of Dr. Joy Joseph Johnson, the Practical Preacher Politician*. Fairmont, N.C.: J.J. Johnson, 1976.

"A Joint Resolution Honoring the Life and Memory of Frank Howe McDuffie, Sr., and Sammie Sellers McDuffie...." General Assembly of North Carolina. Resolution 2005–43, Senate Joint Resolution 1178, 2005. www.ncleg.gov.

Jonsrud, Jarrod. "Harlem's Unsung Hero: The Life and Legacy of Holcombe Rucker." *Journal of Sport History* 38, no. 1 (Spring 2011):. 19–36.

Jordan, Milton C. "Black Legislators: From Political Novelty to Political Force." *North Carolina Insight*, December 1989, 40–58.

Kaliss, Gregory J. "Un-Civil Discourse: Charlie Scott, the Integration of College Basketball, and the 'Progressive Mystique.'" *Journal of Sport History* 35, no.1 (Spring 2008): 98–117.

Keech, Larry. "Laurinburg's McDuffie Put Scott on Road to Success." *Greensboro Daily News*, 11 March 1969.

Kelly, Ross. "Top 40 High Schools that Have Produced the Most NBA Players." https://www.stadiumtalk.com, 20 August 2021, 70–71.

King, Rev. Larkin. Correspondence to Newbold, 1 September 1927. Raleigh: North Carolina Archives, Department of Public Education, Division of Negro Education, Box 4.

Koch, Bill. "Friars legend Jimmy Walker to be inducted into college basketball Hall of Fame." *The Providence Journal*, 30 June 2022.

Ladson-Billings, Gloria. "Landing on the Wrong Note: The Price We Paid for Brown." *Educational Researcher* 33, no. 7 (October 2004): 3–13.

LaFrance, Adrienne, and Vann Newkirk. "The Lost History of an American Coup D'Etat." *The Atlantic*, 12 April 2017.

La Salle, Eriq, dir. Rebound: The Legend of Earl "The Goat" Manigault. 1996. HBO film available on YouTube.

"Laurinburg Charter (Closed 2007)." https://www.publicschoolreview.com. Retrieved 5 December 2021.

Laurinburg Institute (Edited). Film. Available on YouTube and www.laurinburginstitute.org.

"Laurinburg Institute extends a legacy of learning to students." *Laurinburg Exchange*, 12 January 2021.

"Laurinburg Institute, Laurinburg (NC) Players." https://www.basketball.realgm.com. Retrieved 21 October 2021.

"The Laurinburg Normal and Industrial Institute." *Laurinburg Exchange*, 15 December 1932.

Lawrence, Beth. "Inspirational Scotland County educator dies at 101—Family reflects on a life well lived." *Laurinburg Exchange*, 2 January 2018.

Leavell, Ullin W. *Philanthropy in Negro Education.* Nashville: George Peabody College for Teachers, 1930.

Lentz, John. "Students learn as teachers." *Laurinburg Exchange*, 14 May 2009.

Lindsay, Drew. "From Out of a Swamp: A School's Tale of Faith." *Education Week* 13, no. 35 (25 May 1994). http://www.edweek.org.

Logan, Isaac. Interview with Elizabeth Jones. Black Mountain, N.C., 16 March 2023.

Ludlow, Helen W. *Armstong's Ideas on Education for Life.* Hampton, VA: Hampton Institute Press, Reprint, 1945.

Mack, Andre. "Artist Captures Jazz Legend Grachan Moncur III." *Anson Record*, 7 September 2021.

———. "Life and times of Henrietta Davis." *Laurinburg Exchange*, 17 May 2019.

———. "115 Years of Black History." *Laurinburg Exchange*, 14 February 2019.

———. "The Reunion of Laurinburg Institute ." *Laurinburg Exchange*, 12 March 2019.

———. "With Hopes She Remembers Her Experience Here." *Laurinburg Exchange*, 9 September 2021.

Maize, William S. "An Interpretative History of Laurinburg Normal and Industrial Institute, Laurinburg, North Carolina." Master's thesis for Education Department, Rutgers University, June 1948. ProQuest document ID 302064392.

Malcolm, Douglas. "Myriad Subtleties: Subverting Racism through Irony in the Music of Duke Ellington and Dizzy Gillespie." *Black Music Research Journal* 35, no. 2 (Fall 2015): 185–227.

Mallozzi, Vincent. "King of Kings." *SLAM Magazine*, 12 June 2010. https://www.slamonline.com.

Manuel, John. "Charter Schools Revisited: A Decade after Authorization, How Goes the North Carolina Experience?" *North Carolina Insight*, May 2007, 2–71.

"Many Negroes Hear Their Famous Leader." *Laurinburg Exchange*, 19 November 1910.

"Marker Text: Laurinburg Institute." Raleigh: North Carolina Office of Archives and History, cast 2013. https://www.ncculture.com. 10 August 2021.

Maynor, Malinda. "Poor high school resources leave black students unprepared for college." Interview U-0014 with Willa V. Robinson. *Southern Oral History Program Collection* (#4007), 14 January 2004. https://docsouth.unc.edu/sohp/U-0014/excerpts/excerpt_655.html.

McCormick, John. "Impressions and Recollections of Laurinburg in Earlier Days." *Laurinburg Exchange*, 15 December 1932.

McCoy, Shirley McDuffie. Telephone interview with Elizabeth Jones, 1 May 2023.

McDermott, Erin. "MELO's brick masonry class provides life skills for students." *Laurinburg Exchange*, 23 February 2007.

McDuffie, Cynthia. Interview with Elizabeth Jones. Laurinburg, N.C., 3 March 2023.

McDuffie, Emmanuel. Correspondence to Nathan C. Newbold, 15 October 1915. Raleigh: North Carolina Archives, Department of Public Instruction, Division of Negro Education, Box 4.

———. *High School Principals' Annual Report (1931–1932).* Raleigh: North Carolina Archives, North Carolina Department of Public Instruction, Division of Negro Education.

———. *The Ninth Annual Report of the Principal and Treasurer of the Laurinburg Normal and Industrial Institute.* Laurinburg, N.C.: Laurinburg Institute Print, 7 May 1914. Laurinburg Normal and Industrial Institute (Laurinburg, N.C.), n.d. [Announcements, bulletins, programs, etc.]. University of North Carolina, Wilson Library, North Carolina Special Collections.

_____. "Sketch of My Life." *Twenty-Five Years in the Black Belt*. Columbia, S.C.: Reprint, 2021, 39–42. Originally published 1918.

McDuffie, Frances. Interview with Elizabeth Jones. Laurinburg, N.C., 26 February 2023.

McDuffie, Frank "Bishop," Jr. Interviews with Elizabeth Jones. Laurinburg, N.C., 20 May 2021 and 1 March 2023.

_____. "Laurinburg Institute ... 'Deeds Not Words.'" The Mighty Sixth District Omega Psi Phi Fraternity, Inc., 31 January 2021. https://www.oppf6d.org.

_____. "Laurinburg Institute Extends a Legacy of Learning to Students." *Laurinburg Exchange*, 29 November 2021.

McGirt, Roger Martin. "The Development of Public Education in Scotland County." Master's thesis, University of North Carolina at Chapel Hill, 1931.

McLaughlin, Nancy. "Laurinburg Institute/Separate and Equal." *Greensboro News and Record*, 10 December 1994.

McLeod, Leroy. Interview with Elizabeth Jones. Laurinburg, N.C., 1 March 2023.

McNeil, Rena, and Scotland County NAACP Youth Council. *A Diamond Eventually Shines: Scotland County's African -American Pioneers.* Kearney, N.C.: Morris Publishing, 1999.

"MEAC Official Makes Bid For NC House Seat." *The Carolinian*, 21 April 1992.

Melton, J.J. "Our Major Leaguer Wes Covington went from football to baseball career." *Laurinburg Exchange*, 16 April 2021.

_____. "A Story of Success: W. P. Evans Built a Business in the Downtown Area Starting in 1884." *Laurinburg Exchange*, 19 February 2021.

Modlin, Mary. "Walter Parsley Evans, 1863–1937." https://www.usgaarchives.net. Retrieved 15 July 2021.

"Moncur, Grachen III." Wikipedia. https://www.wikipedia.com. Retrieved 11 October 2021.

Moton, Levelle. "Tribute to Sam Jones." Post on Laurinburg Institute Facebook page, 31 December 2021.

Murphy, Mary Katherine. "Educators' legacy honored." *Laurinburg Exchange*, 28 February 2013.

_____. "Film sheds light on Institute." *Laurinburg Exchange*, 21 October 2011.

_____. "Laurinburg Institute to honor alumni." *Laurinburg Exchange*, 18 May 2016.

_____. "Local author publishes philosophical treatise." *Laurinburg Exchange*, 12 August 2011.

_____. "Outreach program targets elementary school students." *Laurinburg Exchange*, 12 August 2011.

_____. "Pastor adds voice to church-state debate." *Laurinburg Exchange*, 8 February 2013.

"Negros Pay Respect." *Laurinburg Exchange*, 18 November 1915.

Newbold, Nathan C. Correspondence to Emmanuel McDuffie, 23 October 1915. Raleigh: North Carolina Archives, Department of Public Instruction Records, Division of Negro Education, Box 4.

_____. Correspondence to G.E. Davis, Supervisor of Rosenwald Buildings, 14 September 1927. Raleigh: North Carolina Archives, Department of Public Instruction Records, Division of Negro Education, Box 4.

_____. Correspondence to Jackson Davis, 18 July 1927. Raleigh: North Carolina Archives, Department of Public Instruction Records, Division of Negro Education, Box 4.

_____. Correspondence to Maxcy John, 24 August 1927. Raleigh: North Carolina Archives, Department of Public Instruction Records, Division of Negro Education, Box 4.

_____. *Report of N.C. Newbold, State Agent Negro Rural Schools for North Carolina, For the Month of December, 1915*. Raleigh: North Carolina Archives, Department of Public Instruction, Division of Negro Education.

The Order of the Long Leaf Pine Society. https://www.longleafpinesociety.org. Retrieved 6 May 2023.

Overfelt, Abbi. "Alumni celebrate installation of Institute's historical marker—Headmaster looks to the future." *Laurinburg Exchange*, 16 May 2014.

———. "Local filmmaker brings 'forgotten' history to life." *Laurinburg Exchange*, 17 December 2013.

Padgett, James A. "From Slavery to Prominence in North Carolina: Preparation." *The Journal of Negro History* 22, no. 4 (October 1937): 433–487.

Peabody, Francis Greenwood. *Education for Life: The Story of Hampton Institute.* Garden City, N.Y.: Doubleday, Page, 1926.

Pembrick, Jael. "Book gives glimpse into local black history." *Laurinburg Exchange*, 22 February 2019.

———. "School starts GoFundMe to help with repairs." *Laurinburg Exchange*, 26 November 2018.

Pollitt, Daniel H. "Interview with Daniel H. Pollitt ." L-0064-4 *Southern Oral History Program Collection* (#4007), *Documenting the American South.* Chapel Hill: University of North Carolina, 15 February 1991.

Quinn, Jim. "In the Gym with Jim—Checking in With Marriott." *Slam Magazine*, 19 December 2003.

Rasmussen, Frederick N. "George W. Collins, pioneering broadcaster." *Baltimore Sun*, 4 August 2014.

Ravitch, Diane. "A Different Kind of Education for Black Children." *The Journal of Blacks in Higher Education* 30 (Winter 2000–2001): 98–106.

"Recognizing Laurinburg Normal Industrial Institute." House Resolution 660. *Congressional Record*, 155, no. 153 (October 21, 2009): H11536–11538. www.govinfo.gov.

Rice, Leon. "The Laurinburg Institute." *Divergents Magazine.* https://www.divergents_magazine.org. Retrieved 10 September 2021.

"Robertson at Heart of Skyliners Win." 4 October 2018. https://www.eurocupbasketball.com.

Robinson, W.A. Correspondence to Walter White, 26 August 1927. Raleigh: North Carolina Archives, Department of Public Instruction Records, Division of Negro Education, Box 4.

———. *Report of School Situation for Negroes in Laurinburg*, 8 July 1926. Raleigh: North Carolina State Archives, Department of Public Instruction Records, Division of Negro Education, Box 4.

Schlabach, Mark. "Memphis Fab Freshmen Run Well Together: Top-Seeded Tigers Are Sparked by Our Players from Same High School." *Washington Post*, 22 March 2006.

"Scotland Has No Farm or Home Agent But I. H. Smith Adequately Fills In." *The Carolinian*, 1 August 1959.

Scott, Charlie, with Mark Wright. "Going Through Hell to Get into the Hall of Fame." 21 October 2019. https://www.OZY.com.

"Sir John Swan." Wikipedia. https://www.wikipedia.com. Retrieved 20 October 2021.

Smart, Zach. "For Chaney, Illustrious Prep Career Continues at Scotland Campus Sports." 21 July 2017. https://www.zachmart.com.

Smith, Isabelle, and Ivory Smith. *Life Lines: A Collection of Inspiring Poetry and Prose.* Laurinburg, N.C.: I. and I. Smith, 1952.

Smith, Matt. "From the Cheap Seats." *Laurinburg Exchange*, 27 July 2011.

Stone, Donald P. *Fallen Prince: William James Edwards, Black Education and the Quest for Afro-American Nationality.* Snow Hill, AL: Snow Hill Press, 1989.

Sturgill, Andy. "Wes Covington." *Biographies.* Society for American Baseball Research. http://www.sabr.org. Retrieved 2 February 2023.

"Successful Institutions of the Colored People." *Laurinburg Exchange*, 15 May 1924.

Swan, Sir John. Video of Sir John Swan. *Laurinburg Institute, Est. 1904* (2009). Viewed on Facebook, October 12, 2021.

"Teachers' Institute." *Laurinburg Exchange*, 12 August 1915.

"Wake Forest Hall of Fame: Charlie Davis." https://www.godeacs.com. Retrieved 28 November 2021.

Walker, Richard. "From N.C. High School Basketball to the NBA: It's a Well-Worn Path that Continues Today." *Carolinas Sports Hubs*, 5 March 2021. https://www.carolinashportshub.com.

Washington, Booker T. *Up From Slavery: An Autobiography*. Reprint: Digireads.com Publishing, 2016. Originally published 1900.

_____, W.E.B. Du Bois, et al. *The Negro Problem*. New York: James Pott and Company, 1903.

West, Hollie I. "Dizzy And the Dean." *Washington Post*, 5 February 1981.

"Whipping Record 1823–1844." Special Collections. Laurinburg, N.C.: Scotland County Memorial Library.

Work, Monroe N. *Industrial Work of Tuskegee Graduates and Former Students During the Year 1910*. Tuskegee: Tuskegee Institute Press, 1911.

Wright, Marilyn *A Sense of Place*. Laurinburg, N.C.: St. Andrews Press, 1991.

_____. *A Sense of Place, Part II*. Laurinburg N.C.: Walsworth Publishing Company, 1996.

_____, ed. "Laurinburg Normal and Industrial Institute." 2006. https://www.ncpedia.org.

Wright, R.B. "Conversations with John Birks "Dizzy" Gillespie, Pioneer of Jazz." *The Black Perspective in Music* 4, no. 1 (Spring 1976): 82–89.

Index

Numbers in **bold italics** indicate pages with illustrations

241